Ways of Saying: Ways of Meaning

Open Linguistics Series

The *Open Linguistics Series*, to which this book makes a significant contribution, is 'open' in two senses. First, it provides an open forum for works associated with any school of linguistics or with none. Linguistics has now emerged from a period in which many (but never all) of the most lively minds in the subject seemed to assume that transformational-generative grammar – or at least something fairly closely derived from it – would provide the main theoretical framework for linguistics for the foreseeable future. In Kuhn's terms, linguistics had appeared to some to have reached the 'paradigm' stage. Reality today is very different. More and more scholars are working to improve and expand theories that were formerly scorned for not accepting as central the particular set of concerns highlighted in the Chomskyan approach – such as Halliday's systemic theory (as exemplified in this book), Lamb's stratificational model and Pike's tagmemics – while others are developing new theories. The series is open to all approaches, then – including work in the generativist-formalist tradition.

The second sense in which the series is 'open' is that it encourages works that open out 'core' linguistics in various ways: to encompass discourse and the description of natural texts; to explore the relationship between linguistics and its neighbouring disciplines such as psychology, sociology, philosophy, artificial intelligence, and cultural and literary studies; and to apply it in fields such as education and language pathology.

Open Linguistics Series Editor
Robin F. Fawcett, University of Wales College of Cardiff

Modal Expressions in English, Michael R. Perkins
Text and Tagmeme, Kenneth L. Pike and Evelyn G. Pike
The Semiotics of Culture and Language, eds: Robin P. Fawcett, M. A. K. Halliday, Sydney M. Lamb and Adam Makkai
Into the Mother Tongue: A Case Study in Early Language Development, Clare Painter
Language and the Nuclear Arms Debate: Nukespeak Today, ed.: Paul Chilton
The Structure of Social Interaction: A Systemic Approach to the Semiotics of Service Encounters, Eija Ventola
Grammar in the Construction of Texts, ed.: James Monaghan
On Meaning, A. J. Griemas, trans. by Paul Perron and Frank Collins
Biological Metaphor and Cladistic Classification: An Interdisciplinary Approach, eds: Henry M. Hoenigswald and Linda F. Wiener
New Developments in Systemic Linguistics, Volume I: *Theory and Description*, eds: M. A. K. Halliday and Robin P. Fawcett; Volume II: *Theory and Application*, eds: Robin P. Fawcett and David Young
Eloquence and Power: The Rise of Language Standards and Standard Language, John Earl Joseph
Functions of Style, eds: David Birch and Michael O'Toole
Registers of Written English: Situational Factors and Linguistic Features, ed.: Mohsen Ghadessy
Pragmatics, Discourse and Text, eds: Erich H. Steiner and Robert Veltman
The Communicative Syallabus, Robin Melrose
Advances in Systemic Linguistics: Recent Theory and Practice, eds: Martin Davies and Louise Ravelli
Studies in Systemic Phonology, ed.: Paul Tench
Ecolinguistics: Towards a New Paradigm for the Science of Language, Adam Makkai
Thematic Development in English Texts, ed.: Mohsen Ghadessy

Ways of Saying: Ways of Meaning

Selected Papers of Ruqaiya Hasan

Edited by
Carmel Cloran, David Butt and Geoffrey Williams

CASSELL

Cassell
Wellington House, 125 Strand, London WC2R 0BB
127 West 24th Street, New York, NY 10011

First published 1996

© Introduction and editorial apparatus, the editors 1996
'The nursery tale as a genre' (revised) and 'Semantic networks: a tool for the analysis of meaning' by © Ruqaiya Hasan 1996

All rights reserved. No part of this publication may be reproduced or transmitted in any form or by any means, electronic or mechanical, including photocopying, recording or any information storage or retrieval system, without permission in writing from the publishers.

Ruqaiya Hasan is hereby identified as the author of this work as provided under Section 77 of the Copyright, Designs and Patents Act 1988.

British Library Cataloguing in Publication Data
A catalogue record for this book is available from the British Library.

ISBN 0 304 33737 4 Hardback
   0 304 33738 2 Paperback

Library of Congress Cataloging-in-Publication Data
Hasan, Ruqaiya.
   Ways of saying, ways of meaning: selected papers of Ruqaiya Hasan / edited by Carmel Cloran, David Butt, and Geoffrey Williams.
      p.   cm. — (Open linguistics series)
   Includes bibliographical references and index.
      Contents: What kind of resource is language? — What's going on: a dynamic view of context in language — The nursery tale as a genre — The grammarian's dream: lexis as most delicate grammar — Semantic networks — The ontogenesis of ideology: an interpretation of mother–child talk — Speech genre, semiotic mediation, and the development of higher mental functions — Ways of saying, ways of meaning.
   ISBN 0-304-33737-4. — ISBN 0-304-33738-2 (pbk.)
   1. Linguistics. I. Cloran, Carmel. II. Butt, David, 1950–
III. Williams, Geoffrey. IV. Title. V. Series.
P125.H35 1996
410—dc20   95-53269
                                                                                                      CIP

Typeset by York House Typographic
Printed and bound in Great Britain by Biddles Ltd, Guildford and King's Lynn

Contents

Acknowledgements and list of sources   vi
Introduction   1

Part One: Text and Context

1. What kind of resource is language?   13
2. What's going on: a dynamic view of context in language   37
3. The nursery tale as a genre   51

Part Two: Tools

4. The grammarian's dream: lexis as most delicate grammar   73
5. Semantic networks: a tool for the analysis of meaning   104

Part Three: Language and Society

6. The ontogenesis of ideology: an interpretation of mother–child talk   133
7. Speech genre, semiotic mediation and the development of higher mental functions   152
8. Ways of saying: ways of meaning   191

Index   243

Acknowledgements and list of sources

The chapters in this volume originally appeared as follows:

'What kind of resource is language?' In *Australian Review of Applied Linguistics*, 7.1. pp. 57–85. 1984.
'What's going on: a dynamic view of context'. In J. E. Copeland and P. W. Davis (eds) *The Seventh LACUS Forum.* pp. 106–121. Columbia, S.C.: Hornbeam Press. 1980.
'The nursery tale as a genre'. In *Nottingham Linguistic Circular*, 13, pp. 71–102. 1984.
'The grammarian's dream: lexis as most delicate grammar'. In M. A. K. Halliday and R. Fawcett (eds) *New Developments in Systemic Linguistics,* Volume I: *Theory and Description.* pp. 184–212. London: Frances Pinter. 1987.
'The ontogenesis of ideology: an interpretation of mother–child talk'. In T. Threadgold, E. Grosz, G. Kress and M. A. K. Halliday (eds) *Semiotics – Ideology – Language*, pp. 125–146. Sydney Studies in Society and Culture, No. 3. Sydney: Sydney Association for Studies in Society and Culture. 1986.
'Speech genre, semiotic mediation and the development of higher mental functions'. In *Language Sciences*, 14, 4, pp. 489–528. 1992. © 1993 Pergamon Press Ltd. Reproduced by kind permission of Elsevier Science Ltd, Oxford.
'Ways of saying: ways of meaning'. In R. Fawcett, M. A. K. Halliday, S. Lamb and A. Makkai (eds) *The Semiotics of Culture and Language,* Volume I: *Language as Social Semiotic.* pp. 105–162. London: Frances Pinter. 1984.
'Semantic networks: a tool for the analysis of meaning' has not previously been published.

We are very grateful to the above-mentioned publishers and journals for permission to reproduce copyright material.

Introduction

1 Overview

> 'I have an idea that there is a continuity from the living of life on the one hand right down to the morpheme on the other'

These words, spoken by Ruqaiya Hasan when asked to reflect on what it is that motivates her linguistic work, succinctly convey what it is in her writings that we (the editors) find so fascinating. With a few exceptions the selection from Hasan's writings included in this volume deal implicitly or explicitly with just this continuity. Those that do not address the issue are those which are concerned, rather, with its corollary, i.e. how to investigate this phenomenon within the framework of the systemic functional model of language.

Hasan is well – even uniquely – placed to write about the relation of language and social life in that she has been forced, through the exigencies of her own life, to observe and reflect on the way in which the different cultures of which she has found herself a member construe the world. In her own words, she has found herself 'iteratively reacculturating' as she moved from the Indo-Pakistani subcontinent to Britain to America and, finally, to Australia. This has meant that, like all such 'nomads', she has had to learn, as an adult, how to successfully transact meaning within each new culture. Few other adult cultural initiates, however, have faced the learning task from the vantage point of a powerful intellect allied with a deep and abiding interest in the use of language in the living of life. A number of the great anthropologists and linguists of this century – Malinowski, Boas, Sapir, Whorf – spring to mind. Unlike Hasan, however, these scholars were temporary visitors to their adopted cultures and their cultural journeys were in the opposite direction to that of Hasan's initial cultural exchange in the sense that they went from within a Western society to a non-Western one.

Perhaps her journeyings convinced Hasan that 'different ways of saying are different ways of meaning' or perhaps her 'iterative reacculturation' predisposed her to the veracity of this view which is a basic postulate within the systemic functional model of language. Her interest as stated above, i.e. in the continuity between the smallest unit of linguistic meaning through to the living of life, has led her to make explicit her view of the concepts and methodology needed in order to go about investigating this continuity. This is most clearly to be seen in her investigation of the semantic styles of English and Urdu (see Chapter 8) which, she argues, reflect different cultural orientations particularly with regard to the social structures of the two speech communities. No community of speakers is homogeneous of course, and Hasan addresses this fact in the same paper, and, in research[1] not explicitly represented in the writings included in this collection, investigates this issue of different orientations to meaning within a single culture/language.

Her idea of the continuity between language and the living of life has meant that Hasan is constantly seeking an explanation of the linguistic phenomena she observes. Thus, in Chapter 8 she states: 'If ... we find a section of the speech community whose predominant orientation is to the implicit style of speaking, we must ask *why*' (emphasis added). For such explanation she does not hesitate to go outside linguistics; indeed, this is essential if language and social life are viewed as dialectically related. Thus, she appeals to the work of anthropologists and sociologists – Benedict, Douglas, Durkheim, Geertz, Hsu. However, it is the work of Bernstein which she finds most compelling in her search for an explanation of sociolinguistic phenomena, and she turns to this body of work again and again (e.g. Chapters 1 and 7). Venturing outside of linguistics for explanations comes naturally to one who holds the view that restricted areas in the practice of linguistics – discourse linguistics, pragmatics, aphasiology – are, in actual fact, undo-able because such restriction separates linguistic phenomena from their explanation.

Hasan's writing agenda includes a commitment to articulating her ideas as explicitly as possible. In her carefully articulated introductions, particularly to her analytic work, she connects with the big questions in linguistics and related disciplines. A commitment to a clear explication of her ideas has the consequence that nothing in her writing is gratuitous or covert. This is most clearly seen in her descriptive work (e.g. Chapters 3–5, 8). In Chapters 4 and 5, for example, where she discusses the use of networks – the tool which is central in systemic functional theory – her strategy involves setting out what it is that counts as the challenge or theoretical motivation for her descriptions and then taking the reader through each step showing how the relations of a network can be proposed and tested. Linguistics thus becomes a mode of strong hypothesis testing in the Popperian sense. At each step of the way she indicates to the reader just what it is that would count as falsification of the hypothesis under discussion. At times, she may verify/falsify the hypothesis herself; for example, in Chapter 8 she asserts:

> If semantic style is a characteristic way of saying and meaning, then the defining attributes of this style should be present in most natural verbal interaction. Exceptions, where the characteristic semantic style is not used, will be significantly fewer; moreover it should be possible to state clearly how these exceptions can be defined.

She then goes on to state the exceptional cases. At other times, her method is to throw down a challenge with respect to the details of her descriptions, e.g.

> In English, the only lexical item capable of functioning as the Event in a clause with the above selection expression is 'scatter'. (Chapter 4)

INTRODUCTION

The interested reader may then follow up the challenge. Her writings are thus a rich source of inspiration not only in the originality of the ideas but also in the more pragmatic sense that interested students are presented with a clearly identified and theoretically motivated research topic.

Hasan's commitment to explicit enunciation of her ideas is also to be seen in the way she provides clear and concise definitions of the terms she introduces, again particularly in the descriptive work where she does not hesitate to exploit redundancy in the interests of clarity. Her writing is, nevertheless, not the kind that is easily accessible on a superficial reading; rather, it is the kind that demands and, indeed, rewards repeated readings.

A third, but implicit component in Hasan's writing agenda concerns her commitment to linguistics as an academic discipline. She urges her colleagues to reflect on their ways of being linguists – of doing linguistics. She has a keen sense of the academic linguist's responsibility to society to reveal the way in which linguistic resources may be used to maintain and defend the social practices of the dominant group. Indeed, in Chapter 1, she suggests that the greatest justification of the entire range of academic disciplines lies in their ability to 'disturb the suspension of disbelief [in reality] which the everyday linguistic practices of a community perpetuate'.

That common-sense reality is created, maintained and defended by a community's everyday linguistic practices has been drawn to our attention by phenomenologists such as Berger and Luckmann (1966). That this superordinate function of everyday linguistic practices is mirrored in the non-common-sense sphere is self-evident: theoretical reality, too, is created, maintained and defended via language and the same resource is also used to examine this reality – to disturb 'the suspension of disbelief' in the theoretical ideas created. Much of Hasan's work has precisely this effect. By her own careful examination, she draws our attention to the need to thoroughly examine ideas in vogue at any particular time, and not only to relate them to their underlying assumptions (implicitly or explicitly stated) but also to follow them through to their logical conclusions. Every one of the papers in this collection demonstrates this rigorous approach. By the same token, ideas that are out of vogue – unfashionable fashions of theorizing – receive her careful scrutiny. Thus, in Chapter 1 – 'What kind of resource is language?' – Hasan appeals to the work of Whorf (1956). Indeed, the ideas of Whorf may be identified as forming one of the major intellectual strands which have inspired Hasan's work[2] even though, at the time she wrote this paper (1983), 'mainstream' linguists had dismissed Whorf's work. In the process of drawing on Whorf's ideas, she clarifies the bases of many of the problems perceived in the so-called Whorfian hypothesis. Her discussion of the misinterpretations of Whorf's view concerning the relativity of reality and the role of language in the creation of that reality is unparalleled even in the context of more recent thoughtful expositions of Whorf's ideas (e.g. Lucy 1985; Lucy and Wertsch 1987).

It seems ironic – or perhaps, on the other hand, it is appropriate – that the social responsibility of the academic community of linguists to reveal the role of everyday language in maintaining and defending the social divisions in society should be highlighted by one who is a member of that sub-community of linguists – the systemic functional community – which is, itself, marginalized in the context of the 'mainstream' linguistic community. Hasan's is, of course, not a lone voice, for the strength of the systemic functional model of language is that it provides the tools necessary for (a) the analysis of differing semantic styles; and (b) the empowerment of the disadvantaged members of society via pedagogic means.

2 The selection

This selection of the writings of Ruqaiya Hasan does not lend itself to a clearcut classification between theoretical and methodological papers. For instance, one of the papers – 'The nursery tale as a genre' – while addressing the theoretical issues concerning the relation between text and context is also a leading example of methodological considerations. We have chosen to organize the collection in three sections. The first section contains papers which discuss the relation between text and context – from culture to situation to text to the realization of these in language. In the second section are the most explicitly descriptive papers. In the systemic functional model language is viewed as a system of systems of interlocking choices and the primary analytic tool arising from this view of language is the network. The two papers in Part Two explore the application (and implications of the use of) the network at two different strata of language – the lexicogrammatical and the semantic strata. The papers in the third section examine aspects of the social structure which are implicated in the way (sub-)cultures express themselves. The decision to include the eight papers selected rather than others was a very difficult one but in the end it was a pragmatic consideration which guided the selection process: we wanted to include those which we regard as invaluable in their relevance to our teaching of linguistics.

The question which forms the title of the paper presented as Chapter 1 is addressed via another question: how is it possible for language to function as a means to so many ends? In elucidating this issue, Hasan discusses language in its role as the means by which we share our experience of physical and social reality. Since, in such sharing we create this reality, it is clear that language is used to deal with what it has been used to create. Therefore, the question is answered thus: language is able to serve as a means to so many ends because the ends were created largely by language. Hasan then illustrates the use of language to create reality with extracts from her corpus of mother–child dialogues.

These dialogues were collected by the mothers who participated in Hasan's research which investigated the role of everyday talk in establishing ways of learning. This project draws on another major intellectual strand informing Hasan's work, the ideas of the British sociologist Basil Bernstein. Like Whorf, Bernstein recognizes the importance of language in the construction of social reality. Unlike Whorf, who was concerned with differing social realities associated with communities of speakers of different languages, Bernstein is concerned with different social realities occurring within communities of speakers sharing a common language. Language is instrumental in creating and maintaining these intra-language differences, according to Bernstein; where social realities differ, these differing realities are associated with variant orientations to meaning and variant 'fashions of speaking'. Bernstein's theory locates the origin of variant orientations to meaning (codes) in the material conditions of social life associated with the social division of labour.

Bernstein's theory had been misinterpreted and dismissed by mainstream linguists. Hasan, however, perhaps recognizing (a) the authenticity of the theory, and (b) that investigations of the linguistic features of coding orientation needed to focus on the semantic stratum rather than the lexicogrammatical – the stratum on which Bernstein's early account of the code features focused – devised semantic networks through which to investigate the hypothesis. The development and use of such networks is discussed in Chapter 5.

Hasan's approach to linguistics has been, from the outset, a quest for meaning. The systemic functional model of language, in its commitment to the unity of form and meaning, is a natural theoretical path for her to follow. Concepts introduced within the framework of the model are subjected to the same careful scrutiny that she brings to other linguistic concepts; perceived shortcomings in, and criticisms of, the model are carefully examined. Thus, for example, the systemic functional model of the text–context relation (Halliday and Hasan 1985/89) has attracted criticism from ethnomethodologists and phenomenologically oriented philosophers on the grounds that, as a normative model of social interaction, it denies individuals the autonomy and freedom to negotiate interactional contexts. In Chapter 2 – 'What's going on?' ... Hasan addresses these criticisms in a characteristically theoretical way pointing out that some environments and certain roles are likely to permit individual negotiation more readily than others. She introduces into the systemic functional conception of context two vectors: degree of institutionalization and extent of social distance between/among the interactants. The former – degree of institutionalization – refers to the description of contexts in terms of a cline from highly institutionalized through to non-institutionalized or individuated; the latter – social distance – is also described as a cline ranging from non-minimal through to minimal. She then proposes that the negotiability of contexts depends crucially on these two variables. Thus, she hypothesizes that it is when minimal social distance is combined with individuated environments that the possibility of individual negotiation of context is highest; only under these conditions are interactants free (at least theoretically[3]) to cooperatively agree on an activity to pursue, to adopt for oneself and assign to other participants particular roles, and to establish how that which is to be done can be accomplished in communicative terms.

The criticism of the systemic functional model as normative is, to a large extent, a function of the view of context held by its critics: context is identified with the material environment of the interaction – what Hasan terms the material situational setting. It is the work of Hasan more than any other writer in the systemic functional model which has clarified the relationship between the pre-existing material (environment) and the semiotic environment brought into existence by language.

In Chapter 3 – 'The nursery tale as a genre' – the notion of context is further clarified, this time in relation to literary genres, and, indeed, applicable to any genre in which the role of language is constitutive. She proposes that for such genres, three orders of context need to be recognized: the (author's) contexts of creation, the (audience's) context of reception and the context reconstituted by the text. With this clarification Hasan is able to elucidate the principles that one might use in proposing structure statements at the level of discourse – what she terms the generic structure potential (GSP) of a text type. The procedure is again based on meaning. The notion of GSP is a theoretical one that can be applied to all genres.[4] A GSP is a statement of the structural resources available to a genre. As an abstract textual structure, it is capable of describing (and therefore generating) the total potential of textual structures available within a genre. Such a structure statement must specify what elements are obligatory and what elements are optional, as well as the ordering of all elements *vis-à-vis* each other. By specifying optional elements, the notion of GSP not only recognizes but incorporates the possibility of text variation. In fact, it is a theory of text variation.

Applying the concept to the genre of nursery tale, Hasan derives a structure potential (SP) for this genre from a representative corpus of nursery tales. The discussion goes further than merely postulating an SP, however, for she works through the chain of realization from SP to lexicogrammar, focusing, for reasons of time and space, on a single postulated optional element – Placement. In the process she demonstrates how it is possible for the description to account for the fact that two texts of the same genre may be identical in their structure without being identical in their realization of this structure.

Hasan's rigorous approach to linguistic principles is illustrated in Chapter 4 – 'The grammarian's dream: lexis as most delicate grammar' – a paper in which the power of the network as an analytic tool is demonstrated. The grammatical description is motivated by Halliday's suggestion that the whole stratum of linguistic form – both grammar and lexis – could be thought of as a continuum of more and more delicate paradigms (or environments of choice). Ultimately, Halliday predicts, lexis might be seen as the output of delicate grammatical paradigms for which there are only unique formal realizations – namely, single words.

With this linguistic principle in mind, then, Hasan makes a 'test case' out of a small lexical domain within verbs of disposal. With this set of nine commonly used items (from 'gather' to 'share'), Hasan sets out the technical aspects of networks – their 'intra-linguistic' justification; their role *vis-à-vis* Saussure's concepts of signification/value and syntagm/paradigm; the six categories of realization statement; the inheritance of features as one follows a path through the network; and the explicit inventory of selection expressions, etc.

Besides the theory proposed by Halliday, one can see in this undertaking the fulfilment of longer-standing goals of linguistic representation, especially: Saussure's injunction that the whole of linguistic form had to be conceived of as relations and relations of relations; Whorf's emphasis on 'reactances', the ways in which, for example, the meaning of words are 'at the mercy of the sentences and the grammatical patterns in which they occur'; Hjelmslev's use of the concepts 'process' and 'system'; as well as the refutation of such unworkable dichotomies as knowledge of the world versus knowledge of language, and even *langue* versus *parole*. Hasan puts the network on notice as a tool for fine semantic distinctions, for example in establishing the uniqueness of 'gather' by contrast with 'collect'. But at the same time, this degree of delicacy is part of a constant pressure to produce greater coherence, relevance, and historical continuity in the practice of linguists.

It is in Chapter 3 that Hasan asserts and argues for the necessity of recognizing the importance of semantic features in the realization of elements of a text's generic structure:

> I suggest that the essential attributes of 'the structurally important units' of any text type will have to be stated in semantic terms.

The identification of semantic properties is not, however, sufficient, for it is only via wording that meaning is accessible. Thus, 'the range of lexicogrammatical patterns which are capable of realizing these specific semantic properties' must also be specified. The specification of the lexicogrammatical patterns which realize semantic features, together with the use of networks at the semantic stratum, is explicated in Chapter 5 – 'Semantic networks: a tool for the analysis of meaning'. Choices at the semantic stratum, while activating choices at the lexicogrammatical stratum, are themselves activated by choices at the stratum of context. Hasan first devised semantic networks in order to relate the semantic options selected by speakers to the social situation, in particular to the social class attributes of the speakers. This research explicitly addresses the relation between language and the social system postulated by Bernstein (e.g. 1971).

Networks at the semantic stratum were originally introduced in the systemic functional model in the early seventies by Halliday (1973) and Turner (1973) for this same purpose. These networks are context-specific, i.e. they refer only to the range of semantic options available in a particular context, the regulative context. Fawcett (1980) also introduced networks at the semantic stratum which were relatively context-free. However, what seems to be lacking in Fawcett, and indeed, in Halliday and Turner, is a theory of discourse units – units of language at the semantic stratum – which may serve as the point of entry in the networks presented. Hasan's networks are not only relatively context-free; they are based on a notion of a basic constituent unit at the semantic stratum which serves as the environment for semantic choices. This unit which forms the point of entry to the semantic networks is the message.

As outlined above, under the influence of the sociological theory of Bernstein, the early seventies saw a flurry of research into the relation between language and the social attributes of speakers. Why, it may be asked, did Hasan find it necessary to re-engage with these research problems in the eighties? The answer to this question is twofold. First, Bernstein's earlier research tended to focus on lexicogrammatical features, with the exception of the work of Halliday and Turner cited above. And secondly, the data which formed the basis of Bernstein's research was restricted in that people were asked to say what they would say in a particular situation. In Hasan's research, by contrast, mothers audio-recorded themselves in everyday interaction with their preschool children. The data thus consisted of naturally occurring talk between mothers and children in the context of their daily routine interactions. These conversations are represented in Chapter 6 where Hasan is able to show how through everyday talk children are implicitly introduced to stereotypic ideas of women's work. However, she does not stop there; rather, she extends related feminist work of the early eighties, and shows how Whorf's notions of 'fashions of speaking' and of linguistic features in 'configurative rapport' are invaluable in beginning to understand how everyday talk in the home contributes to the ontogenesis of ideology. She further argues the necessity of developing accounts of the relations between linguistic and other semiotic modalities adequately to describe conditions for the development of ideological orientations in young children.

The development of orientations to ways of saying and meaning which may result in the development of variant forms of consciousness is the basis of the paper in Chapter 7 – 'Speech genre, semiotic mediation and the development of higher mental functions'. Here, her concern is to resolve some long-standing theoretical and methodological difficulties in Vygotsky's theory of development. She agrees with Vygotsky that verbal semiosis may be a necessary condition for the development of higher mental functioning; she argues, however, that it is not just any form of verbal semiosis which will produce the particular forms of that functioning in which Vygotsky and Luria were interested – for example, the ability to categorize using abstract criteria – and which are valued and rewarded by society generally. The problem, rather, is to describe the specific forms of verbal semiosis which give rise to variant functioning and, as importantly, to identify the social conditions which are the basis for the development of variant forms.

INTRODUCTION

Neo-Vygotskian scholars (e.g. Wertsch 1991) have proposed Bakhtin's concept of speech genre as an appropriate analytic tool for the description of the effects of semiotic mediation. While acknowledging that social situations are crucial to the selection and reproduction of speech genres – indeed, this insight is basic in Bernstein's theory of coding orientation – Hasan nevertheless rejects the use of Bakhtin's concept as a solution. Her most general objection is that the concepts of 'social situation' and of 'speech genre' as formulated by Bakhtin remain theoretically undeveloped and may only be used for *ad hoc* explanation. However, she points out that concepts similar to these are theoretically developed within the systemic functional model of language. She then proceeds to outline how the resources of this model may be pressed into service in order to describe semiotic mediation in situated occasions of language use with Bernstein's theory providing the sociological explanation for the development of variant forms of human consciousness.

The final paper in the collection – 'Ways of saying: ways of meaning' – sets out the basic design for a cultural theory of the future – one in which the functional description of grammar provides the core of the description of the meaning potential. Nevertheless, as the core, the grammar itself can only be described because of the systematic accounts of contexts of situation and of culture.

In the paper, Hasan establishes a basis for characterizing a culture's semiotic style – i.e. the characteristic way of meaning – and semantic style – i.e. the characteristic way of meaning verbally. She argues for a single crucial dimension – a cline of degrees of implicitness. In the graded variation between explicit and implicit, Hasan provides a bridge between statements about social structure and about meaning-making in language.

The first component of the bridge consists of the contrast between explicit and implicit in relation to grammatical systems. Hasan shows how two implicit ways of saying are characteristic of middle-class Urdu speakers: (1) the high rate of use of a special 'restricted' form of exophoric reference (i.e. reference that can only be interpreted through shared cultural experience); and (2) the rate of Subject ellipsis which is, in fact, another form of implicit device. The argument for the implicit style in middle-class Urdu is enhanced by the fact that in a number of ways, the interpretative possibilities in Urdu are apparently greater concerning Subject ellipsis and the immediate situation – exophoric Subject ellipsis need not be interpreted as *I* in statements and *you* in questions – as is the case in English. Overall then the Urdu speaker, on the basis of the grammatical system alone, would seem to run the risk of misinterpretation and/or ambiguity. This, however, is not the case because, despite the high order of implicitness, his/her role and cultural identity are more clearly defined by shared cultural experience.

The contrast with English is, in the first place, a comparison with what the system does and does not require of the middle-class English speaker. The 'logical necessity' of shared knowledge, with the 'implicit style' in Urdu, is not so apparent. The English system has fewer settings for instantial, indeterminate and restricted exophorics; the semantic style makes less use of implicit devices. And the speaker, when an implicit device is selected, can more often resolve the indeterminacy through access to the material situational setting and assumptions concerning formal Subject ellipsis – namely, that *I/you* are the relevant meanings.

The detailed examination of lexicogrammar across English and Urdu provides the basis for understanding that most difficult of cultural issues – the mutual penetration/construction of language and culture – the reciprocal development of social order and linguistic patterning. Here we see what Whorf struggled to clarify with his concept of 'fashions of speaking' and 'constellations of meanings in configurative rapport'. The bond between culture and language may be like that between Saussure's signifier and signified – a relationship in which neither member can be isolated out. But Hasan finds a way of putting the processes of meaning in the system of culture – the ensembles of semiotic values – on display. Furthermore, a number of concepts at the centre of sociological debate are brought into relief: for example, the contrast between localized (restricted) and universalistic (elaborated) codes of meaning in Bernstein's work; so too, the contrast of middle-class Urdu and middle-class English pressures to mean, a contrast between maintaining clear boundaries, on the one hand, and the need to renegotiate roles and identities, on the other. This argument about differing 'regulating principles' in the social life of two communities addresses the decades of cynicism concerning the tractability of Whorf's work – it clarifies the culture–language relationship without the assumption that the two concepts need to be isolated.

Assessing her own work, Ruqaiya Hasan would seem to have some reservation concerning the success (to date) of her programme of writing about the continuity between the living of life and the morpheme; in conversation with us she has commented: ' ... this sort of continuity is not something that I have managed to convey in any writing.'

This assessment is one with which we (the editors) respectfully beg to disagree.

C. C.
D. B.
G. W.

Notes

1 See, for example, Hasan (1987; 1989; 1991; 1992a; 1992b); Hasan and Cloran (1990).
2 Discussions of Whorf are also to be found in the papers constituting Chapters 7 and 8 in this volume.
3 Cloran (1982) has shown, in an experiment, that individuated contexts are no less resistant to individual negotiation than institutionalized contexts. Indeed, it was found that individual freedom to negotiate a context for interaction is strictly proscribed even in individuated contexts where the social distance between/among interactants is minimal.

4   Hasan's idea of GSP is originally proposed in the 1978 paper 'Text in the systemic functional model'.

References

Berger, P. and Luckmann, T. (1966) *The Social Construction of Reality: A Treatise on the Sociology of Knowledge*. New York: Doubleday.

Bernstein, B. (1971) *Class, Codes and Control*, Volume 1: *Theoretical Studies towards a Sociology of Language*. London: Routledge & Kegan Paul.

Cloran, C. (1982) *The Role of Language in Negotiating New Contexts*. Unpublished BA honours thesis, Macquarie University.

Fawcett, R. P. (1980) *Cognitive Linguistics and Social Interaction*. Heidelberg: Groos.

Halliday, M. A. K. (1973) *Explorations in the Functions of Language*. London: Edward Arnold.

Halliday, M. A. K. and Hasan, R. (1985/89) *Language, Context, and Text: Aspects of Language in a Social-Semiotic Perspective*. (1985) Deakin University, Victoria: Deakin University Press; (1989) Oxford: Oxford University Press.

Hasan, R. (1978) 'Text in the systemic functional model'. In W. Dressler (ed.) *Current Trends in Textlinguistics*. Berlin: de Gruyter.

Hasan, R. (1987) 'Reading picture reading: invisible instruction at home and in school'. In *Proceedings from the 13th Conference of the Australian Reading Association*. Sydney, July 1987.

Hasan, R. (1988) 'Language and socialisation: home and school'. In L. Gerot, J. Oldenburg and T. van Leeuwen (eds) *Language in the Process of Socialisation: Home and School*. Proceedings from the Working Conference on Language in Education, 17–21 November 1986. Macquarie University.

Hasan, R. (1989) 'Semantic variation and sociolinguistics'. *Australian Journal of Linguistics*, 9.

Hasan, R. (1991) 'Questions as a mode of learning in everyday talk'. In T. Le and M. McCausland (eds) *Language Education: Interaction and Development*. Launceston: University of Tasmania, pp. 70–119.

Hasan, R. (1992a) 'Meaning in sociolinguistics theory'. In K. Bolton and H. Kwok (eds) *Sociolinguistics Today: International Perspectives*. London: Routledge.

Hasan, R. (1992b) 'Rationality in everyday talk: from process to system'. In J. Svartvik (ed.) *Directions in Corpus Linguistics*. Berlin: de Gruyter.

Hasan, R. with Cloran, C. (1990) 'A sociolinguistic interpretation of everyday talk between mothers and children'. In J. Gibbons, M. A. K. Halliday and H. Nichols (eds) *Learning, Keeping and Using Language* Volume I: *Selected Papers from the 8th World Congress of Applied Linguistics*, Sydney, 16–21 August 1987. Amsterdam: John Benjamins.

Lucy, J. A. (1985) 'Whorf's view of the linguistic mediation of thought'. In E. Mertz and R. J. Parmentier (eds) *Semiotic Mediation: Sociocultural and Psychological Perspectives*. Orlando: Academic Press.

Lucy, J. A. and Wertsch, J. V. (1987) 'Vygotsky and Whorf: a comparative analysis'. In M. Hickmann (ed.) *Social and Functional Approaches to Language and Thought*. Orlando: Academic Press.

Turner, G. (1973) 'Social class and children's language of control at age five and age seven'. In B. Bernstein (ed.) *Class, Codes, and Control*, Volume II: *Applied Studies towards a Sociology of Language*. London: Routledge & Kegan Paul, pp. 135–201.

Wertsch, J. V. (1991) *Voices of the Mind: A Sociocultural Approach to Mediated Action.* Cambridge, Mass.: Harvard University Press.

Whorf, B. L. (1956) *Language, Thought and Reality* (J. B. Carroll, ed.). Cambridge, Mass.: MIT Press.

Part One: Text and Context

1 What kind of resource is language?

It seems to me that there are some advantages in stating the title as I have done – in the form of a question. Of course, we all know that this is not a genuine question – just one of those tainted speech acts we are given to producing in everyday life. Thus, this speaker would not like the hearer(s) to provide an answer. In fact, if someone now started answering this question, I would be more than surprised; I would feel deprived. After all I have come here, prepared in my own humble way, to say something about what kind of resource I think language is. Nor do I think that by raising a question, I have run an enormous risk, since, being familiar with conventions of behaviour at conferences, I feel justified in my belief that no one is going to steal my turn. But I realize – with hindsight, to be frank – that there were good reasons for presenting the title as a question, rather than as a description. A descriptive title might have been 'The kind of resource that language is'. But that sounds altogether too final. I do not wish to take it upon myself to *pronounce* upon *the* kind of resource that language is. I simply wish to present an opinion – what *I* think is a possible answer to this question. Opinions are open to debate; they initiate a conversation in a manner that pronouncements may not. Naturally I do not wish to imply that the opinions I am about to offer are entirely my own. I am indebted to many scholars from whose work I have derived inspiration. It would be too tedious to mention all these names since the list is long, except for one – Michael Halliday – simply for the reason that he, if I am not mistaken, is the originator of the expression 'Language as a resource' (Halliday 1974).

Let me now turn to the question that I have posed myself: what kind of resource is language? One way of approaching this question might be to try to enumerate the many ways in which language plays a crucial role in the life of a community – the uses to which we put language, from the humble everyday activities such as those of greeting friends, or entering into conversations motivated solely by 'sociability' (Goffman 1981), to those guided by a distinct purpose – be it that of buying a newspaper or buying petrol or the more awesome one of being interviewed for a job or a still more awesome one of educating the young – there is nowhere that language does not come in. In fact, it is not possible to present an exhaustive list of the range of uses for which we employ language. This is not a discovery made by linguists the other day – it is the common-sense perspective shared by most members of a community, who have had the occasion – for some reason or other – consciously to think about it. I say 'for some reason or other *consciously* to think about it' simply because the ubiquity of language is such that we go about the business of living, making use of it and taking it for granted in much the same way as we take it for granted that eyes are for seeing and ears are for hearing. As the great Danish linguist, Hjelmslev, remarked

> It is in the nature of language to be overlooked – to be a means and not an end. (Hjelmslev 1961)

I mention this fairly obvious sense of the phrase 'language as a resource' simply as my way into asking some other questions. For example: Why is it possible for language to function as a means? How is it that language constructs an empire to which, virtually, no limits can be set? I am suggesting there is a chance we might understand better what kind of resource language is by examining these questions rather than by the simple affirmation of the ubiquity of language. But, of course, to do justice to these questions, one must examine many aspects of language. That could take weeks, if not longer. So what I propose to do is to rush in where angels might fear to tread. Thus, I will declare that the reason language can be means to so many ends is because the ends were created largely by language. I am saying no more and no less than that a language is a shaper of reality for those who use it. I am aware that a claim of this kind, generally, does not go down well; at the least it engenders scepticism. However, I intend to stay with this claim, for I know of no better hypothesis for answering the questions I have just raised. Still, and particularly remembering the fate of Whorf, it appears necessary to expand on the claim that language is a shaper of reality.

The greatest problem that has arisen in regard to this claim derives from an assumption which I do not share – namely that there is one ultimate Reality, written with a capital R – a view which makes one cry out, in the words of Royce (1964) who expresses the attitude as follows:

> If you cannot convince me that there is some kind of knowable ultimate reality, or if you cannot convince me that there are certain absolute values by which I can live my life, I shall commit psychological suicide. Either convince me that there is 'one truth' or one right way of doing things, or I shall conclude that everything is meaningless and I will not try any more. (4)

The quest for ultimate reality rests upon assumptions about both the nature of the universe and the nature of the human mind, whereby it is assumed that there is one immutable ultimate reality and that human minds are

WHAT KIND OF RESOURCE IS LANGUAGE? 15

innately fashioned to the perception of that reality. To use David Butt's phrase (1983), this is the hypothesis of the 'mirrorites'.

The rise of science and technology has created the illusion that such ultimate reality actually exists; and the reason we are being held back in our goal of discovering it, is simply because we are bad behaviourists, or incurable empiricists – or whatever might be the academic term of abuse current at the time. To such an attitude, the thought is not daunting that the last century's cherished beliefs turn into this century's lamentable superstitions. Tracing the success of modern science to Galileo, Rorty (1981) chides 'modern philosophy' as follows:

> The tradition we call 'modern philosophy' asked itself 'How is it that science has had so much success? What is the secret of this success?' The various bad answers to these bad questions have been variations on a single charming but uncashable metaphor: namely, the new science discovered the language which nature itself uses. When Galileo said that the Book of Nature was written in the language of mathematics, he meant his new reductionistic, mathematical vocabulary didn't just *happen* to work, but that it worked *because* that was the way things *really* were. He meant that the vocabulary worked because it fitted the universe as a key fits a lock. (191–192)

Rorty argues that such bad answers to bad questions led to – and I use his phrase – 'the neurotic Cartesian quest for certainty' (Rorty 1979, 161), to the triumph of 'pure reason' and to conceptions of the 'natural language of the mind'. He suggests that, instead of giving these answers

> We shall just say that Galileo had a good idea and Aristotle a less good idea; Galileo was using som terminology which helped, and Aristotle wasn't. Galileo's terminology was the *only* 'secret' he had – he didn't pick that terminology because it was 'clear' or 'natural' or 'simple', or in line with the categories of the pure understanding. He just lucked it. (193)

This view is highly reminiscent of Whorf, who raised the question:

> Are our concepts of 'time', 'space', and 'matter' given in substantially the same form by experience to all men, or are they in part conditioned by the structure of particular languages? (Whorf 1941, 138)

Whorf suggested that when we find no similarity in our concepts of time, space and matter, it is wrong to lay the blame, as some have done, on the slowness of our intuitions; or to say, as some have said, that we are lacking in clarity of thought or in rationality. These explanations do not account for observed phenomena. He suggests that

> The right answer is: Newtonian space, time and matter are no intuitions. They are recepts from culture. That is where Newton got them. (153)

Whorf maintained:

> all observers are not led by the same physical evidence to the same picture of the universe, unless their linguistic backgrounds are similar or can in some way be calibrated (1940, 214)

I would quibble with Whorf here only with regard to the phrase 'the same physical evidence'. If your view of reality is physicalistic, it opens the door to the ultimate goal of the *discovery* of this same physical universe. But as I shall argue later, physical universe, *per se*, is unknowable; only the socially constructed reality has a chance of getting known. Nor is it helpful to attempt to salvage the situation, by postponing the attainment of Ultimate Reality to a distant future as Peirce (1878) seems to, when he says:

> Finally, as what anything really is, is what it may finally come to be known to be in the ideal state of complete information, so that reality depends on the ultimate decision of the community. (189)

I am no philosopher; but from the point of view of a layman, this could be interpreted in one of two ways. First, that when all members of a community believe a thing to be so, then that thing is 'the truth', 'the reality', for that community. In which case, it would seem, we are saying no more than what Whorf said when he talked about our being 'parties to an agreement' (Whorf 1941). The second interpretation would be in line with the Cartesian argument that rationality will ultimately win; that since, as Peirce pointed out, 'our efforts are self-corrective' (Weiss 1952, 174) we would eventually end up seeing Nature as it wants to be seen. I have considerable difficulty with this interpretation, for it assumes not only that there will be a time when we shall know all that there is to know, but also that at the same time we shall know that we know all that there is to know. Such a hope, it seems to me, replaces the hope of that 'millennium' which the weakening of religious faith has taken away. As rigorous as the methods of science are said to be, the history of science, even in that corner of the world whose ideology is now the most dominant – namely, the Western culture – does not appear to agree with this view. Newton was as certain of his facts as Einstein; and, perhaps, a future Einstein would be as certain of *his* facts as Newton or Einstein. I would be in agreement with Rorty (1980) that to suggest that there can be an end of enquiry is a reactionary move, reminiscent of the role of the Church in the matter of Galileo.

But once the notion of ultimate reality is taken away, what remains? What remains is not a void, but an affirmation that reality is relative – it is relative to time, to place and above all to people. The physical universe in which people live may be independent of its inhabitants, but the picture of it that communities operate with is as much an artefact as a work of fiction. To maintain effect, fiction demands a suspension of disbelief. My hypothesis is that to say that language is a shaper of reality is to say that language is instrumental in sustaining this suspension of disbelief.

Whenever the question of language in relation to reality has been raised, there have been cries of despair. To understand some of the causes of this despair, I would recommend Fishman's (1960) exegesis of the Whorfian hypothesis. I will add briefly that amongst the linguists of this century Whorf was perhaps the most resolute attacker of the 'ethnocentricity' through which the findings of the Western cultures could be presented as the only ultimate infallible truths. 'We do not know', he said, 'that civilization is synonymous with rationality' (1956, 81). Since I consider Whorf one of the major thinkers on the subject of the relationship of language to reality, I will spend some time in the discussion of how Whorf's sayings have been interpreted. I hope that in the course of doing this, I shall also have pointed out some of the ways in which such a relationship should not be interpreted.

Whorf has often been understood as literally saying that language determines the perception of reality. It is quite likely that Whorf has actually used the phrase 'perception of reality'. But the spirit of Whorf's writing is quite opposed to the way in which the phrase has been interpreted by even such eminent scholars as Brown and Lenneberg (1954) or Lenneberg (1964), who read it as a term synonymous with 'sense perception through the eye'. They proceed then to check whether or not the speakers of two distinct languages with differing colour terminologies would 'perceive' colours differently. That this interpretation of the Whorfian phrase is not coherent with the structure of his argument does not appear to worry them. Lenneberg, moreover, comes to the conclusion that

> Since the use of words is a creative process, the static reference relationships such as ... are recorded in a dictionary are of no great consequence for the actual use of words. However, the differences between languages that impressed Whorf so much are entirely restricted to these static aspects. (1975, 554)

He goes on to add that

> it is not appropriate to use the vocabulary meanings as the basis for an estimation of cognitive capacities. (1975, 555)

The irony here is that none of this has much to do with Whorf, who would have agreed largely with Lenneberg on the question of vocabulary. Whorf warned that

> the error made by most people who attempt to deal with ... social questions of language (is that) they naively suppose that speech is nothing but a piling up of lexations, and that this is all one needs in order to do any and every kind of rational thinking; the far more important thought materials provided by structure and configurative rapport are beyond their horizons. (1956, 83)

And almost as if anticipating the kind of misinterpretation to which he was to be subjected, for claiming that

> Languages differ not only in how they build their sentences but also in how they break down nature to secure the elements to put in those sentences. (1941, 240)

He went on to comment on the linguistic naïveté of logicians who

> tend to pick out tables and chairs and apples on tables as test objects to demonstrate the object-like nature of reality and its one-to-one correspondence with logic. (1941, 240)

It may be true that vocabulary from the domain of physical experience is easily manipulable for the type of laboratory experiments Lenneberg and Brown had designed, but it remains to be demonstrated that it was differences of this kind 'that impressed Whorf so much'. It is this mode of interpreting Whorf that Hoijer (1954) described as the 'vulgarization of the Whorfian hypothesis'.

What this discussion shows is that naïve arguments about cultural preoccupations on the basis of a handful of vocabulary relating to the domain of physical experience can neither confirm nor disprove the claim about language as a shaper of reality (Hasan 1975; 1978). Moreover, it highlights *that* conception of reality – and cognition – wherein physicalistic elements are imbued with a significance which is rarely, if ever, accorded to social phenomena. The physical reality of each one of my listeners is a fact that transcends language, but my view of you as an audience is a different matter altogether. This latter presupposes a certain kind of social practice, which without language could not easily have come about.

Cole and Scribner (1974), again discounting 'Whorf's thesis' – which, of course, is not his thesis as I have just argued – deny that the 'absence or presence of a lexical distinction can be taken as an indicator of a corresponding perceptual or conceptual distinction'. Now, Whorf was inevitably interested in the relation between thought and language; as Fawcett (1983) remarked, Whorf believed that semiotic systems were essential to thinking. Turning to Whorf's conception of the relationship of language to thinking, Cole and Scribner have this to say:

> The reasoning and thinking processes of different people in different cultures do not differ ... *just* their values, beliefs, and ways of classifying differ.
> (Cole and Gay 1972; quoted in Cole and Scribner 1974, 25)

Their main thesis, then, is that thought processes are universal; 'the basic difference is in the material for thought' (1974, 26). But in expressing their position thus, they seem to me to act as an excellent example of precisely that quality of Western intellect which Whorf so brilliantly related to 'an aggregate of phenomena' in standard Average European languages. He argued that the overall design of these languages is admirably suited to the creation of an illusion – or a theoretical fiction, if you prefer – whereby it is possible to think of form without content, and content without form, thought process without thought material and thought material without thought process. It is, indeed, hard to imagine how 'thought process', as such, could ever be examined, without involving an examination of 'thought content' as well. Nor is it easy to see why the difference between values, beliefs and classification can be shrugged off into insignificance as '*just* values, beliefs and ways of classifying' (my emphasis), as if *that* is not as important as the process itself! Here is Whorf's own account of the assumptions about language and thought, underlying the approach exemplified by Cole and Scribner:

> According to natural logic, the fact that every person has talked fluently since infancy makes every man his own authority on the process by which he formulates and communicates. He has merely to consult a common substratum of logic which he and everyone else are supposed to possess. Natural logic says that talking is merely an incidental process concerned strictly with communication, not with formulation of ideas. Talking ... is supposed only to 'express' what is essentially already formulated ... Formulation is an independent process, called thought or thinking and is supposed to be largely indifferent to the nature of particular languages. Languages have grammars which are assumed to be merely norms of conventional and social correctness, but the use of language is supposed to be guided ... by correct, rational or intelligent thinking.
> Thought, in this view, does not depend on grammar but on laws of logic and reason which are supposed to be the same for all observers of the universe – to represent a rationale in the universe that can be found independently by all intelligent observers. (1940a, 207–208)

Whorf continues his argument:

> Natural logic contains two fallacies. First, it does not see that the phenomena of language are to its own speakers largely of a background character and so are outside the critical consciousness and control of the speaker who is expounding natural logic. Hence, when anyone as a natural logician, is talking about reason, logic, and the laws of correct thinking, he is apt to be simply marching in step with purely grammatical facts that have somewhat of a background character in his own language ... Second, natural logic confuses agreement about subject matter, attained through use of language, with knowledge of the linguistic process by which agreement is attained: i.e. with the province of the despised (...) grammarian. Two fluent speakers reach a point of assent ... Because they thus understand each other ... they think ... that it is simply a matter of choosing words to express thoughts ... The amazingly complex system of linguistic patterns and classifications ... is all background ... (211) (*But*) ... the background phenomena ... are involved in all our foreground activities of talking and of reaching agreement, in all reasoning and arguing of cases, in all law, arbitration, conciliation, contracts, treaties, public opinion, weighing of scientific theories, formulation of scientific results. Whenever agreement or assent is arrived at in human affairs, THIS AGREEMENT IS REACHED BY LINGUISTIC PROCESSES, OR ELSE IT IS NOT REACHED. (1940a, 212, original emphasis)

I have quoted Whorf at enormous length for three reasons. First, it articulates an emphatic rejection of the notion that the lexicogrammatical categories of language are receptacles into which are poured intentions, meanings and values. As for Halliday, so for Whorf, the system of language is a meaning potential; it is not simply, to use Hjelmslev's terminology, the 'plane of expression', with the 'plane of content', as an external reality. Fawcett (1983) talks about the inadequacies of the Chomskian conception of language. There is not enough time to develop the theme that these inadequacies arise quite inevitably from pursuing the Cartesian notion of Rational Man, even if Aarsleff (1970) is right in claiming that Chomsky is guilty of the misinterpretation of Western intellectual history. When we take Reason as God-given, mirroring Nature, and think of the language system – not just the ability to learn language but the system itself – as innate, inevitably, the categories of language appear to be just a formalism; the profundity of Man is seen as a function of his Natural Rationality, the language as simply its expression.

Secondly, and in sharp contrast to the latter position which I have just outlined, the extract denies the possibility of establishing forms of reasoning in the absence of language. Thus, if we ever came across a human organism – not a *person*, note, because persons are created through semiosis – lacking totally any form of language, it would not be possible for us to say anything about her/his forms of reasoning. Reasoning man is talking man; such a person is a being who has participated in semiosis. As Whorf said ' "Talk" OUGHT TO BE a more dignified and noble term than "think" ' (1940b, 220). Thirdly, and last, this discussion has brought my argument full circle to the point where the claim is being reiterated that language is instrumental in *sustaining the suspension of disbelief with regard to the artefact of constructed reality*. It is perhaps obvious that these three points are closely related to each other. More specifically, I would argue that the first point about the system of language as meaning potential is a necessary postulate for arguing the relationship of language to forms of reasoning and for its ability to operate as an instrument in the suspension of disbelief. I will, therefore, look at the first point a little more closely.

In his *Philosophical Investigations*, Wittgenstein (1958) comments

> When we say: 'Every word in language signifies something' we have so far said nothing whatever. (7^e.13).

For, this view of meaning can very easily be reduced to 'naming'. A natural language is not simply a 'naming-game'. If it were the idea that language simply expresses or names categories of content would be justified. In that case, categories of content would be established totally in independence from language, as the human body exists independent of its clothes. I am aware that even those scholars who reject the naming theory find the denial of the physical reality of existents worrisome. My own approach to this problem is to refuse to buy into it. To ask if we would or would not see a tree as a tree and a mountain as a mountain, even in the absence of language, is to raise what Rorty would describe as 'bad questions'; and we should avoid the temptation of giving bad answers. It is important to recognize that, in the nature of things, we can never answer such questions with any certainty; none of us knows a world without any language. It is doubtful if we shall ever find out how the world of physical reality appeared to the earliest group of *homo sapiens* as it struggled to create the various systems of semiosis.

Rather than speculate about the 'real' nature of physical reality as it must appear to a mind uninformed by semiosis and hence unevolved by culture, it seems far more helpful to say that confronted with the world – both the world outside and the one inside the organism – human beings proceeded to make sense of these phenomena; they developed means of communicating about these phenomena. It is doubtful if to do this they only used the modality of language. Recent work in developmental linguistics points more and more to the continuities between the various semiotic systems (Halliday 1975; Shotter 1978; Newson 1978; Trevarthen and Hubley 1978; and many others). Nor can it be said that communication developed in independence from sense perception. But the acknowledgement, that there exists sense perception, does not necessarily lead to the view that language 'mirrors' this sensed reality. Let me develop this point, which is an important one.

Sense data, by its very nature, is private. Consider that the question: 'Is your pain as bad as mine?', in that form, is not susceptible to an answer, except with a 'Well, I don't know how bad your pain is!', which amounts to saying that sensation is private. The various semiotic systems enable us to 'talk' about our experience of ourselves, our fellow beings and our environment. From this point of view, the expressions of language are *not* vocal replications of that which the senses experience. In fact we do not know what it would mean to say that the language sign replicates or presents an exact correspondence to the world, thus sensed. Instead all we can claim is that linguistic signs function as a necessary step to the creation of intersubjectivity.

With regard to intersubjectivity, I wish to raise two related points. One of these will take me directly to Saussure and Hjelmslev, the other to Halliday. In the first place it is a necessary condition of any system capable of creating intersubjectivity that it should possess the attribute of what Berger and Luckman call 'detachability' (Berger and Luckman 1966, 51). What I understand by this term as it would apply to language is that the linguistic sign does not name raw experience, irrespective of how we define that term. Any given sign is distanced from raw experience, to the extent that it must apply, and is so applied, by the members of the community, to distinct instances of a class of 'raw experiences' each of which is, in some sense, non-identical with the others. When we create the correspondence theory of meaning, we create a fiction that is essentially circular; all we can show is that the categories of language correspond to that which is created by language. It is for this reason that Saussure, and following him Hjelmslev, maintained that raw reality is unknowable. Hjelmslev, reasoning very closely, argued that language *forms* meanings; meanings are not to be found lying around, like apples on tables. Both the expression and the content of the signs in the system of language are already abstractions; they are not coextensive with certain classes of humanly producible sounds or with what 'is in the world'.

The notion of 'truth', in the sense of correspondence with raw reality is alien to language. In fact, whatever aspect of raw reality has not been articulated semiotically remains unknown. This is the reason for suggesting that reality is not *found* but *shaped*, not *mirrored* but *constructed*. This construction is largely an artefact of the verbal sign system. Perhaps there are sayable things, none of which is being said in any language anywhere; but, if so, there is no way in which we could come to talk about them except to the extent that the system of language itself may be a resource in enquiry. As F. P. Ramsey said in response to Wittgenstein: 'What we can't say, we can't say; and we can't whistle it either' (quoted in Skinner 1981). I would go one step further and say that one can't even know that one can't say it, because 'it' is not '*it*' yet; in order to attain 'it-ness' it stands in need of linguistic articulation. *The ability of language to function as a means to so many ends arises from the fact that, for the most part, it is used to deal only with what it, itself, has created.*

This potential of language to give satisfaction in all situations is made possible, as Hjelmslev remarked, by the fact that language is not a *collection* of expressions, but a *system* of signs, such that each sign is related to others, and precisely by virtue of these relations – the configurations and the rapports – each sign is the union of expression and content. The fact must also be recognized that the sign system, as a system, possesses certain 'structural peculiarities', which permit

> the unlimited possibility of forming signs and the very free rules for forming units of greater extension. ... (This) makes it possible for a language to allow false, inconsistent, imprecise, ugly and unethical formulations as well as true, consistent, precise, beautiful and ethical formulations. The grammatical rules of language are free of any scale of values, logical, aesthetic or ethical; and, in general, language is independent of any specific purpose. (1961, 109–110)

Thus I am arguing that it is a gross misunderstanding of the nature of language to think of the sign simply as expression; the sign is a composite of meaning *and* expression.

The second point that arises from a consideration of intersubjectivity is what I would like to describe as the notion of 'validation'. Language grows not in isolation – not intra-organically, but inter-organically, to use Halliday's terms. This view entails the concept of validation. Shaped reality is validated reality; it is that which gets comprehended by the listeners and by doing so, achieves validation. Whatever the nature of my experience – and it is bound to be in some respects unique to me – only that part of it is validated which is expressible and is, thus, seen as expressed. I believe that it is this idea of validation that George Herbert Mead (1910, 23) talks about as follows:

> It is only through the response that consciousness of meaning appears, a response which involves the consciousness of *another self* as the presupposition of the meaning in *one's own attitude.*

Unless the formed meanings are thus validated through the practices of other members of the community, there would be no possibility for the creation of intersubjectivity. For example, what passes as 'question' could not pass as 'question' unless its question-ness has been validated by the characteristic provision of answers; what passes as 'honesty' could not pass as 'honesty' unless it were recognized as 'honesty' by other members of the community. The selfsame pattern of behaviour could conceivably pass as 'stupidity' in another place, at another time, by another community; and by the same token, by different subcommunities at the same time, in the same place. The notion of validation is essential to the success of language in operating as an instrument for the suspension of disbelief. Beliefs are not personal in origin; they have to be socially legitimated. The pre-condition for this legitimation is the concept of validation. When I say: 'I am very tired', and my saying is validated by others in treating me as a person who is very tired, then my use of that statement to describe that condition is validated. When a community has validated, through its linguistic practices, the belief that the earth is flat, then for that community the earth is flat. They will go to enormous lengths to retain that belief, not because it is false and they are obstinate and stupid, but because, by their lights, it is *the* truth. This suspension of disbelief towards the linguistically shaped reality is capable of being disturbed only to the extent that within the language also lies the possibility of raising questions, of constructing arguments, of demanding proofs. For today's truths to turn into tomorrow's untruths, there has to be conversation. From the point of view of validation, the *community* is the central fact.

Once we have reached this point, we are forced to recognize the very fundamental role that the *use* of language plays in the creation, maintenance and change of the *system* of language. No matter how anthropomorphically I may talk of the language system, the fact remains that neither could the system create itself, nor could it evolve intra-organically. On the one hand, the possibility of communication denies the possibility of such solipsistic origins for language; on the other hand, it demands both detachability and validation, without which communication could not take place. But the recognition of the latter two properties as central to the linguistic sign takes us back to the obvious answers with which I started. This is because there is no special *forum* for the creation and evolution of the system of language. It has got created – and has evolved over the period of human history – simply by the fact that it has been pressed into service in the interests of doing 'other things' – things such as greeting, conversing, buying, interviewing, educating and a host of others. It would be a tautology to say that as the use of language extends, so the domain of 'formed meanings' extends; for, from the point of view I have been presenting, the two expressions mean one and the same thing. It is in this manner that I interpret Halliday's saying that

> The nature of language is closely related to the demands that we make on it, the functions it has to serve. (1970, 141)

Language is able to cope with our demands because it is in meeting these demands that its origin is rooted; it is able to give satisfaction in all situations because it is largely by and with language that these situations were created in the first place. We can see this principle at work clearly in the development of communication in children. Children do not first 'acquire' language and then use it; there is a dialectic between the process, i.e. use, and the system whereby the successful acts of communication beget the *potential* for communicating. Somewhere in the early stage, which Trevarthen (1979) describes as 'primary intersubjectivity', the baby must recognize that interaction with the other is a possibility; and that this interaction can take specific forms, such as smiles, gurgles, eye contact and bodily movements. It is hard to imagine that these specific forms of behaviour could be associated with communication by a baby in the absence of the care-giver's response. With the onset of 'secondary intersubjectivity' (Trevarthen and Hubley 1978) which coincides with the emergence of protolanguage, communication really takes off. But because of the internal structure of protolanguage which differs qualitatively from adult language (Halliday 1975), the child's meanings cannot be viewed as 'formed content'. That is why the care-giver's interpretation of the protolingual baby must rely on situational clues, a point to which Malinowski (1923), de Laguna (1927), Halliday (1975), Bruner (1978) and others have drawn attention. 'Formed content' – the kind of meaning that is specific to natural human languages – appears only with the emergence of adult language, since it is at that time that the structure of the system itself evolves to develop a means whereby 'formed content' becomes possible, namely through the emergence of the lexicogrammatical level. The systematic relations of the signs are essential to their status as signs.

Two remarks appear pertinent here. First, from the developmental point of view there is a continuity in communication as communication, especially if we see communication as meaningful behaviour. This meaningful behaviour must, in some sense, be related to the communicator's needs. In saying this, I am very conscious of the fact that 'need' is a term frowned upon in developmental linguistics, where it has been criticized vigorously by, for example, Lenneberg (1964). But if we take into account Lenneberg's assumptions about the nature of language, this would explain the basis of his criticism. To recognize needs as the mainspring of language and communication is to recognize that the system for communication has a teleological origin. If our basic postulate is that language is God-given and is innate, we cannot entertain the hypothesis that its emergence might arise simply as a response to human needs. I have argued, by contrast, for a conception of language as rooted in community and communication, a hypothesis which is a necessary step in accounting for the ubiquity of language. But if it is accepted that language is used as means to ends, it seems difficult to deny its teleological aspect. Thus my argument is that language could not develop as a means to the many varied ends unless its origin were rooted in the satisfaction of the user's needs. The continuity in the child's communication can be seen as a development and a refinement of the means whereby the child's needs can be attained. All we need is a wider, more socially viable concept of need than in Lenneberg (1964), where it gets restricted to a bottle of milk or a cookie. So, the first point I am making is that both 'purpose' and a society where purposes get recognized are essential to the growth of language.

At the same time – and this is the second point – it is important to focus on the role of the adult in these early processes. This role can be seen as that of providing 'validation'. We have no definite way of knowing exactly what it is that the infant is attempting to communicate. It is just possible that there are certain bits of putative information, which are never validated by the care-giver. From this point of view the expansions that a care-giver returns to the immature expressions of the child could be as much a limiting of his universe as an enabling of the emergence of his social self. The word *socialization* is the learned name for the practices whereby a novice is brought to share the shaped reality; and for the most part it is reality shaped by the systematic operation of language. Minds are created by brainwashing. If children grow up believing the beliefs of their speech community, this is not because such beliefs are transcendentally available to all of us as rational beings – it is because these beliefs are enshrined in the language of their community. So on the one hand I am arguing that language is purpose-free *qua* meaning potential (cf. p. 23), while on the other hand I am suggesting that the development and attainment of a meaning potential for an individual can only come about through the continued and extended use of the resources already at that individual's command, which implies orientation to purpose.

It has become a commonplace of developmental linguistics to claim that by their fourth year, children have acquired a mastery of their mother tongue. But if so, the phrase *mastery of mother tongue* stands in need of close scrutiny. Let me share with you my own experience here. For the last few years I have run a course under the label of *Language and the Child*, where the students have the option of submitting a mini-research which calls for the examination of language data collected from children engaged in the performance of some naturalistic task. I have learned much from the data collected by my students. A pertinent set of researches to mention here is one that requires the student to compare the 7-year-olds' 'mastery of mother tongue' in describing their participation in such events as a holiday or a visit to the zoo, or a trip into the city, and the same child's description of the making of, say, a model, to someone who was not present at the time the model was made. The data from this set of researches is an eye-opener.

The child who is voluble and almost unstoppable in describing the former, produces language in the latter case that is halting; unfinished structures, even 'ungrammatical sentences' occur all over the place. And the greatest differences are to be found in the manifestation of the textual function, ranging from awkward schematic structure to the disruption of cohesive ties. To my mind, there cannot be clearer evidence for the hypothesis that the growth of language in an individual is the function of that individual's engagement in a varied set of activities, calling for the use of language. You can only learn how to mean, by attempting to mean. There is a continued dialectic between the process – the use of the meaning potential – and the system – the community's or the individual's meaning potential, as such, at any given point in time.

This takes me to the final phase of my discourse. I claimed earlier that if the child grows up believing the beliefs of his speech community, this is because, as Whorf said, these beliefs are enshrined in the language of his community. To learn language is to learn to suspend disbelief with regard to these beliefs; to behave as if these beliefs have *sui generis* status. In the words of Douglas:

> The forms of knowledge most taken for granted in any group come to be seen as absolute – as independent of the knowing minds, as out there.(1971, 27)

But what is the paradigm environment in which such knowledge and belief become the growing child's reality? Clearly not a situation of direct debate on the matter. As Halliday points out:

> nobody teaches him [the child] the principles on which social groups are organized, or their systems of beliefs, nor would he understand it if they tried. It happens indirectly through the accumulated experience of numerous small events, insignificant in themselves, in which his behaviour is guided and controlled and in the course of which he contracts and develops personal relationships of all kinds ... The striking fact is that it is the most ordinary everyday uses of language, with parents, brothers and sisters, neighbourhood children, in the home, in the street and the park, in the shops and the trains, and the buses, that serve to transmit, to the child, the essential qualities of the society and the nature of social being. (1974, 4)

It seems then that the paradigm environment both for learning language and for learning through language, for the child, is the environment of casual conversation. So I will now turn my attention to some cases of mother–child talk to provide some indication of how individuals' 'worlds' are created, how reality is spun out of language, because *that* reality is already the domain of language.

First, the cases where the object of enquiry is the linguistic sign itself. I will present three cases. Each differs from the others in some respects, while each is alike in that the attention is focused on some linguistic sign.

WHAT KIND OF RESOURCE IS LANGUAGE? 27

Case 1: Kelly and mother are busy getting ready to cook corn bread. The incessant talk is about getting ingredients and utensils, and about measuring and mixing and chopping. Kelly is 3 years 7 months old.

M: Now I'll cut up the onions and capsicums.
And I'll get you to grease the dish.
K: What's grease?
M: I'll put a little bit of oil in that dish.
K: Mm.
M: And then I want you to rub it around with your fingers ...
K: Mm.
M: All over the dish ...
Only on the inside.
That's right ... Lovely.
Yeah, that's right. With the tips of your fingers.
And do it all down the sides as well.
And get it all over there.

This was a direct enquiry: what's grease? and was tied to a specific activity. The mother's explanation takes these facts into account. Unlike the *Oxford Learner's Dictionary*, which states the following definition

vt put or rub grease on or in (especially parts of a machine)

the mother ties her answer to the specific activity. Kelly has had her first 'go' at the validation of the sign 'grease' – she will need many more to arrive where her mother is.

Case 2: Carol, 3 years 6 months old, and mother are getting together their snack to take it outside in the garden; Annie, Carol's younger sister, is also included in the plan, but is too young to assist. The mother has announced and Carol has agreed tacitly that they are 'about to get morning tea and take it outside'.

M: I'll put the grapes in a bowl and then everybody can share those.
C: Mum will you share those?
M: Yes I will ...
C: Mum will Annie share those?
M: Hope so.
C: Will I share them?
M: Hope so ...

It seems to me that the point of this interaction for Carol is to get the linguistic signs *everybody* and *share* straight. Just what is *everybody*? But Carol's enquiry is indirect. Does sharing mean that everyone gets to have a go? Carol's enquiry is again indirect. But in asking these questions Carol displays a fairly mature understanding of the nature of meaning in language. Her hidden assumption is that the answers to her questions will provide a satisfactory account of the course of conduct that would arise if 'everybody' is 'everybody' and 'to share' is 'to share' as we understand these words. And note that she does not extend her enquiry about participants beyond the closed set that is pertinent to the planned sharing. And why should she? After all, she is not in the business of writing a paper on quantifiers!

Case 3: Nigel and mother are playing with Nigel's trains. Nigel is at this time 3 years 8 months old. The talk moves back and forth from the toy trains on the board to Revd Awdry's engines. Revd Awdry has written a series of stories about the railway in which each of the engines is a character perhaps larger than life, capable of jealousies, intrigues, enmities and friendships. Suddenly Nigel turns to mother with a serious expression:

N: What's enemy, Mummy?
M: (somewhat taken off guard) oh – um – enemy, well enemy is someone you think might hurt you. [A pause follows this response, and then Nigel pronounces with great conviction.]
N: But stone is not enemy.
M: No stone is not enemy though it can hurt you.

This example is particularly interesting. It shows quite clearly a quality that Carol's questions had also contained – namely that to say that something is a linguistic sign is to grant it a set of implicational relations. In fact, this is part of what it means to say that language is a sign system – not a collection of words, 'not a piling up of lexation'. Nigel's comment to mother's response shows an awareness acquired – almost on the spot – of the rapport between *stone, enemy* and *hurt*. You must guard against stones and enemies because both can hurt. None the less enemies are different; they don't just *happen* to hurt you – they *mean* to hurt you; they are intentional beings like yourself. And yet this is not the view that the traditional Azande of Africa would necessarily share (Evans-Pritchard 1973). There, a stone does not just happen to hurt you, it *means* to hurt you. And if you want proof, that *too* can be supplied. After all, the stone was always there; if its being there was sufficient cause for its ability to hurt, why did it do it on one particular occasion and not on the others? The conclusion is arrived at almost inevitably: it is acting as an accomplice in the machinations of a malefactor.

This takes me to the larger example presented below.

224–5	C:	Mum do pussy-cats die when people die? ...
226	M:	Do pussy-cats what, love?
227	C:	Die when people die?
228–9	M:	Well pussy-cats die when their time comes. ...
230		Everything dies, one day.
231	C:	Do dogs do they one day?
232	M:	Do what?
233	C:	Do dogs die one day when ...
234	M:	Yes dogs die, too. ...
235	C:	Do fruit die?

WHAT KIND OF RESOURCE IS LANGUAGE?

236–7	M:	Fruit dies, yes. In a different sort of way.
238	C:	How?
239	M:	Well, see how the fruit up there on the tree's green?
240	C:	Mm.
241	M:	See, how down here, it's gone all yellow and squashy and horrible?
242	C:	Aa.
243	M:	That means it's died, it's …
244–5		Well, we don't call it, we don't *say* it's died, we say it's gone bad.
246	C:	Mummy
247	M:	Mm …
248–50	C:	Mum, see where the persimmons have dropped off the tree … cos um cos they're sick, and they've got germs.
251	M:	Yes, that's right.
252–3	C:	They're sick and they've got germs.
254	M:	Mm.

I will leave it to you to decide whether this discussion between Carol and her mother is about language or about facts. Indeed, I find it difficult to draw a line between the two; the arguments that I have presented point to an inextricable mingling of the two. Let me set the scene for this larger example. It follows as a distant sequence of Case 2. Mother, Annie and Carol are *now* in the garden eating their snack. Suddenly Carol notices a cat that has wandered into their garden:

| 185 | C: | Oh, a pussy-cat! |
| 186 | M: | It's up in the tree, isn't it? |

There ensues a discussion on whether people mind pussy-cats in their houses, whether cats are shy like birds or whether they are different. Mother and child turn to their snack when Carol notices that the cat has disappeared as silently as it had arrived. Some more discussion of cats' desirability follows. Carol says:

| 220–1 | C: | But sometimes when pussy-cat goes into people's garden, some people say 'Come back, pussy-cat! Come back!' |
| 222–3 | M: | (is amused) Do they? Is that what they do? |

They both laugh and there is a relaxed pause in the conversation, when Carol begins again, and this is where the text starts

| 224–5 | C: | Mum do pussy-cats die when people die? |

You might say that the mother's

| 226 | M: | Do pussy-cats what, love? |

arises because of the form of Carol's question. Or you might say that she is suitably impressed by the largeness of that enquiry. She wishes to be quite certain that Carol has asked the question which she did ask. Carol provides the essential answer (227). The mother handles that question very seriously.

228–9   M: Well, pussy-cats die when their time comes.

As I listen to this reply, I am reminded of the song 'There is a season turn, turn' ... with the lines 'There's a time to live, and a time to die'. The mother is voicing the same belief that the song voices; and the song is voicing a belief from the most outstanding religious text for Christians. Do all communities in the world believe that you only die when 'your time has come'? How well does this belief accord with our faith in medicine, our practices in protecting ourselves from unnecessary risks? What is the 'right conduct', to use Peirce's phrase, that arises from a belief of this kind? The mother is not deflected by any of these considerations. She continued after a small pause with a generalization:

230   M: Everything dies, one day.

Now Carol has to find out what that means.

231   C: Do dogs do they one day?

Note the mother's response. She is not particularly hanging on every word of Carol's. So far as she is concerned she has really dealt with Carol's question: *Everything dies, one day*. But, nonetheless, she must attend to Carol; after all, they are engaged in a conversation. She asks for a repeat of the question:

232   M: Do what?

Carol specifies

233   C: Do dogs die one day when ...

It appears that Carol is about to add either *when people die* or *when cats die* or even possibly *when their time comes* but she doesn't get there; the mother cuts in. That does leave open the question whether the notion of independent deaths – each organism dying when *its* time comes – has actually sunk in. The mother's answer is affirmative:

234   M: Yes dogs die, too ...

Note the pause. For Carol – as for most children in the Western world – cats and dogs must share some critical similarities. Still cats and dogs is not

WHAT KIND OF RESOURCE IS LANGUAGE?

'everything'. How can this part of the statement be tested? Obviously, by moving further away from the category to which cats and dogs belong. Carol does just that:

235   C: Do fruit die?

Fruit is sufficiently different from the category into which cats and dogs can be subsumed. Does 'everything' include fruit? Carol is not disappointed; the mother again takes that question seriously. But her answer supports an opinion which arises from her: *Everything dies, one day.* She appears to work with a general framework wherein 'death' is only one form of mutability; other manifestations of mutability are death-like, such as 'going bad'; to the mother 'dysfunction' is 'death'. For Carol, this is a far goal to reach; she is still groping towards this super-generalization, which permits the mother to reply quite comfortably:

236–7   M: Fruit dies, yes. In a different sort of way.

This rider about manner is a more or less open invitation to further enquiry. It is not surprising that Carol should come back with a:

238   C: How?

This involves the mother in an elaborated and staged explanation, each part of which is expressed as a question, since to make a demand is to demand attention. By employing this device the mother secures the child's attention, waiting at each stage for the child's cues as an indication that her child is moving with her:

239	M:	Well, see how the fruit up there on the tree's green?
240	C:	Mm.
241	M:	See how down here, it's gone all yellow and squashy and horrible?
242	C:	Aa.
243	M:	That means it's died, it's …
244–5		Well, we don't call it, we don't say it's died; we say it's gone bad.

Mutability is fearsome; death is not beautiful – every step that takes you closer to mutability represents an undesirable stage. W. B. Yeats's *Old Men Admiring Themselves* sit staring into the water as it flows by – their hands are like claws, their knees are twisted like old thorn-trees while they lament that everything that's beautiful drifts away. I am definitely not suggesting that the mother is creating poetry; I am implying, though, that art too draws upon the same rich fund of knowledge which is the social possession of the community by courtesy of language. Contrast Yeats with a truly fatalistic culture, such as the Indian one. Here the poet has this to say:

> The point of perfection, the acme of a drop of water is to 'die into' the ocean; when pain has passed the stage of endurance, it turns into its own cure.

I could not lay claim to a wide knowledge of Western literature but I suggest it would be difficult to find there such an expression of contentment – resignation yes, but contentment no – at the idea of mutability. This mother, with her 'yellow and squashy and horrible' certainly does not think of mutability as the point of perfection.

It is doubtful that Carol has grasped the finely finished notion of mutability which the mother has presented to her. But that something in that direction has taken place is perhaps obvious from Carol's own essay into the area. As she picks up the mother's theme and tries it out, we can almost see her groping to find her way:

246	C:	Mummy.
247	M:	Mm [a medium pause].
248–50	C:	Mum see where the persimmons have dropped off the tree ... cos umm cos they're sick and they've got germs.
251	M:	Yes, that's right.
252–3	C:	They're sick and they've got germs.
254	M:	Mm.

Note the child's covert connection between sickness and death; and the overt one between sickness and germs. No doubt she has had many goes at this latter connection; children are always catching germs and mothers are always talking about this experience. Its extension to the case in hand thus presents little problem for Carol; but it is doubtful if she has quite seen the connection between fruit going bad and animals dying. But there is no need to worry, for Carol will engage in other conversations and for the novice – such as the child – conversations are pregnant with 'facts about the world' because language is the main fact-builder about the world.

I have done no more than scratch on the surface of this conversation. Much more could be said, specifically about the forms of reasoning that are learned through conversations such as these. The examination of a statement, the structuring of argument, inferential relations amongst the sayings, are also being learned at the same time as language is being learned. Holding the view that I do, I am only able to agree with half of what Rorty says about Sellars' view of what language means to social man. I quote:

> What is special about language is not that it 'changes the quality of our experience' or 'opens new vistas of consciousness' or 'systematizes a previously unconscious manifold' or produces any other sort of inner change. All that its acquisition does is to let us enter a community whose members exchange justifications of assertions, and other actions with one another. (Rorty 1979, 85)

It is meaningless to ask whether language changes the quality of our experience; for the experience that cannot be articulated is like the Einsteinian thesis from the point of view of Newton: it is not an 'impossibility' *per se*, but to those located at a particular point, it is the unknowable, the unsuspected. I may object to the flowery style of 'opens new vistas of consciousness' and the philosophical hang-ups underlying 'systematizes a previously unconscious manifold', but I have attempted in my own very sketchy analysis to show that language is instrumental in creating awareness, in articulating the similarities and the differences between whatever categories its speakers operate with. The trouble is that all of this becomes background phenomena. Philosophers behave as if they – and they alone – know anything worth knowing not only about our systems of knowledge but also about our language, although their work is not exactly distinguished either for linguistic expertise or the deep-going social orientation that is necessary to appreciate the role of language in the creation of social man and of his world.

I have not left myself any time to develop the implications of the hypothesis that language is a shaper of reality, that it is above all the instrument through which we maintain a suspension of disbelief against the recepts of our own culture. These implications are many, but I would like to say a word about the one that appears more urgent to a multiethnic community such as ours. The search for an ultimate reality – for one right way of being, doing and saying – in a country such as ours is, in the last analysis, a power-game; the winners will be those who, in the colloquial phrase, are sitting pretty. One should not be misled by universalistic arguments which present the attractive hypothesis of finding Man's common factor through a set of reductionist techniques. To appreciate the bond of human brotherhood, the unity of the species – their alikeness – it is not necessary to reduce them to banality; to see our common heritage, it is not necessary to affirm 13 or 15 or 42 semantic universals. Rather, to honour human creativity, we should join Whorf in saying that

> Linguistic knowledge entails understanding many different, beautiful systems of logical analysis. Through it, the world as seen from the diverse viewpoints of other social groups, that we have thought of as aliens, becomes intelligible in new terms. Alienness turns into a new, and often clarifying way of looking at things. (1942, 264)

And what is true across ethnic communities may be equally true of subcommunities within the same larger community. If these are characterized, among other things, by differing 'fashions of speaking', then the well-intentioned but misguided effort to show that underneath we are *all* alike does not help those whose fashions of speaking are the main factor in holding them back. It again helps only those who are already in an advantaged position. No one tells me that standard educated English is beautiful, so why do they need to convince me that Black English too is beautiful and logical? In tribute to Labov (1969), we would accept that *qua* system both are equal, in so far as they both possess the internal coherence and interrelatedness which is characteristic of all human language. The reasons for which substandard varieties of language stand in need of championship lies ultimately in the social divisions, the hidden and ugly nature of which Basil Bernstein (1971) has explored. It is ugly precisely because while one *can* claim the two to be equal, while one *can* suggest that the fashions of speaking in the two polarized subcommunities are two legitimate fashions, the socio-economic institutions of the middle-classes ensure that one and only one of these fashions of speaking, namely their own, affirms the values – the orientation to meaning – which are invariably associated with what counts as success in the macro-community. The argument that the lower socio-economic classes wish to stay where they are because of their spiritual values of friendship cuts about as much ice as the view that socio-economic frustration creates good poetry.

Language is a fearsome resource through which we not only do seemingly trivial things, e.g. greeting, gossiping or buying a loaf of bread, but through it we can also have the power of doing enormously momentous things, e.g. monopolizing resources, putting others down, cutting them off from the road to personal fulfilment. We not only use language to shape reality, but we use it also to defend that reality, against anyone whose alternative values might threaten ours. But, if language can be used to defend a reality, then by the same token, it can be used to examine the very reality created by it. Such examination is not to be found in habitual thinking and behaviour; it can only arise by the disturbance of daily habits and communal beliefs. The greatest justification for technical disciplines – e.g. for linguistics, for poetics, for chemistry, for physics, for the entire range of expert disciplines, in fact – is that they can disturb the suspension of disbelief which the everyday linguistic practices of a community perpetuate.

References

Aarsleff, H. (1970) 'The history of linguistics and Professor Chomsky'. In *Language*, 46. Also reprinted in H. Aarsleff (ed.) *From Locke to Saussure*. University of Minnesota Press, 1982.

Berger, P. L. and Luckman, T. (1971) *The Social Construction of Reality*. Harmondsworth: Penguin.

Bernstein, Basil B. (1971) *Class, Codes and Control*, Volume I. London: Routledge & Kegan Paul.

Brown, R. and Lenneberg, E. H. (1954) 'A study in language and cognition'. *Journal of Abnormal and Social Psychology*, Vol. 49, No. 3. (Reprinted in R. Brown (ed.) *Psycholinguistics: Selected Papers*. New York: Free Press, 1972).

Bruner, J. L. (1978) 'Learning how to do things with words'. In J. L. Bruner and A. Garton (eds) *Human Growth and Development*. Oxford: Clarendon Press.

Butt, D. G. (1983) 'Ideational meaning and the mirror of nature'. Paper presented at the VIIIth ALAA Congress, La Trobe University.

Cole, M. and Scribner, S. (1974) *Culture and Thought: A Psychological Introduction*. New York: John Wiley and Son.

Douglas, J. D. (1971) 'Understanding everyday life'. In J. D. Douglas (ed.) *Understanding Everyday Life: Toward the Reconstruction of Social Knowledge.* London: Routledge & Kegan Paul.
Evans-Pritchard, E. E. (1973) 'For example, witchcraft'. In M. Douglas (ed.) *Rules and Meanings.* Penguin. (Excerpt from Evans-Pritchard *Witchcraft, Oracles and Magic Among the Azande.* Oxford: Clarendon Press, 1937.)
Fawcett, R. P. (1983) 'Language as a resource'. Keynote Address to the VIIIth ALAA Congress, La Trobe University.
Fishman, J. A. (1960) 'A systematization of the Whorfian hypothesis'. *Behavioural Sciences,* 5(4). (Reprinted in J. W. Berry and P. R. Dasen (eds) *Culture and Cognition: Readings in Cross-Cultural Psychology.* London: Methuen, 1974).
Goffman, E. (1981) *Forms of Talk.* University of Pennsylvania Press.
Halliday, M. A. K. (1970) 'Language structure and language function'. In J. Lyons (ed.) *New Horizons in Linguistics,* Harmondsworth: Penguin.
Halliday, M. A. K. (1974) *Language and Social Man.* (Schools Council Programme in Linguistics and English Teaching: Series II, Vol. 3). London: Longman.
Halliday, M. A. K. (1975) *Learning How to Mean.* London: Edward Arnold.
Hasan, Ruqaiya (1975) 'Ways of saying: ways of meaning'. Paper presented at Bourg Wartenstein Symposium No. 66 on *Semiotics of Culture and Language.* In R. Fawcett, M. A. K. Halliday, S. M. Lamb and A. Makkai (eds) *Semiotics of Culture and Language.* Frances Pinter, 1984. (Chapter 8 of this book).
Hasan, R. (1986) 'Some implications of semantic distance for language in education'. In A. Abbi (ed.) *Studies in Bilingualism.* New Delhi: Bahri Publications.
Hjelmslev, L. (1961) *Prolegomena to a Theory of Language* (trans. F. J. Whitfield). University of Wisconsin Press.
Hoijer, H. (1954) 'The Sapir-Whorf hypothesis'. In H. Hoijer (ed.) *Language and Culture.* University of Chicago Press.
Labov, W. (1969) 'The logic of non-standard English'. *Georgetown Monographs on Language and Linguistics,* Vol. 22. Georgetown University Press.
de Laguna, G. A. (1927) *Speech: Its Function and Development.* Indiana University Press.
Lenneberg, E. H. (1964) 'A biological perspective of language'. In E. H. Lenneberg (ed.) *New Directions in the Study of Language.* MIT Press.
Lenneberg, E. H. (1975) 'Language and cognition'. In D. D. Steinberg and L. A. Jakobovits (eds) *Semantics.* Cambridge University Press.
Malinowski, B. (1923) 'The problem of meaning in primitive languages'. Supplement I in C. K. Ogden and I. A. Richards *The Meaning of Meaning.* Routledge & Kegan Paul.
Mead, G. H. (1910) 'What social objects must psychology presuppose?'. *The Journal of Philosophy,* Vol. 7. (Reprinted in T. Luckman (ed.) *Phenomenology and Sociology.* Penguin, 1978).
Newson, J. (1978) 'Dialogue and development'. In A. Lock (ed.) *Action, Gesture and Symbol: The Emergence of Language.* Academic Press.
Peirce, C. S. (1878) 'Consequences of four incapacities'. *Journal of Speculative Philosophy,* 2. (Reprinted in C. Hartshorne and P. Weiss (eds) *Collected Papers of C. S. Peirce* Volumes V & VI. Harvard University Press, 1960).
Rorty, R. (1979) *Philosophy and the Mirror of Nature.* Princeton University Press.
Rorty, R. (1980) 'Pragmatism, relativism and irrationalism'. *Proceedings of the American Philosophical Association,* 53. (Reprinted in R. Rorty *Consequences of Pragmatism*).

Rorty, R. (1981) 'Method, social science and social hope'. *The Canadian Journal of Philosophy*, 11. (Reprinted in R. Rorty *Consequences of Pragmatism*. Harvester Press).

Rorty, R. (1982) *Consequences of Pragmatism*. Harvester Press.

Royce, J. R. (1964) *The Encapsulated Man*. Van Nostrand Co.

De Saussure, F. (1966) *Course in General Linguistics*. McGraw-Hill Paperback.

Shotter, J. (1978) 'The cultural context of communication studies: theoretical and methodological issues'. In A. Lock (ed.) *Action, Gesture and Symbol: The Emergence of Language*. Academic Press.

Skinner, Q. (1981) 'The end of philosophy'. (Review of R. Rorty *Philosophy and the Mirror of Nature*.) In the *New York Book Review* (19 March).

Trevarthen, C. (1979) 'Communication and cooperation in early infancy: a description of primary intersubjectivity'. In M. Bullowa (ed.) *Before Speech: the Beginning of Interpersonal Communication*. Cambridge: Cambridge University Press.

Trevarthen, C. and Hubley, P. (1978) 'Confidence, confiding and acts of meaning in the first year'. In A. Lock (ed.) *Action, Gesture and Symbol: The Emergence of Language*. London: Academic Press.

Weiss, P. (1952) 'The logic of creative process'. In P. P. Weiner and F. H. Young (eds) *Studies in the Philosophy of C. S. Peirce*. Cambridge, Mass.: Harvard University Press.

Whorf, B. L. (1940a) 'Science and linguistics'. *Technological Review*, 42, April. (Reprinted in J. B. Carroll (ed.) *Language, Thought and Reality*. MIT Press, 1956, pp. 207–219.)

Whorf, B. L. (1940b) 'Linguistics as an exact science'. *Technological Review*, 43, December. (Reprinted in J. B. Carroll (ed.) *Language, Thought and Reality*. MIT Press, 1956, pp. 220–232.)

Whorf, B. L. (1941) 'The relation of habitual thought and behaviour to language'. In L. Spier (ed.) *Language Culture and Personality: Essays in Memory of E. Sapir*. Sapir Memorial Publication. (Reprinted in J. B. Carroll (ed.) *Language, Thought and Reality*. MIT Press, 1956).

Whorf, B. L. (1941) 'Language and logic'. *Technological Review*, 32, April. (Reprinted in J. B. Carroll (ed.) *Language, Thought and Reality*. MIT Press, 1956, pp. 233–245).

Whorf, B. L. (1942) 'Language, mind and reality'. *Theosophist*, January–April. (Reprinted in *Language, Thought and Reality*.)

Whorf, B. L. (1956) 'A linguistic consideration of thinking in primitive communities'. In J. B. Carroll (ed.) *Language, Thought and Reality*.

Wittgenstein, L. (1958) *Philosophical Investigations*. (Trans. by G. E. M. Anscombe). Basil Blackwell (2nd edition).

2 What's going on: a dynamic view of context in language

My basic concern is with the relationship between text and context of situation. But 'context of situation' – and sometimes just 'context' or 'situation' – mean different things to different people; I believe my use of the term to be in keeping with the Malinowski – Firth – Halliday tradition. The half century between Malinowski (1923) and Halliday (1974a) has seen a radical shift in the notion, in precisely the direction in which Firth (1950) seems to have pointed it. For Malinowski context of situation was just that: the situation context. For Halliday, following Firth, it is an abstraction; and if situation may be said to accompany the text, then this is more by virtue of the functional nature of language than by virtue of any physical spatio-temporal co-occurrence of the two. The word 'accompany' has undergone an important reinterpretation. Halliday's context of situation (1977; 1978) captures what Goffman (1975) refers to as the 'motivational relevancies' inasmuch as they bear upon the talk in all its aspects. The interaction as it unfolds through the mediation of the various modes of meaning – verbal and non-verbal – is an evidence of such relevancies. It, therefore, provides a direct or indirect account of its creators' answer to the question: What is it that's going on here?

The racy idiomaticity of everyday usage might here deceive us into thinking that the question is a simple one, calling for an answer obvious to all. But as several scholars have pointed out we are faced with an inherent indeterminacy; at any time that the question is raised, the answer to it can always be some other than that which is given, for there is a considerable latitude in the interpretation of 'what', of 'here' and of 'going on'. Obviously, then, none of the answers is a 'slice of reality' as is physically present here and now at the time of asking; rather the answer must refer to some elements abstracted from some slice of reality somewhere in some domain of experience. The reality captured by the answer is filtered reality, and the active agent, here, is the interactant – it is his focus that informs the answer. So, although the answer may be rooted in the objective, its point of departure is the subjective one. According to this line of reasoning, then, the word 'situation' in the expression 'context of situation' refers to that part of reality which is filtered through the interactant's focus upon some aspect of his environment. Were we to leave the story off at this point, each context of situation would appear to be a unique creation by a unique individual, and what could be more gratifying than the belief that one's self is indeed the centre of the universe?

However, we do have to take into account the fact of interaction, the presence of which argues that the subjective must somehow be turned into the intersubjective. Perception, individual focus, one's own view of what is relevant – these are private things. To be shared they must be made public; and some form of sharing there must be as that is a necessary condition for the unfolding of interaction even where deception is involved. The means whereby the private is rendered public is provided by the semiotic codes. My focus on the situation can become your focus on the situation – if I so wish – because common to us is some means of representing that focus. A shared situation is by definition a coded situation – a fact to be kept in sight whenever we are reminded of the uniqueness of individual experience. For if emphasis on the subjectivity of focus highlights uniqueness, the need for coding functions as a corrective, indicating the limits on this uniqueness: whatever can generally function as a medium of communication must necessarily be a system of social conventions. So what is shared between individuals is conditioned not only by the unique identities involved; rather the filtering of reality is twofold. Reality is thus and thus because *I* see it thus and thus but the *other's* perception of my perception of the thus-ness of reality must be filtered through the coded message, being in this process conditioned by the nature of the code. And more important still, this sharp division between the individual and the social, the unique and the conventional, is perhaps only an artefact of our analysis. For even though we may choose to begin with the individual, there is an important sense in which he can be seen as a being that is actively shaped by the sum of his own interactions and hence by the nature of the semiotic codes prevalent in his community (Bateson 1942; Whorf 1956; Bernstein 1971).

The total set of semiotic codes in a community serve to define the nature of the 'world' for its members. Each code has a role in the mediation of meanings but it would be naïve to imagine that there are no differences between the codes. I would suggest that distinct semiotic codes carry distinct representational capacities; the accounts of recent research in non-verbal communication would certainly appear to support this hypothesis (Argyle and Kendon 1967; Argyle 1972). Clearly, despite overlaps, what can be said through the resources of the verbal code is not coextensive with what can be 'said' through the gazing code or the gesture code or the code of dress. But in my view the difference between the codes goes beyond the matter of 'how much' can be said; it extends to what may be described as the partiality of a code to certain kinds of relevance (Bateson 1968). For it would appear that the functional nature of each code predisposes one to the encoding of certain relevancies rather than others. So, the gazing code *must* convey an interpersonal type of meaning, and it would be a mistake to imagine that either gaze-avoidance or the 'impersonal look in the eye' fail to convey some meaning. Certainly when it comes to the filtering of the interactive situation through the verbal code, there would appear to be certain aspects which – by the nature of the code – are treated as being relevant – as being a part of the interactant's subjective focus. Whatever else an interactant may attend to or not, these are factors which he cannot choose to ignore; his conception of what is relevant to the interaction must contain these elements within it:

I   the nature of the social process – what is being achieved through the acts of verbal meaning;
II the nature of the relationship between the interactants;
III the nature of the mode for message transmission.

These factors correspond to Halliday's terms – field, tenor and mode of discourse. In principle it is possible to break up this tripartite set in different ways (Gregory and Carroll 1979; Martin 1979; Hymes 1968; 1972; Hasan 1973); I have followed the Halliday schema because it appears to be the most highly motivated, being placed simultaneously in relation to both the social system and the verbal code, as displayed in Figure 2.1.

The figure presents some of the most important elements which influence verbal interaction, while providing a theoretical context for the interpretation of the expression 'context of situation'. In what follows I shall restrict myself to a small corner of this broad canvas, dealing only with certain aspects of context and text as if all else were equal.

If we accept the view of context of situation which I have presented above and which is schematically presented in Figure 2.1, certain things follow. In the first place, we must make a distinction between what I am referring to as 'context of situation' and the actual physical setting in which a text might unfold. Let me refer to the latter as '*material situational setting*'. The material situational setting always includes elements that are not part of the context of situation; this is the reason why the question: What is it that's going on here? has so many legitimate answers. The overlap between the two can vary according to the role that the language plays in the unfolding of the social process; when the process is defined by reference to language – e.g. *seminar, lecture, lyric* – then the material situational setting in which the text actually gets produced may be largely irrelevant to the text. Someone producing an advertisement for publication must sit somewhere at some time in or out of others' company; but these aspects of the material situational setting need not impinge upon the text in any way. By contrast, if the role of language is subsidiary, the social process being defined without reference to language – e.g. moving furniture around in a room – then elements of the material situational setting are likely to be actively picked up as the ingredients of the context of situation. In principle we can think of the material situational setting as a dormant source for affecting the verbal goings-on. Elements of this dormant source are available for activation; it is a different matter

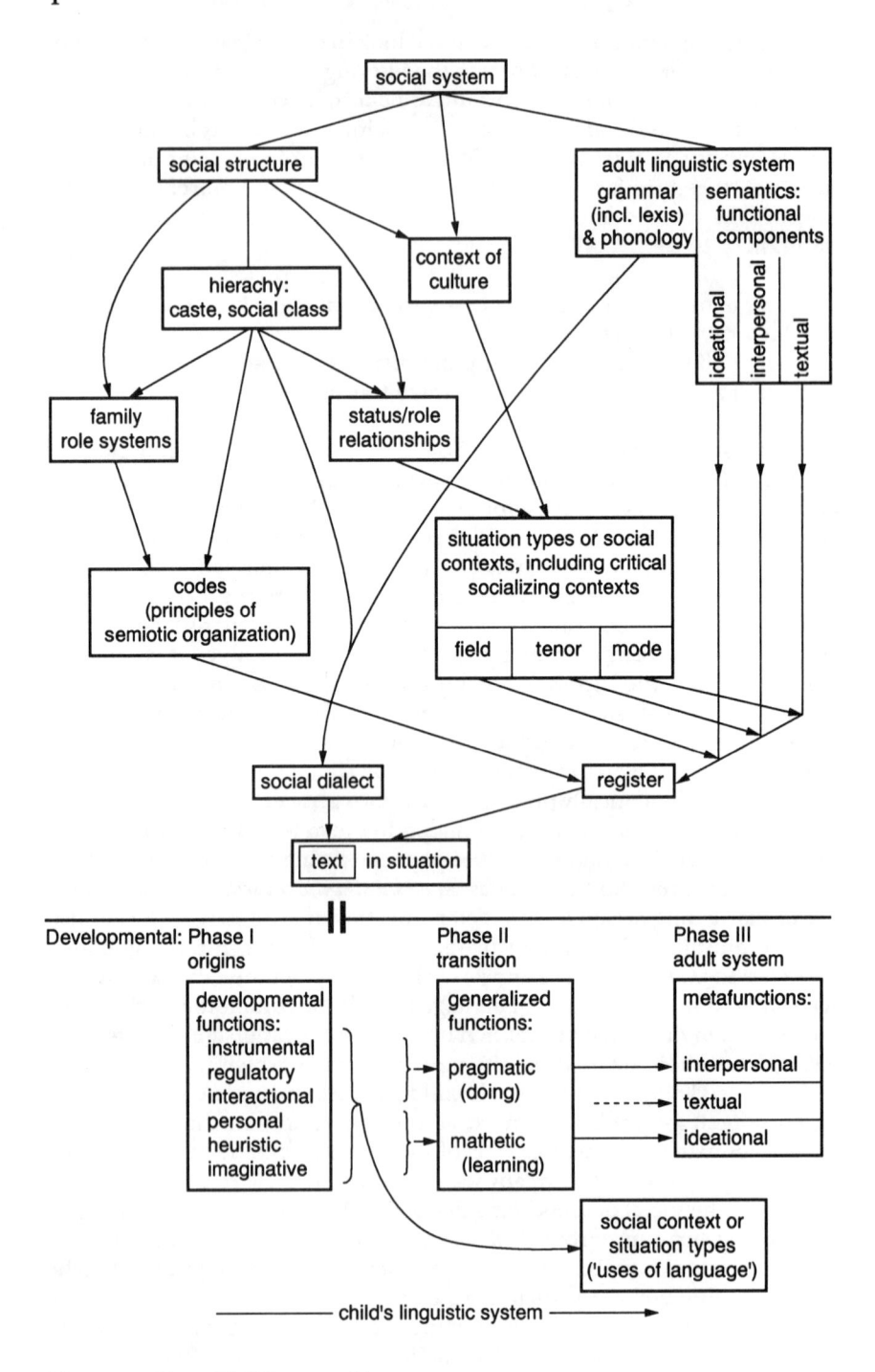

Figure 2.1 (from Halliday 1974b)

whether such activation would entail a change in the context of situation or not (Hasan 1980). I shall return to the role of the material situational setting in determining the nature of the context of situation for the observer at a later point.

The second thing that follows from my view of the context of situation is the nature of the relationship between it and text. If context of situation is an account of the interactant's motivational relevancies, then it must be seen as a dynamic force both in text creation and text interpretation. It is a prerequisite of all language use, not an *ad hoc* a-theoretical notion that one can appeal to when it suits one's convenience or inasmuch as it suits one's convenience, as in most speech act analyses (Sbisa and Fabbri 1980). I would like to dissociate myself from that use of the term *context* which treats it as the explanation of whatever cannot be explained through the analysis of the form of the message; for such a use of context is hardly any more viable than that of performance. And in any event there exists a catch-all phrase in the expression 'knowledge of the world' which is surely a wide enough basket to take in any number of failures of analysis. That context is pertinent to interaction is a widely held view; in recent years its relevance to specifically the verbal aspects of interaction has received a great deal of attention. However, most studies have approached the analysis in terms of the sequencing of speech acts, thus concentrating on what is often referred to as micro-analysis of interaction (Dore 1980; Labov and Fanshel 1977; McTear 1979). Yet another recent development is the attempt to synthesize both the micro- and macro-analysis (Sinclair and Coulthard 1975). Such studies have contributed a great deal to our understanding of text construction and text interpretation.

In my own work I have argued that context can be seen as the major determinant of the defining characteristics of text genres (Hasan 1973; 1978; 1979; 1980); given the nature of the context of situation – the contextual configuration – we can predict the crucial semantic elements of the embedded text as well as the permitted range for the overall message form. For example if we know that the social process is that of advertising, this simple fact permits us to predict that the message form must contain an element of structure whose function it is to attract attention. Let us refer to this element of text structure as Capture; it is this element that is realized in the written mode through the management of the visual layout, the typeface patterns and/or the presence of pictures; and in the spoken mode through the introduction of music or other acoustic effects. Further, the tendency of advertisements to use pun – *Go to Work on an Egg*, alliteration – *Top People Take The Times*, and such apparently preposterous locutions as *Go jump in a New Zealand Lake* – is functionally motivated; they are there as (part of) the realization of the element Capture. A second obligatory element of structure may be referred to as Focus. The crucial semantics of this element is to single out that which is being advertised. The caption *Go Jump in a New Zealand Lake* adorns the top of a picture of a beautiful lake; underneath the picture a discrete legend announces *Air New Zealand*. This is the Focus of this particular advertisement. The beauty of New Zealand as displayed by the picture constitutes the Justification for the Focus. Space does not permit a more detailed account of other elements of structure for an advertisement; but hopefully this brief introduction lends support to the hypothesis that the contextual configuration can be used to predict the structural potential for texts belonging to specific genres. The notion of appropriacy would be inapplicable to text without the prior assumption that the meanings of the text are controlled by context. And by the same token, the ability to infer the contextual configuration of a text is an essential part of its interpretation; if we read *Go Jump in a New Zealand Lake* as a gratuitous insult, we are certainly far from interpreting the text successfully. Thus the relationship between text and context is twofold for the acculturated reader: if we have access to the context, we can predict the essentials of the text; if we have access to the text, then we can infer the context from it. In both cases we proceed from that which is present to that which is not present but which stands in some causal relation to the former.

The above view of context is often seen as normative (Sbisa and Fabbri 1980; Cicourel 1980) and as such undesirable for the following reasons:

I   that it implies the presence of a social contract;
II   that it postulates an ideal for human behaviour;
III that it does not permit variation;
IV   that it denies individual autonomy; and
V   that it presents context as a fully evolved object prior to the creation of the text, while the fact of the matter is that contexts and texts evolve together.

Let me deal with the first two objections very briefly. The recognition of a norm does imply the presence of a social convention; we may use the metaphor of social contract to refer to the fact that members of a community follow a set of conventions which are essentially arbitrary in nature, but in saying this we claim no more than that the actual practices of a community indicate how a convention should be read – and this includes the reading of all its values, not just one. A convention is made legitimate through practice, not through amicable discussion as the metaphor of social contract might sometimes mislead us into thinking. The actual practices of a community are often a means for the categorization of its members; this is borne out by the researches of anthropologists of very different ideological persuasions. I would suggest that the concept of power in sociology is closely related to the concept of norm; however, to describe norms is not to side with the group wielding power any more than to describe working-class dialects is to bring about a social revolution whose benefits are reaped by the downtrodden. The recognition of norms would be misleading if, for one reason or another, a scholar chose to ignore the presence of conflicting norms; but such shortcoming does not invalidate the concept of norm itself; what it does invalidate is that particular account of it.

Nor does it appear to me that norm entails idealization of relevant behaviour. Some idealization must always exist in any general statement, and when we talk about occasions of talk and how people tend to act verbally on such occasions we must make an effort to distinguish between what is inside the frame, what outside (Bateson 1955; Goffman 1975). But with reference to the occasion itself, it is not necessary to postulate one invariant mode of behaviour as the only correct possibility. In fact the question of evaluation need not enter into the concept of norm, for a norm may be established on a purely statistical basis; to say that something happens typically is not to claim that it is therefore good, or beautiful, or correct. Nor does it necessarily entail a monolithic view of 'it' whatever that may be: variants do occur, i.e. are normal but it is also normal for variants to occur systematically. These points have been argued admirably by Labov with specific reference to language (Labov 1966; 1972); and there seems little reason to suspect that behaviour in other semiotic codes – or at a different level – is radically different. Norms of behaviour have little to do with the kind of idealization entailed by theories of innate competence, which logically involves but one blueprint; instead norms of behaviour in specific contexts of situation are more readily relatable to the notion of acculturation. In not a few communities, bargaining is the norm for the occasion of buying and selling; in others the fixed price prevails. Neither is ideal behaviour; but we would think that a buyer who tried to bargain in Saks is certainly being atypical while refusal to bargain in an African shop was once described to me as 'somewhat insulting to the shopkeeper' by one of the shopkeepers himself. Thus in my view, the confusion of norm with idealization is based on a misconception: the typical is only the most frequent – it therefore is bound to be socially significant – but it is not obligatory as a reflex action is or as behaviour which is genetically pre-programmed might be. Judgements about the appropriacy of some piece of behaviour always make appeal to a culture and this appears entirely consistent since specific contextual configurations are only culturally validated (Goffman 1975; Bateson 1955; Hasan 1975; 1980; Malinowski 1923; Firth 1950; Halliday 1974b).

Obviously then if context is being employed as the rationale for a prediction of the *typical* patterns of behaviour, this is not tantamount to a claim of *absolute* determinism. Although invariance may be said to imply typicality, the reverse is not true; typical behaviour is not invariant behaviour even within the context of the same culture. But to claim that variation can happen anywhere, anyhow, any time or that the individual is equally free to negotiate a situation in all environments is to vulgarize the notion of both variation and individual freedom. Even those scholars who talk most about the individual's negotiation of context, use the habitual tense, which one might argue gives a lie to the overt rejection of norm! But it may be useful to think of variations as falling into two major categories: those which are within the system and those which are external to it. Examples of the latter type are such happenings which are often interpreted by the members of the community as 'disruption', 'interruption', 'postponement', etc. while a subcategory of this type of variation is composed of pathological behaviour, arising from whatever cause. Of these, disruption – or at least some forms of it – would appear to be the most complex as it is here that distinct foci on the situation have to operate side by side, with the participants inhabiting distinct universes simultaneously. Variations which are within the system have been described (Hasan 1980) as arising from the local, non-criterial properties of both the text and the context. What one says now influences what one might go on to say next; this is obvious from the readiness with which we note mixed metaphors, inconsistencies and 'forgettings' in our own speech even as we are speaking. There is a sense in which the processual nature of the text is an important source of its uniqueness. Equally important is a second fact: each contextual configuration is indicative of a range of possible behaviours; it 'tells the organism among what *set* of alternatives he must make his next choice' (Bateson 1964); it does not detail what each particular choice must be. A third point that needs to be taken into account in the consideration of variation in behaviour is the flexibility of the notion 'context'. It is perfectly obvious that specific contexts cannot be hermetically sealed off one from the other; none the less, it is also an empirical fact that we recognize 'different' contexts. I have argued that each particular category of context contains elements whose presence or absence is non-criterial to its identity (Hasan 1980): for example, the identity of the context 'shopping for food in a personal service store' does not alter either because of how well one knows the store-keeper or what particular goods one buys. But these are certainly the elements in the context of situation whose presence or absence correlates with difference in typical behaviour. If the store-keeper is well known to us, we would normally – i.e. without 'good reason' – not start off on our business of shopping without some sociability (Hasan 1978; Ventola 1979), though of course there is nothing to prevent us from being unpleasant, snobbish or eccentric – except perhaps the weight of social opinion and the part it plays in the formation of our egos. Thus it is obvious that there are variations in behaviour within the same context which are susceptible to systematic explanation in terms of more delicate details in the field, tenor and mode of discourse.

Let me turn now to the question of individual autonomy. It is well to recognize that there is a close relationship between individual autonomy, variation and acculturation: variation is a constant of learned behaviour and individual autonomy operates only in the realm of learned behaviour, not in that of automatic, genetically controlled activities. A hypothesis about the relationship between text and context must provide a systematic account of both variant norms and individual autonomy not because failure to do so is reactionary, but because these concepts are essential to our understanding of how contexts, behaviours and cultures are related to each other, and how any change ever occurs in any of these. But what does individual autonomy mean? None of us is ever totally free (Douglas 1966); this is truer still in interaction. The very recognition of the other's identity is a constraint on our own; and while it is true that to have the speaking turn is to have power, it is perhaps no less true that to be speaking is to be vulnerable: there is good folk wisdom in the saying that if speech is silver, silence is golden. To speak is to declare our relationship to our social universe; even if we flout authority, ignore peer relation, construct a new set of rights and obligations for roles with old labels, we still take cognizance of the social mores around us, for these roles and relations have already been defined without reference to our own specific individualities. Thus individual autonomy cannot mean total lack of social constraint. However, in the present context it may be reasonable to suggest that individual freedom consists in freedom to negotiate a frame of relevance – a context of situation – for interaction. That one has this freedom is quite evident. But to claim just this much is not sufficient since it is equally evident that this freedom to negotiate contexts is not equally available to all at all times. Rather, there are certain environments which permit such negotiation more readily than others and certain roles allow one to exercise this privilege more than others. So the more interesting question is: how can these environments be characterized? Obviously the answer would bear relevance to whether text and context evolve together or whether some perception of relevancies must precede text construction in real time. If it is true that the subjective focus is made intersubjective through the mediation of the semiotic codes, then it would follow that wherever the context is individually negotiated, it must evolve with the text, since the verbal code would itself play a crucial role in mediating the frame of relevance.

Before answering the question raised above, let me first say what I understand by individual negotiation. For me this concept centres round two considerations. In the first place, negotiation implies face-to-face interaction; thus the concept of negotiation is not applicable to those contexts which have a monologic mode. Secondly, negotiation of context implies that one party to the interaction could not have predicted the nature of the context with a significant probability of being correct without the benefit of access to what the other party is saying. Individual negotiation is a meaningful concept only if the negotiated context is not directly supported by the weight of conventionally interpreted environment. Therefore, if we can characterize those environments which as they stand permit us to predict with a significant probability of being correct what the frame of relevance is likely to be for the embedded interactions, then we shall have located the very domain in which individual negotiation of context has the lowest probability of occurrence. This is where by implication individual autonomy would be under strain; and variation in behaviour would be highly systematic. I suggest that such characterization of environments is possible; and that it can be made in terms of the three factors – field, tenor and mode – which were introduced earlier.

Recall that in contexts with monologic mode, the possibility of individual negotiation does not arise. Interactions embedded in such contexts do not present a genuine possibility of turn-taking; hence there is no cooperative negotiation; rather, there is from the interpreter's point of view a presentation of the context as a *fait accompli*. Typically the text is so constructed here as verbally to encapsulate its own context maximally, and barring the inherent indeterminacies of the verbal code, the reader/listener is presented with a frame of relevance which is now an integral part of the text. I would suggest that for texts in the monologic mode, the maker of the text must proceed from some notion of his frame of relevance. That is to say, in real time, context must precede the text. I do not imply by this that all the details of the text are as it were pre-planned by the speaker; this would be a reification or an overburdening of the speaker's already too overburdened mind! I mean simply that the speaker must have some notion of what he is attempting to achieve, who his audience is and what strategy he is about to employ to achieve his end. It is a common mistake to imagine that the 'what' in question has to be of a practical, informational kind; this is by no means necessary. The saying of sweet nothings or even of non-sweet nothings is just as much directed to an achievement of something as the writing of a manual for the repair of a machine. Nor is there any implication of explicit awareness any more than there is of an awareness of meaning as distinct from verbal realization in normal, everyday speaking.

In contexts with dialogic mode, the possibility of genuine turn-taking exists; therefore, a cooperative negotiation of context can occur. But not all contexts are equally amenable to this; as I suggested above only those contexts genuinely lend themselves to negotiation where the environment is interpretatively neutral. To state this more explicitly we have to introduce certain attributes by reference to which both field and tenor can be further subcategorized. One such attribute is *institutionalization*. We may think of this as a continuum extending from most institutionalized to least institutionalized – or *individuated*. I believe that my use of these terms is in keeping with that of Bernstein (1971). Thus a process may be ranged anywhere on a cline from most institutionalized to most individuated. Social processes which are institutionalized would logically be multiply coded semiotically; that is to say, the fact that they are institutionalized would be indicated by the fact that the different modes of meaning would single them out, and the boundaries set for a process by one mode would be commensurate with those set by another mode of meaning. As example consider the social process of marrying or dispensation of justice. Both these processes are toward the institutionalized end of the continuum and accordingly both are multiply coded through ways of dressing, ways of conducting oneself, performance of a set of ritual actions, the presence of a set of recognized locations for the carrying out of these ritual actions and by a communally recognized set of the rights and obligations accruing to participants who enter the various stages of these processes in various capacities. These non-verbal codings become diagnostic of the nature of the process, and this has a serious consequence for the prediction of frames of relevance. The unfolding of insitutionalized processes involves *convergent coding*, with several modes of meaning operating visibly and at once so that there is a great deal of redundant information. And what, from the point of view of verbal coding, may be seen as just a material situational setting, can from the point of view of the social process be seen as situation semiotically coded through a series of distinct codes. Whenever there is evidence of convergent coding, we tend to interpret the context for verbal interaction by reference to it and our interpretation has a significant probability of being correct. This is true even when an institutionalized process is under strain, since the erosion of multiple convergent codes is of necessity slow; whatever the crisis for marriage as a social process may be, even today if we find a young woman in a wedding dress walking to the church the common inference is that a wedding is about to take place; and this common inference has a high probability of being correct. It is not outside the realm of possibility that she is on her way to, say, a fancy-dress party but few people would infer this; and what is more such inference would have a considerably low probability of being correct. Equally, when we see someone enter a shop or a bank and walk up to the counter and engage in a verbal exchange, we infer this to be a service encounter and there is a very high probability of our being correct in this inference, although again it is not entirely impossible that the person is at that moment engaged in threatening the assistant in a quiet, non-histrionic way. Let me add in passing that the different participants of a social process do not have the same 'attitude' to the process: the priest does not feel the same way about this wedding as the bride and groom do, just as the golfer does not feel the same way about the game as the caddy does (Goffman 1975); but in my view this does not mean that two distinct processes are going on side by side. We must see the tension of distinct views as inherent in the nature of that process; and these tensions contribute to the form of verbal interaction if and when it takes place. We can say then that when the material situational setting displays a series of convergent codes, then the probability of the individual negotiation of context is appreciably reduced.

This prediction can be made even more accurate if we consider the remaining factor: tenor of discourse. Recall that tenor is concerned with role relations. Roles can also be subcategorized by reference to the institutionalized–individuated continuum. Institutionalized roles are normally hierarchic, while the individuated ones even if hierarchic permit greater discretion to the role-holder. If the role is hierarchic this implies non-reversibility of functions: the two roles have distinct rights and obligations and the line is drawn sharply. The carriers of the two hierarchic roles cannot just assume any role except under a certain condition. This is provided by reduced *social distance* (Hasan 1973; 1978; 1980). The social distance between the interactants is determined by reference to the range and frequency of their interaction. The wider the range and the more frequent their interaction with each other, the less the social distance between them. We get close to the personal attributes of the carriers of roles through this attribute. The greatest degree of role reversibility is possible where the role is individuated and the social distance between the interactants is minimum. Such a role might be *friend* or *close colleague* or *close sibling* (of possibly the same sex). Whatever one can do, the other can do too; their rights and obligations are balanced. The reduction of social distance and the reversibility of rights and obligations implies that a great deal of discretion is available to both interactants. The lowest degree of role reversibility is permitted where the roles are hierarchic and institutionalized while the social distance is at its maximum; an example would be an interviewer and an interviewee for a job.

We are now ready to make the final generalizations. In any situation of interaction in the dialogic mode, whatever other information is available to the interactants or not, this much they must know for this pertains to their personal history: what kind of social distance obtains between them, and therefore how far along the institutionalized end of the continuum they would be. If the material situational setting is convergently coded, and if the social distance is tending to the maximum, then we have an environment which is hostile to individual negotiation of context. This is not to say that one cannot attempt it, but such attempts are viewed with suspicion or anger or explained away as a joke in bad taste. If I go to get a visa at a foreign consulate and am called to an interview with the Assistant Consul, I really do not have the privilege of negotiating a context of casual chat with him; that dance is led by him. Of course I could always try leading, but if I did it would either say something about my intelligence, if you are uncharitable, or about my ideological stance, or cast doubt upon my real motive in applying for the visa. The environment in which cooperative negotiation of context is genuinely achieved most often, can be described as one where the material situational setting is not convergently coded as pertaining to some specific social process and where the social distance between the interactants is near minimum. For example upon meeting a close colleague in the Central Quad of my Campus, I can negotiate a context so that we may end up either going to the bar for a drink or we may settle down to a discussion of the latest manifestation of academic bureaucracy or whatever. Seeing us together in the Central Quad gives one no ground for predicting what our specific frame of relevance might be at that moment. It is, however, worth pointing out that even in such an open and potentially variable environment, the form of our interaction is still generally predictable (Ventola 1979). When the context is cooperatively negotiated, the text and the context evolve approximately concurrently, each successive message functioning as an input to the interactants' definition of what is being achieved.

I hope that I have succeeded in showing how within a conception of contextual norms, both variation and individual autonomy can be systematically treated so that they become useful theoretical tools in the discussion of text creation and text interpretation. The nature of interaction is inherently social, no matter how personal the ends it is made to achieve.

References

Argyle, M. (1972) *The Psychology of Interpersonal Behaviour*. Harmondsworth: Penguin.
Argyle, M. and Kendon, A. (1967) 'The experimental analysis of social performance'. In J. Laver and S. Hutcheson (eds) *Communication in Face to Face Interaction*. Harmondsworth: Penguin.
Bateson, G. (1942) 'Morale and national character'. In G. Watson (ed.) *Civilian Morale*. Society for the Psychological Study of Social Issues, Second Yearbook. New York: Houghton Mifflin.
Bateson, G. (1955) 'A theory of play and fantasy: a report on theoretical aspects of the project for the study of the role of paradoxes of abstraction in communication'. In *Approaches to the Study of Human Personality*, American Psychiatric Association, Psychiatric Report No. 2.
Bateson, G. (1964) 'The logical categories of learning and communication', submitted as position paper to the 'Conference on World-View' sponsored by Wenner-Gren, 1968; reprinted in *Steps to an Ecology of Mind*. New York: Ballantine (1972).
Bateson, G. (1968) 'Redundancy and coding'. in T. A. Sebeok (ed.) *Animal Communication: Techniques of Study and Results of Research*. Bloomington: Indiana University Press.
Bernstein, B. (1971) *Class, Codes and Control*, Volume I: *Theoretical Studies towards a Sociology of Language*. London: Routledge & Kegan Paul.
Cicourel, A. V. (1980) *Language and Social Interaction*. Working Paper No. 96, Centro Internazionale di Semiotica e di Linguistica, Università di Urbino.
Dore, J. (1980) 'Linguistic forms and social frames in interpretation'. In *The Sixth LACUS Forum 1979*. Columbia, S.C.: Hornbeam Press.
Douglas, M. (1966) *Purity and Danger*. London: Routledge & Kegan Paul.
Firth, J. R. (1950) 'Personality and language in society', *The Sociological Review*, 42. Reprinted in Firth, *Papers in Linguistics*. London: Oxford University Press (1957).
Goffman, E. (1975) *Frame Analysis*. Harmondsworth: Penguin.
Gregory, M. and Carroll, S. (1978) *Language and Situation*. London: Routledge & Kegan Paul.
Halliday, M. A. K. (1974a) *Language and Social Man*, Schools Council Program in Linguistics & English Teaching, Series II, Paper 3. London: Longman.
Halliday, M. A. K. (1974b) 'Language as social semiotic: towards a general sociolinguistic theory'. In A. Makkai and V.B. Makkai (eds) *The First LACUS Forum*. Columbia, S.C.: Hornbeam Press.
Halliday, M. A. K. (1977) 'Text as a semantic choice in social context'. In T. A. van Dijk and J. S. Petofi (eds) *Grammars and Descriptions*. Berlin: de Gruyter.
Halliday, M. A. K. (1978) *Language as Social Semiotic: The Social Interpretation of Language and Meaning*. London: Edward Arnold; also Baltimore, Maryland: University Park Press (1979).
Halliday, M. A. K. and Hasan, R. (1976) *Cohesion in English*. London: Longman.
Hasan, Ruqaiya (1973) 'Code register and social dialect'. In B. Bernstein (ed.) *Class, Codes and Control*, Volume II. London: Routledge & Kegan Paul.
Hasan, Ruqaiya (1975) 'Ways of saying: ways of meaning', paper presented at Conference on Semiotics of Culture and Language, sponsored by Wenner-Gren; mimeo. (Chapter 8 of this book).

Hasan, Ruqaiya (1978) 'Text in the systemic-functional model'. In W. U. Dressler (ed.) *Current Trends in Text Linguistics*. Berlin: de Gruyter.

Hasan, Ruqaiya (1979) 'On the notion of text'. In J. Petofi (ed.) *Text vs. Sentence: Basic Questions of Textlinguistics*, Papers in Textlinguistics, Vol. 20.2. Hamburg: Helmut Buske.

Hasan, Ruqaiya (1980) 'The structure of a text; the identity of a text', Chs. 2 and 6 in M. A. K. Halliday and R. Hasan *Text and Context: Language in a Social Semiotic Perspective*. Tokyo: Sophia University.

Hymes, D. (1968) 'The ethnography of speaking'. In J.A. Fishman (ed.) *Readings in the Sociology of Language*. The Hague: Mouton.

Hymes, D. (1972) 'On communicative competence'. In J.B. Pride and J. Holmes (eds) *Sociolinguistics*. Harmondsworth: Penguin.

Labov, W. (1966) *The Social Stratification of English in New York City*. Arlington: Centre for Applied Linguistics.

Labov, W. (1972) *Sociolinguistic Patterns*. Philadelphia: University of Pennsylvania Press.

Labov, W. and Fanshel, D. (1977) *Therapeutic Discourse*. New York: Academic Press.

McTear, M. F. (1979) ' "Hey! I've got something to tell you" etc.'. *Journal of Pragmatics*, Vol. 3, No. 3/4. Amsterdam: North-Holland.

Malinowski, B. (1923) 'The problem of meaning in primitive languages'. In C.K. Ogden and I.A. Richards *The Meaning of Meaning*, 8th edn. New York: Harcourt Brace and World (1946).

Martin, J. R. (1979) *Conjunction and the Structure of Conversation*. University of Sydney, mimeo.

Sbisa, M. and Fabbri, P. (1980) *Models (?) for a Pragmatic Analysis*, Working Paper No. 91, Centro Internazionale di Semiotica e di Linguistica, Università di Urbino.

Sinclair, J. McH. and Coulthard, M. (1975) *Towards an Analysis of Discourse: The English Used by Teachers and Pupils*. London: Oxford University Press.

Ventola, E. (1979) 'The structure of casual conversation in English'. *Journal of Pragmatics*, Vol. 3, No. 3/4. Amsterdam: North-Holland.

Whorf, B. L. (1956) *Language, Thought and Reality* (J.B. Carroll (ed.)). Cambridge, Mass.: MIT Press.

3 The nursery tale as a genre[1]

For those occasions of talk where several semiotic codes act convergently, the role of language is ancillary and the environment pragmatic, it is possible to state a structure potential for an infinity of texts capable of occurring appropriately in that environment. This is a direct consequence of the fact that the relevant factors of the environment – i.e. the contextual configuration – are causally related to the elements of the text structure; the text is, here, a verbal expression of the social activity, and so by reference to the social activity, a generalized statement of text structure can be achieved.

How far are these general statements applicable to the nursery tale? A doubt about their applicability arises because at least in one important respect the nursery tale differs markedly from those categories of texts embedded in pragmatic environments: in the case of the nursery tale, the role of language is constitutive precisely because it plays such a crucial role in the determination of the tale's genre that it may be regarded as the primary source of its definition. This is true whether we examine it from the point of view of text construction or from that of text recounting or reception. We observe that a given text may or may not be assigned to this genre only on the basis of the presence or absence of certain properties; but these properties themselves become accessible to the audience only through language. While it may be true that the criteria for the evaluation of tales will vary over centuries (Eagleton 1983), I doubt if the basis for what is or is not a tale can be provided independent of language. None of the other semiotic codes may substitute the role of language in the realization of the elements of its structure. Paralinguistic codes such as those of gesture and voice quality, if introduced – as in a 'lively' recounting – are totally parasitic on the language of the text. Their appropriacy is judged not by anything lying outside the text in the actual environment of text construction or reception but primarily by reference to the language of the text.

I see these features as the direct consequence of the role of language in the definition of the genre. To say that this role is constitutive is tantamount to the claim that, unlike texts embedded in pragmatic environments, the language of the tale is not responsive to factors of the material situational setting within which the creation or the recounting of the tale takes place.

So the messages of the text present theses (Ellis 1966) the experiential content of which is, as a rule, unrelated to the immediate surroundings. Therefore, the extra-linguistic characterizations of this genre are much weaker than the linguistic ones. In this respect the nursery tale is very much like the other genres of literature, on whose periphery it lies (Vygotsky 1971). This is not to claim that texts of the literary genres are suspended *in vacuo*, having nothing to do with the life of the community. Rather it is to argue that for this entire range of genres we must recognize at least three distinct orders of context. First, we must recognize the context of creation, whereby the artistic conventions of the author's community are reflected – directly or indirectly – in the created texts; the author's conception of the audience finds an expression there and the author's own individual pre-occupations are built into the text. Secondly, there is the context of the audience's contact with the text, wherein responses to the meanings of the text at one and the same time reflect communal attitudes and personal orientations. Thirdly, and most relevant to arguments here, there is the reconstituted context which is specific to that one text – what it is about, in what relations the characters and events are placed *vis-à-vis* each other, how do the theses hang together and what are the strategies through which the text achieves a generally recognizable generic shape (for a more detailed discussion see Hasan 1976; 1985a; 1985b). Although these remarks are made with specific reference to the literary genres, I would suggest that they apply to a greater or lesser degree to all genres where the role of language is constitutive. For example, the seemingly simple but deeply interesting question of what renders a textbook obsolete in, say, chemistry, biology, physics or linguistics cannot be handled effectively except by some such conception of multiple contexts.

I would suggest that the nature of the factors which motivate the elements of structure in such genres is relatively opaque. This is because the environments in which such texts are either created or received bears only a tangential relationship to their inner unity. It follows then that the elements of the structure of the nursery tale can neither be seen as fully governed by the author–audience interaction nor by the fact that the nursery tale has the purpose of socializing young children into the culture, of entertaining them constructively or of soothing them to pleasurable slumber. The single salient fact that appears most relevant is the overall adherence to an array of existing conventions. But to say that the structure of the nursery tale is controlled by artistic conventions is to explain nothing, unless alongside of this assertion we can also provide a convincing account of how artistic conventions themselves originate and how any change is successfully introduced into a body of pre-existing conventions. Even if I were capable of throwing light on these questions, this would require a paper by itself; so at least for the time being, I shelve a more detailed discussion of the question of what motivates the elements of the structure of the nursery tale. I shall take as my starting-point the earlier assertion that the structure of the nursery tale conforms largely to a pre-existing convention.

THE NURSERY TALE AS A GENRE

This would imply that, to construct a concept of the criterial properties of the tale one must be exposed to the data which consists of nursery tales. It occurs to me that at least in so far as the child is concerned, perhaps storying is not so very different from shopping; within their own terms of reference both represent universes of discourse which antedate the child, and both can be accepted, rejected or modified in keeping with the experiences to which the child is exposed as social maturity is achieved. To my mind, the significance of this discussion lies in the fact that all current accounts of the structure of the nursery tale – mine included – are very much more clearly beholden to the linguistic corpus of the genre than is the case with shopping or being interviewed by a doctor. None the less, I hope to draw attention to the growth of a convention for the construction of the tale, which would go some way towards upholding the general approach I have favoured.

Let us turn now to the first question: are there any properties that a text must possess in order to be seen as an instance of the genre 'nursery tale'? In order to save space, I must assume familiarity with the framework I have presented in earlier writings (Hasan 1978; 1979; Halliday and Hasan 1980), though most of it grew originally from my efforts to grapple with the notion of stories for and/or by children. The most relevant notion here is the Generic Structure Potential (SP or GSP for short). The GSP is an abstract category; it is descriptive of the total range of textual structures available within a genre G. It is designed to highlight the variant and invariant properties of textual structures within the limit of one genre; and to achieve this, the GSP must be capable of specifying the following facts about text structure:

I it must specify all those elements of structure whose presence is obligatory, if the text is to be regarded as a complete instance of a given genre by the members of some sub-community;
II in addition, it must enumerate all those elements whose presence is optional, so that the fact of their presence or absence, while affecting the actual structural shape of a particular text, does not affect that text's generic status;
III the GSP must also specify the obligatory and optional ordering of the elements *vis-à-vis* each other, including the possibility of iteration.

Meeting these requirements, a GSP would represent the total potential of structures for a genre G, while the actual or schematic structure of any one instance of G would represent a particular configuration permitted by the GSP itself. The GSP is thus analogous to a system, while the actual structure of some individual text is just one possible instantiation of some particular path allowed by the GSP. It is important to underline the fact that the GSP is a statement of the structural resources available within a given genre. Just as a lexicogrammatical network itself carries no implications about which of its options would be selected in any given clause or group, so the GSP carries no implications about which of the permitted configurations will be manifested in a given text. A text is perceived as complete if it realizes all the obligatory elements. Since such elements are crucial to the generic status of the text, the greater the proportion of such elements realized (verbally), the easier it is to judge correctly the text's generic status (in displacement). The recognition of optionality – both for the elements and for their order *vis-à-vis* each other – builds in the possibility of text variation from the start. From the point of view of structure alone – i.e. ignoring the lexicogrammatical realization of the elements – two texts may vary either because each is systematically relatable to a distinct SP, or because each represents a distinct set of selections permitted by the same SP. This statement captures our experience that not only is there structural difference between texts of distinct genres but also texts belonging to the same genre are not necessarily identical in their structure. Note that the entire discussion has been couched in general terms. What has been said about the GSP above is true for all genres, so that we may claim general applicability for the theoretical framework, even though the specific details will vary from one genre to the next.

With these preliminary remarks I shall turn my attention to the structure potential of the nursery tale. The data on the basis of which the SP is constructed consists of such anthologies as Grimms, Jacobs, Aesops and more recent tales for children. For the SP to be valid, it must prove adequate for the description of these and other existing tales; further, any newly constructed text which conforms systematically to the SP should be recognized as an instance of the genre by socialized readers today. I suggest that the SP presented below would meet both these criteria.

[(<Placement>^)Initiating Event^] Sequent Event ^ Final Event [^(Finale)•(Moral)]

Figure 3.1 SP of the nursery tale

The round brackets in the above representation enclose elements which are optional; the claim of the SP is that we can find nursery tales in which there may be no element Placement and/or Finale and/or Moral. I hope to show below that the optionality of the element Placement is a development whose roots lie in a much older convention relating to the presence of myths. The elements NOT enclosed in round brackets are obligatory; in the absence of any one of these elements the tale would be considered incomplete. The angled brackets enclose elements whose lexicogrammatical realization may be included or interspersed with the lexicogrammatical realization of some other element(s). The raised dot • between elements refers to the fact that the order of the elements on the two sides of the dot is reversible, while the carat sign ^ indicates relative fixity: the element to the right of the carat sign cannot precede the element on the left of the sign. Since mobile elements are mobile within a certain limit, the boundaries of

THE NURSERY TALE AS A GENRE   55

such a limit are indicated by enclosing the relevant elements in a square bracket. In the SP above two such brackets exist. The first encloses Placement and Initiating Event; the second encloses the elements Finale and Moral. The latter bracket is simpler, claiming that Moral might precede Finale or vice versa but that neither can precede Final Event. By contrast, the first square bracket refers to a more complex state of affairs. Here the claims of the SP can be read as follows:

I   the element Placement is optional; (hence the round bracket);
II if it occurs two alternatives are available:
   a   either it will precede Initiating Event (hence the ^ between the two);
   b   or it will be included/interspersed in the Initiating Event (hence the angled bracket).

The possibility that the realization of the Placement may follow that of the Sequent Event is not permitted. In this respect the nursery tale differs from literary short stories where today no such restriction is to be observed. The remaining symbol in the SP is the curved arrow appended to some element(s); this symbolizes the possibility of iteration for that element. Since the labels for the elements were selected on the basis of their mnemonic value, they are hopefully self-explanatory, though a word must be added regarding the difference between Final Event and Finale. The former stands in a logical relation to some event(s)/state(s) of affairs; it represents a culmination, or what Labov refers to as Resolution (Labov 1972). Finale, on the other hand, is the highly conventionalized 'return to altered rest' statement about the main protagonists, intimating a habitual tenor of existence for them, which can then logically function as the Placement for another tale. This is precisely what happens in serial stories of the type exemplified by Revd Awdry's Railway stories.

The significance of such a GSP is twofold. On the one hand, if valid, it will describe adequately the existing tales and function as the grammar representing the resources for the creation of new tales; on the other hand, if the metalanguage for this SP is the same as that for SPs set up to account for markedly different genres, this could be taken as some substantiation for the assertion made above that generic structures as a whole are subject to the same general conditions, and that the same metalanguage is generally applicable. The reader might care to compare Figure 3.1 with the following – Figure 3.2 – which represents the GSP for shopping transactions.

I have attempted to argue above that a shopping transaction is far removed from a nursery tale. If any relations are observed between the two, they are likely to be largely general (see, for example, O'Toole and Butt 1984). Note, though, that so far as the statement of the generic structure potential is concerned, we need the same kinds of notions that apply to the generic structure potential for the nursery tale: our concern is with obligatory and optional elements; with obligatory and optional ordering of the

[(<Greeting>)•(Sale Initiation)^] [(Sale Enquiry•) {Sale Request ^ Sale Compliance}•Sale^] Purchase ^ Purchase Closure (^ Finis)

Figure 3.2   after Hasan (1979; 1980; 1985a)

elements; with iteration and inclusion. In both cases the GSP is a system-like object whose potential product is an 'array of actual structures' (Hasan 1978). The genre, as conceived of here, is fluid; it is not represented simply by a number of texts, each of which is the realization of but one schematic structure.

In recent years, especially in the analysis of the structure of dialogic discourse, it has been suggested that units such as 'exchange structure' or 'adjacency pair' or a sequence of messages such as Initiate ^ Respond ^ Acknowledge should be thought of as elements in the structure of 'conversation', where the term 'conversation' should effectively be read as 'non-monologic discourse'. Some of the best examples of such analyses are to be found in Sinclair and Coulthard (1975), Coulthard and Montgomery (1981); and of course there is the always inspiring work of Goffman (1981). To me it seems that the status of these units is not that of the elements of generic structure. Note, in the first place, that exchange structures, adjacency pairs and triads, etc. are not universally applicable across genres. For example, it is not easy to postulate such relations between messages in a monologic discourse (Hasan 1984a). This brings me to the second observation that the status of such units *vis-à-vis* text structure is the same as that of clause complexes; the only difference between the two is that one is based on adjacency pairing, the other on joining through cause, effect, sequentiality, etc. And although both play a part in the realization of the elements of textual structure, these latter type of elements or their configuration cannot be specified by reference to the categories of adjacency pairs or clause complexes. This claim is not very different from saying that *the boy* is not a function in the structure of the sentence *the boy ran*; rather it is a realization of the conflation of the functions Subject, Theme, Actor. The functions Subject, Theme and Actor are not set up by reference to what nominal groups are like, even though a statement of how these functions may be realized is an essential part of the overall description of the structure of the sentence, and will necessarily involve reference to groups such as *the boy*.

To judge the adequacy of the SP postulated for the tale it is necessary to discuss each of the elements and the crucial realizational features associated with each. Since this requires a good deal of time and space, instead of dealing with all elements superficially, I shall concentrate on an in-depth discussion of the element Placement. I shall also attempt to hypothesize how the optionality of Placement has developed in nursery tales of European origin. First a few general comments on the realization of the elements of a

GSP. Any description of the lexicogrammatical realization of textual structure must at once focus both on variance and invariance. It is possible for two texts of the same genre to be exactly alike in their structure without being exactly alike in the realization of this structure (Hasan 1985a); in fact, realizational variance must occur if they are two distinct texts rather than two distinct tokens of the same text. The crucial question is that of locating the sources of variance and invariance. For example, according to the GSP in Figure 3.1 above, tales may vary structurally with specific regard to the element Placement, since three possibilities are open:

Table 3.1   The options open to nursery tale for Placement

> (i)   tale has no Placement;
> or (ii) tale has a discrete Placement, which must precede Initiating Event;
> or (iii) tale has a non-discrete Placement, so that its realization is interspersed or included with the realization of Initiating Event.

But, two tales in which the same option is selected, say, the second one above, are not necessarily identical in all respects; they may differ in the actual meanings and wordings which realize discrete Placement in the two tales. And, what is equally important, even from the point of view of realization, the two tales may be alike without being entirely identical.

Experience in textual analysis will bear out the hypothesis that the invariant aspects of the realization of story – or for that matter any text type – can be handled better by appeal to semantic properties. Thereafter, a semantically motivated model of language description will provide specification of the range of lexicogrammatical patterns which are capable of realizing these specific semantic properties. Thus statements about the invariant aspects of the realization of some textual element may take a standard form, requiring that any stretch of language capable of realizing a specific element of textual structure must 'have' the semantic property this or that. The approach I am suggesting is somewhat different from Longacre's (1974; 1977) who postulates a deep and a surface structure. His framework leads to a reification of entities without contributing to explicitness of criteria. For example, it is not clear what is achieved by the claim that 'Aperture ("once upon a time") is considered to be a feature of the surface only'; the corresponding deep structure element for Longacre (1974) is Exposition. But when it comes to practical analysis of a text, the question is precisely: How is the element Exposition realized? The answer that it is realized by the surface feature Aperture is not exactly revealing. In the last resort, the chunk of language that one says corresponds to, realizes or is the bearer of a deep structure element of Exposition has to be recognizable in some way that can be stated explicitly in unambiguous terms. In the words of Mandler and Johnson (1977), what is needed is a theory which would 'provide a clear and unambiguous parsing system which can be used for dividing the story in structurally important units'. I suggest that the essential attributes of 'the structurally important units' of any text type will have to be stated in semantic terms. But this by itself is not sufficient, otherwise Rumelhart's schema (1975) would be quite unambiguous, which, according to Michaelis (1983) is not the case. For this strategy to be successful, we also need a model of language description, which can be used for making non-ambiguous statements about the realization of the semantic attributes by reference to which the structurally important units of text types can be identified. Thus any discussion of the realization of textual structures will involve at least three types of abstraction. These abstractions are shown in Table 3.2.

Table 3.2 The realization of the elements of generic structure

> *Type 1*: an element of a GSP, e.g. Placement.
> *Type 2*: its crucial semantic attribute(s), e.g. person particularization.
> *Type 3*: The lexicogrammatical pattern(s) capable of realizing person particularization, e.g. indefinite modification.

Table 3.2 is not presented as a complete statement of how Placement in nursery tales can be analysed. In applying these principles to the realization of this element, I shall proceed from the simplest case, i.e. option (ii) (see Table 3.1) where it is realized discretely.

The crucial semantic property relevant to the realization of the element Placement is that of 'character particularization'. Whatever else is or is not achieved at this element, this much of meaning must be conveyed. However, this semantic property itself may be manifested lexicogrammatically either *explicitly* or *inexplicitly*. I shall describe the former mode first; so, the focus of the discussion at present is a discrete Placement whose realization is explicit. The most frequent, almost formulaic linguistic manifestation of character particularization is achieved through a declarative clause, in which the Process is relational – either existential, intensive or possessive – and the role of Participant is mapped on an indefinite nominal group where the modifier must be realized either by the indefinite article or by a cardinal numeral. These linguistic features are exemplified by the following:

1   Once upon a time there was a woman ... (Jacobs: *Tom Tit Tot*)
2   There was once upon a time a good man who had two children a girl by a first wife, and a boy by the second. (Jacobs: *The Rose Tree*)
3   Once upon a time when pigs spoke rhyme
    And monkeys chewed tobacco,
    And hens took snuff to make them tough,

And ducks went quack, quack, quack, O!
There was an old sow with three little pigs ...
(Jacobs: *Three Little Pigs*)

An examination of a wider range of corpus shows that the important lexicogrammatical fact here is not the nature of the Process but the characterization of the nominal group which realizes some Participant role. So it can be stated quite categorically that character particularization when explicitly realized must involve the presence of nominal group(s) the Thing word of which must be an animate – or quasi-animate – noun modified by the indefinite article as in *a woman, a good man, an old sow* or by a cardinal numeral as in *two children* and *three little pigs*. Definite modifiers, e.g. *the, this, her* etc. can be used only when they can be interpreted by reference to an already particularized person. The Process, on the other hand, does not have to be relational as the following example shows:

4   A wolf used to raid a farmer's hencoop every night.

Why is it that indefinite modification achieves character particularization? The rationale is extremely simple: an indefinite modification always implies that there exist other entities of the class named by the noun so modified. What achieves particularization is precisely the contrast between those singled out by mention and those left aside unmentioned (Butt 1984). I see character particularization as the one single crucial semantic property relevant to explicit realization of Placement.

Apart from this crucial property, there are two associated ones. The difference between the two kinds of semantic properties is that the former has to be present if Placement is discrete and explicit; the latter do not have to be present, but often are. These may be referred to as 'temporal distance' and 'impersonalization'. Through temporal distance, the events and characters of the tale are placed at a point in time far removed from that of the tale's creation or reception. The congruent, and again, almost formulaic formal realization is through a Temporal Adjunct with the feature 'far', e.g. *Once upon a Time, (Long) long ago* or just *Once*. Its non-congruent, metaphorical (Halliday 1994) realization is achieved by diverse means: either a Locative Adjunct is used with the feature 'far', or reference is made to some mythical being or to an improbable (set of) event(s). In example 3, we find both the congruent and metaphorical realization of temporal distance, where the metaphorical realization takes the form of a series of events each of which is equally improbable. In 5, the metaphorical realization takes the form of invoking a mythical being; and introducing a Locative Adjunct:

5   When good King Arthur reigned, there lived near the Land's End of England, in the country of Cornwall, a farmer who had one only son called Jack.
    (Jacobs: *Jack the Giant-killer*)

I would draw attention to the use of the myth in the nursery tale. Mythical characters, places and events are treated as common knowledge standing in no need of introduction. The treatment of myth as common shared knowledge has significant consequences for the optionality of the element Placement, as I shall argue at a later stage.

Impersonalization refers to the convention whereby neither the narrator nor the audience can be assigned the role of *dramatis personae* in the tale. Even when Kipling addresses his audience as *Best Beloved*, this form and all others co-referential with it, relate to the outer contexts of creation and reception; they do not pertain to the inner reconstituted context of the tale itself. Milne's *Winnie-the-Pooh* is of some interest from this point of view. Christopher Robin, introduced into the tale as one of the characters therein, is unrecognizable to Christopher Robin the audience, as the extract below shows:

6   He crawled out of the gorse-bush, brushed the prickles from his nose, and began to think again. And the first person he thought of was Christopher Robin.
    ('Was that me?' said Christopher Robin in an awed voice, hardly daring to believe it.
    'That was you.'
    Christopher Robin said nothing but his eyes got larger and larger, and his face got pinker and pinker.)
    So Winnie-the-Pooh went round to his friend ...
    (Milne: *Winnie-the-Pooh*, text in bracket from the original)

On finding out that he is in the inner context of the tale, Christopher Robin's eyes grow 'larger and larger' and his face gets 'pinker and pinker'; and well it might, since the experience of listening to tales does not generally prepare one for such an eventuality. The semantic property of impersonalization shows the tale's unmistakable affinity to literature, where the *I* of the poem, the story or the novel is best not interpreted as referring to the person of the author. This permits us to add one more observation to the realization of character particularization: the Thing-noun of the realizing nominal group should have the speech role 'other' (Halliday and Hasan 1976). Both the associated properties – temporal distance and impersonalization – have essentially the same function: they both remove the events and the characters of the tale from the axis of the biographical to that of the general and hypothetical. Thus the tale with explicit Placement is clearly marked off from narratives of personal experience such as analysed by Labov (1972).

These three properties – particularization, impersonalization and temporal distance – can be seen as forming the semantic nucleus that is relevant to the realization of Placement. In addition, two other semantic properties need mention; these are 'attribution' and 'habitude'. By attribution I refer to the fact that the particularized character may be assigned certain characteristics; these may pertain to quality, status, possession or relationship. The formal realization of attribution is achieved by clauses with intensive, circumstantial or possessive Process where Carrier is a particularized nominal, and/or by the presence of appropriate Modifying/Qualifying elements in nominal groups. Habitude refers to the assignment of habitual acts/states to the particularized character(s). A linguistic unit capable of realizing this property must refer to an even tenor of existence, which can later function as the background to the set of events which constitute the various stages of the tale. The habitual nature of actions can be indicated through the selection of simple past tense where the lexical verb of the Process is non-punctiliar; however, with punctiliar verbs the use of iterative expressions, e.g. *often, for many years* and/or such exhaustive expressions as *whenever, wherever, nobody, anybody* and/or a modal auxiliary is required. Thus examples 2 and 5 cited earlier continue as follows and constitute Placement of the two stories:

2a There was once upon a time a good man who had two children: a girl by a first wife, and a boy by the second. The girl was as white as milk, and her lips were like cherries. Her hair was like golden silk, and it hung to the ground. Her brother loved her dearly, but her wicked stepmother hated her. (Jacobs: *The Rose Tree*)

5a When good King Arthur reigned, there lived near the Land's End of England, in the country of Cornwall, a farmer who had one only son called Jack. He was brisk and of a ready lively wit, so that nobody or nothing could worst him.
   In those days the Mount of Cornwall was kept by a huge giant named Cormoran. He was eighteen feet in height, and about three yards around the waist, of a fierce and grim countenance, the terror of all the neighbouring towns and villages. He lived in a cave in the midst of the Mount, and whenever he wanted food he would wade over to the mainland, where he would furnish himself with whatever came in his way. Everybody at his approach ran out of their houses, while he seized on their cattle, making nothing of carrying half-a-dozen oxen on his back at a time; and as for their sheep and hog, he would tie them round his waist like a bunch of tallow-dips. He had done this for many years, so that all of Cornwall was in despair. (Jacobs: *Jack the Giant-killer*)

Attribution and habitude have the function of foregrounding those characters which are most central to the development of the tale. In 'filling out' the character(s), they set up a certain expectation of typical behaviour in a range of circumstances. Or to put it another way, the events of the tale retrospectively justify the attributes and habitual behaviours assigned to the character(s). Thus, at least in well-made tales, the presence of these properties is fully motivated. However, so long as their realization continues, the tale is 'arrested' at the element Placement. In order to move to the element Initiating Event, the cycle of the habitual has to be broken by a one-time-occurring event. I refer to both these properties of attribution and habitude as 'elaborative'. So the semantic properties associated with the element Placement fall into two categories: those which are nuclear, and those which are elaborative. Particularization, temporal distance and impersonalization are nuclear while attribution and habitude are elaborative.

I would suggest that potentially all elements of the nursery tale have these two general types of semantic properties associated with them. The difference between the two is that at least some selection from among the nuclear properties is essential to the movement of the tale, while the tale can progress without any selection from the elaborative properties. For this reason the latter can be viewed as optional. Moreover, the overall structure of the tale has a way of getting round the absence of the optional category. For example, if attribution is not built in at Placement, the later developments of the tale would still permit the audience to infer such an attribute retrospectively. In Jacobs' *Tom Tit Tot* we are not told first that the old woman's daughter was stupid; however, we infer this from the girl's inability to interpret an idiomatic expression of her own mother tongue which leads her to make a gaffe. In this respect the tale is like a certain kind of literature, where it is truer than in everyday life that handsome is he who handsome does. The behaviours – verbal and non-verbal – of a character in a story or novel become a means of symbolically articulating (Hasan 1979; 1985b) its value in the text, and ultimately relate to the entire thematic development of the literary artefact.

Table 3.3 presents a summary of the semantic properties relevant to the element Placement and their typical lexicogrammatical realization; Table 3.4 presents an informal analysis of 2a, using the categories summarized in Table 3.3.

This completes our account of the explicit realization of a discrete Placement. How is inexplicit realization of discrete Placement achieved? The semantic property central to this distinction is of person particularization. Hopefully, the above account has demonstrated that when the realization of discrete Placement is explicit, then person particularization is made explicit within the text. Inexplicit realization is built upon the assumption of common, shared knowledge. Thus it immediately raises the question of allusion to other texts, whether spoken or written, that are supposed to be current in the community. When person particularization is achieved through the use of a proper noun, I refer to this as inexplicit realization. The use of a proper noun implies that the person mentioned thus is known; this in turn implies the existence of other texts, and brings allusion into play. The body of knowledge that is assumed as available, independent of the text under focus, may be the property of large sections of the community, as is the case with characters from mythologies. For the members of their own community neither Zeus, nor Indra, nor King Arthur, nor St. Paul need be explicitly particularized. Their identity has been created cumulatively through the mythic system absorbed by large sections of the culture so that the assumed familiarity can be used as a point of departure as in example 5 and again as follows:

THE NURSERY TALE AS A GENRE 63

Table 3.3 Summary of realizational categories for explicit discrete Placement

NUCLEAR	ELABORATIVE
Crucial –Person particularization: realized by indefinite modification, e.g. *a, some, one, two, three*... of animate/quasi-animate noun as Thing. **Associated** –Impersonalization: realized by third person noun as Thing in nominal group with indefinite modification. –Temporal distance: realized by locative adjunct (temporal/spatial) with semantic feature 'far'; metaphorically, location identified by the improbable, the exotic and the mythic.	–Attribution: realized by intensive, possessive or circumstantial process; Carrier particularized person; attribute, identity, possession, relation or by Epithet, Ordinal, Classifier and/or Qualifier modifying particularized person as Thing. –Habitude: realized by simple past if lexical verb is non-punctiliar; otherwise by modals *used to, would* and/or locative adjunct (temporal) with feature 'frequent', e.g. *often, every now and then,* and/or conditional expressions, e.g. *whenever, whoever, whatever,* etc.

7 When King Arthur's glory was at its best, his sister, the Queen of Lothian lived at her lonely castle in the north ... (Hope-Moncrieff: *The Young Unknown*)

At a more restricted level, a quasi mythology may be created by a succession of tales themselves. Here the mythology is not so pervasive, and must be regarded the property of a much smaller section of the community as a whole. The creation of such restricted mythologies perhaps provides an insight into the nature of the widely accepted myths. Some examples would be *Dr Who, Tintin, Asterix, Babar, Winnie-the-Pooh, Christopher Robin,* Revd Awdry's various engines named *Gordon, Thomas, Edward, Percy,* etc. or the dinosaur *Desmond.* Each tale in such a saga augments the mythology, and to the devoted young audience the characters thus created might possess a particularization which might well exceed their perception of the particularization of King Arthur and his valiant knights. Today's child is far more likely to ask: who is Merlin? than: who is Dr Who? A well-established saga of tales can take a lot for granted as is evident from 8, which the uninitiated have difficulty in following. Those sagas still struggling to establish themselves may have to resort to a reminder as in 9:

8 Henry and Gordon were lonely when Thomas left the yard to run his Branch Line. They missed him very much.
   They had more work to do. They couldn't wait in the shed till it was time, and find their coaches at the platform; they had to fetch them. They didn't like that... (Revd Awdry: *Troublesome Engines*)

Table 3.4 The semantics and lexicogrammar of the realization of Placement in example 2a. Jacobs: *The Rose Tree*

There was once upon a time a good man who had two children: a girl by a first wife, and a boy by the second. The girl was as white as milk, and her lips were like cherries. Her hair was like golden silk, and it hung to the ground. Her brother loved her dearly, but her wicked stepmother hated her. (Jacobs: *The Rose Tree*)	
once upon a time	**temporal distance** realized by temporal adjunct, with feature 'far'
a good man	**person particularization** realized by indefinite modifier: *a* + animate Thing: *man* **impersonalization** realized by third person noun as Thing: *man* **attribution** realized by Epithet: *good* modifying *man*
two children: a girl; a boy	**person particularization** realized by modifier *two, a, a* + animate Thing: *children, girl, boy*
had	**attribution** realized by Possessive Process; Carrier: *a good man* Possession (relation) *two children: a girl . . . a boy*
a first wife	**person particularization** and **attribution** realized by *a* and *first*, respectively; (note relation between *man, wife*)
the second wife	**person particularization** and **attribution** realized by *the* and *second* (both interpreted by reference to *first wife*)
The girl was as white as milk	**attribution** realized by intensive, attributive process; Carrier: *the girl* (particularized)
her lips were like cherries	**attribution** realized by intensive, attributive Process; Carrier: *her lips* (note introduction by reference to particularized person)
her hair was like golden silk	**attribution** as above
it hung to the ground	**habitude** (= metaphorical attribution) realized by simple past *hung* non-punctiliar lexical verb
Her brother loved her dearly	**habitude** realized by simple past *loved* non-punctiliar lexical verb
her wicked stepmother hated her	**habitude** realized as above; **attribution** realized by Epithet *wicked*

THE NURSERY TALE AS A GENRE 65

9   I wonder how many of you know Sammy? I expect some of you have heard the story of how he saved the express from an accident. In those days he was only a rather unhappy little shunting engine, but ever since that adventure he has been a proud passenger engine on the line between Sleeping Sunbury and Little Bumbledon ... (Gibbs: *Sammy Meets Father Christmas*)

I suggest that the modern practice of using proper nouns to refer to the *dramatis personae* without a textual person particularization has its origin in the above-mentioned phenomena. But in many modern nursery tales, we do not have even a quasi myth to fall back on; so the effect of this practice is quite different from that which it has in the intertextually supported saga. At this moment we are probably witness to the stabilization of a change in the conventions of the nursery tale. Be that as it may, the door to the optionality of Placement is opened partly through the possibility of inexplicit realization. But before I turn to this, a word about non-discrete Placement.

Non-discrete Placement is included or interspersed within the realization of the Initiating Event. Let me first provide examples of non-discrete Placement, whose realization is explicit:

10 A girl once went to the fair to hire herself for servant. At last a funny-looking old gentleman engaged her, and took her home to his house. (Jacobs: *Master of all Masters*)
11 A woman was sitting at her reel one night;
    And still she sat, and still she reeled, and still she wished for company.
    (Jacobs: *The Strange Visitor*)

In both these cases the particularization is explicit, but it is presented along with (some part of) the Initiating Event. This is borne out by the fact that the event(s) mentioned relate to a particular occasion rather than habitual doings. Lying at the border of explicit and inexplicit non-discrete realization are openings of the following type:

12 Once upon a time when pigs spoke rhyme ...
    All the birds of the air came to the magpie and asked her to teach them how to build nests. For the magpie is the cleverest bird of all at building nests. (Jacobs: *The Magpie's Nest*)
13 The cat and the mouse
    Play'd in the malt-house:
    The cat bit the mouse's tail off.
    (Jacobs: *The Cat and the Mouse*)

In 12 an entire superordinate species *all the birds* is mentioned, followed by what appears to be mention of a subspecies *the magpie*. Then, within the same message, one specific member of the subspecies is mentioned, i.e. *her*, with a return to the whole species of *the magpie* immediately after. The specific member is not explicitly particularized for the audience. In 13, this toing and froing between species and member is absent; simply one specific member from each of the two species is mentioned, but the specificity of the two members is not explicated textually. However, in both cases the inter-

66   PART ONE: TEXT AND CONTEXT

action between the characters builds upon some characteristic attribute of the species, so they can be treated as prototypes. In 12 such knowledge is not just presumed, but explicitly stated in the last sentence of the example: *For the magpie is the cleverest* ... etc. In 13, where the interactive patterns of behaviour for the two species are supposed to be common shared knowledge no such explicit explanation is provided. The relation between cat and mouse is treated on a par with the wider mythic systems; both kinds of knowledge are seen as pervasively shared by members of the community. What cats do to mice is not something one needs to be told about explicitly just as what Merlin or King Arthur can achieve needs no specific mention. If 12 and 13 are compared with 10 and 11, it will be seen that while the latter have a vestigial manifestation of Placement in the initial indefinite nominal groups, *A girl* and *A woman*, the persons of *the* (specific) *magpie*, *the cat* and *the mouse* are not particularized textually. Although neither contains the crucial semantic property of person particularization, in 12 at least the associated property of temporal distance and the elaborative property of attribution are present; and this permits us the possibility of treating the opening as 'some sort of' Placement. Of course the 'sort' that it is, is 'inexplicit', non-discrete Placement, not containing the crucial characteristic of the element. This makes 12 a 'fuzzy' case. But even 13 is somewhat fuzzy. True that it does not have either the nuclear or the elaborative properties, but the ambiguity of the reference of *the cat* and *the mouse* as either species or as prototype, as well as the possibility of assumed knowledge of their attributes, etc. makes it doubtful whether we can think of it as a story entirely without Placement. This fuzziness is removed when a character is brought in as a proper noun with the role of a participant in a once-occurring event. In such cases the associated and elaborative properties alone can be used as a means of determining whether the tale contains the element Placement. In 14, 15 and 16 it cannot be maintained that there is any indication of the element Placement:

14   One day, when Christopher Robin and Winnie-the-Pooh and Piglet were all talking together, Christopher Robin finished the mouthful he was eating and said carelessly: 'I saw a heffalump today, Piglet.' (Milne: *Winnie-the-Pooh*)

15   One day Henny-Penny was picking up corn in the cornyard when – whack! – something hit her upon the head. 'Goodness gracious me!' said Henny-Penny; 'The sky's a-going to fall; I must go and tell the king.' (Jacobs: *Henny-Penny*)

16   Janet was looking in the window of the sweet-shop. It was full of Easter eggs.
'Which would you like, darling?' asked her mother. Janet had already made up her mind. Right in the middle of the window was a chocolate egg with a blue ribbon ... (Wilson: *Chocolate Kittens*)

Although there is no Placement in 14–16, at a more delicate level they differ from each other. The identities of the characters mentioned in 14 have already been carefully constructed through other texts. Someone unfamiliar with the Pooh saga will fail to appreciate this fact. However, in 14 and 15 the tale establishes itself as a tale by invoking a fictional environment, which does not run parallel to the events of everyday life. Little boys do not talk to piglets, though a piglet with a capital P is different; hens do not carry messages to kings, but a hen that is quasi human (note the *her*) is different. In 16, this fictional quality is absent; it could very well be the description of a day's doing for Janet, which is being presented from the point of view of a third party. Given the sentence *Peter was going to the carnival and on the way he lost his pocket money*, we do not immediately react to it as an event in a tale as we do when told *A girl went to the fair to hire herself for servant* or *An old women was sweeping her house, and she found a little crooked sixpence*.

It seems to me that tales opened by examples 14–16 cannot be said to have 'taken up' the option of Placement. And if 8 is seen as part of the Placement for *Troublesome Engines*, this is purely on the basis of the myth of Railway Engines and by virtue of the elaborative properties of attribution and habitude.

This discussion of the options for Placement and their realization may be summed up as in Figure 3.3 below.

Hopefully, the figure is self-explanatory, especially when read in conjunction with the examples cited for each quadrant, and the information provided in Figure 3.3 (a) and (d) are diametrically opposed; (a) is the clearest case of the selection of Placement, while (d) is the clearest case of the non-selection of Placement. If (a) and (d) are seen as the endpoints of a continuum, (b) and (c) represent two midstages on it. In (b) the Placement is discrete but inexplicit as for example in:

17 Mr and Mrs Vinegar lived in a vinegar bottle. Now one day ... (Jacobs: *Mr Vinegar*)
18 Tommy Grimes was sometimes a good boy, and sometimes a bad boy; and when he was a bad boy, he was a very bad boy. Now his mother used to say to him: 'Tommy, Tommy, be a good boy, and don't go out of the street, or else Mr Miacea will take you.' But still when he was a bad boy he would go out of the street; and one day, ... (Jacobs: *Mr Miacea*)

In these cases the Placement is discrete; neither the attribution nor the habitude 'run into' the realization of the Initiating Event. But note that characters are not explicitly particularized, being mentioned by name as if they were already known. (c), on the other hand, is realized explicitly, but is included within the realization of another element, Initiating Event. A certain degree of confusion can arise here, the source of which is discussed below. Before leaving Figure 3.3, note the incomplete square, which lies on the periphery of quadrants (b), (c) and (d). The examples here are of the type in which 'placing' the character appropriately would depend upon the degree and kind of socialization that the reader has had. This is where fuzzy cases such as *the magpie, the cat and mouse, Henny-Penny, Winnie-the-Pooh, Gordon, Henry, Thomas, Milly Molly Mandy* and *King Arthur* belong.

68   PART ONE: TEXT AND CONTEXT

DISCRETE | **NON-DISCRETE**

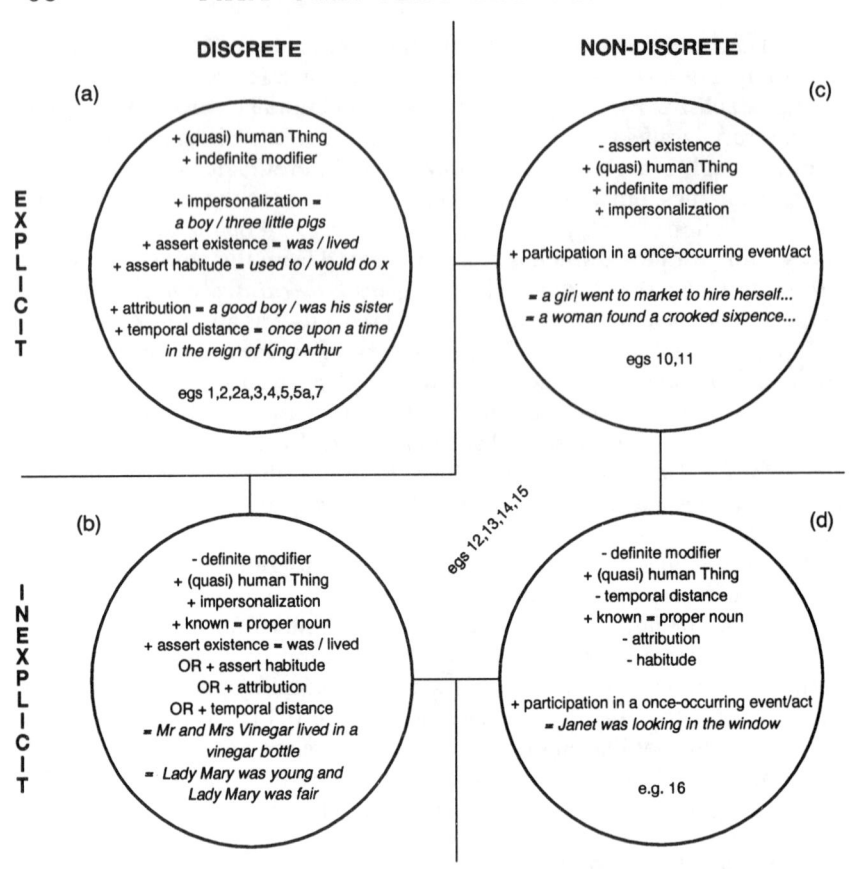

(a) EXPLICIT:
- \+ (quasi) human Thing
- \+ indefinite modifier
- \+ impersonalization = *a boy / three little pigs*
- \+ assert existence = *was / lived*
- \+ assert habitude = *used to / would do x*
- \+ attribution = *a good boy / was his sister*
- \+ temporal distance = *once upon a time in the reign of King Arthur*

egs 1,2,2a,3,4,5a,7

(c) EXPLICIT:
- − assert existence
- \+ (quasi) human Thing
- \+ indefinite modifier
- \+ impersonalization
- \+ participation in a once-occurring event/act
  = *a girl went to market to hire herself...*
  = *a woman found a crooked sixpence...*

egs 10,11

(b) INEXPLICIT:
- − definite modifier
- \+ (quasi) human Thing
- \+ impersonalization
- \+ known = proper noun
- \+ assert existence = *was / lived*
- OR + assert habitude
- OR + attribution
- OR + temporal distance
  = *Mr and Mrs Vinegar lived in a vinegar bottle*
  = *Lady Mary was young and Lady Mary was fair*

(d) INEXPLICIT:
- − definite modifier
- \+ (quasi) human Thing
- − temporal distance
- \+ known = proper noun
- − attribution
- − habitude
- \+ participation in a once-occurring event/act
  = *Janet was looking in the window*

e.g. 16

egs 12,13,14,15

Figure 3.3   The realization of the options of Placement

I do not propose to discuss the realization of the Initiating Event with the same degree of detail – this would require a paper to itself – but it is important to comment briefly on this element of the tale, since the difference between discrete and non-discrete Placement is often not appreciated. Some confusion arises from the fact that, at a more delicate level, the Initiating Event can potentially be seen as made up of three parts. Elsewhere, I have referred to these as 'setting', 'event' and 'culmination' (Hasan 1984b); perhaps, it would have been more appropriate to use the terms 'frame', 'main act' and 'sequel'. The justification for these alternatives will hopefully become obvious as the discussion continues. 'Frame' is a part of the Initiating Event which may or may not be present. In 1a it is not selected, whereas in 15 it is:

1a: (i) Once upon a time there was a woman,
     (ii) and she baked five pies. (Jacobs: *Tom Tit Tot*)
15:   (i) One day Henny-Penny was picking corn in the cornyard

(ii) when – whack! – something hit her upon the head.
(iii) 'Goodness Gracious me!' said Henny-Penny;
(iv) 'the sky's a-going to fall;
(v) I must go and tell the king.'

Clause (i) of 15 has the function of frame. Frame refers to a state of affairs which acts as the background for the main act. So the semantic property essential to it is anteriority OR concurrence with main act. Lexicogrammatically, the clause realizing frame may have a progressive tense to indicate concurrence, but this is, of course, not the case if anteriority is indicated. Consider the following example:

> 19 (i) One day the master was out, (ii) and then the lad, (iii) as curious as could be, hurried to the chamber where his master kept his wondrous apparatus for changing copper into gold ... (Jacobs: *The Master and his Pupil*)

Here frame is realized by (i); the tense is a simple past and (i) is anterior to the main act, realized by clause (ii).

Main act is an essential part of the Initiating Event. Semantically, it is characterized as punctiliar process, a one-time happening or doing. Often the one-time-ness is realized by the selection of a Temporal Adjunct, e.g. *one day* in 15 and 19; but such underlining is not essential. In 1a, we simply have *and she baked five pies*; the punctiliar nature of the main act is sufficient by itself to indicate oneness. But how do we pick out the one-time happening and doing which functions as the main act? This has been perceived as a serious problem. So, for example, Longacre comments

> I have been unable to find any surface structure features which distinguish an episode which encodes the Inciting Moment from any other Episode. (Longacre 1974)

Although his Inciting Moment is not exactly identical with what I refer to as main act, there is a good deal of overlap. Both Labov (1972) and Rumelhart (1975) appear to rely on the one-time-ness of the act, but this requires a contrast with Placement or frame; and I have attempted to show that both Placement and frame are optional. A tale could begin with *A woman baked five pies* just as we have *A girl once went to hire herself for servant*. If the Initiating Event consisted of only one such action or happening, one could always stipulate that the first action or event with the semantic features 'actualized time' and 'one-time-ness' is the critical one; but this is not the case. For example, in 14 we find two progressive and three simple past tenses:

> 14 (i) One day, when Christopher Robin and Winnie-the Pooh and Piglet *were talking*, (ii) Christopher Robin *finished* the mouthful he *was eating* (iii) and *said* carelessly: (iv) 'I *saw* a heffalump today, Piglet.'

Here it would be quite wrong to suggest that (ii) *finished* is the main act in the Initiating Event since nothing much hangs upon the act of finishing. It is really the *saying* (iii) that sets the whole story going. So the main act is where it all begins to move. And we can make some generalizations about its lexicogrammatical realization:

Table 3.5   The lexicogrammar of main act

(i)   Process be punctiliar;
(ii) Process be Non-relational (i.e. Material or Mental or Verbal);
(iii) The tense of the verbal group be non-progressive;
(iv) If (i)–(iii) are equal for two (or more) processes, occurring in a clause-complex then the one that is temporally posterior-most will realize the main act of the Initiating Event.

The main act is followed by sequel. These are states of affairs which are related to the main act in specific ways. At least three kinds of relations can be found: (i) (purely) temporal sequence: (ii) causal dependence; and (iii) tangential relations. It is an interesting fact that most of the relations between the states of affairs in the Initiating Event are of the causal type. Temporal sequence which is generally favoured as the most frequent relation within the story turns out to be the outcome of the fact that effects follow causes temporally. Sequel again poses a problem. The fabric of a tale appears seamless; and in this integrated whole each happening or action is related in some way to some other. The best criterion I have found for the closure of the Initiating Event – which is logically the closure of sequel as well – is to relate it to the main act. The main act sets up an expectancy. Thus (1a) *baking* sets up an expectation of eating/selling/giving the baked goods; (19) *hurrying* into a chamber sets up an expectation of getting out of that chamber; (15) being *hit* on the head sets up an expectation of a safety measure or a retort. An Initiating Event closes where an expectation that has been set up by the main act is frustrated. Thus within its own organization the Initiating Event is like a metaphor for the whole tale just as a clause may be said to be a metaphor for the text (Halliday 1981). The part frame (or setting) appears to resemble Placement; and, in fact, so far as I can see, neither Labov (1972) nor Rumelhart (1975) make a distinction between what I have called Placement and frame. There are, however, crucial differences between the two concepts: frame is only locally relevant, while Placement is relevant to the whole tale. To say that the story of *The Rose Tree* (example 2a) and of *Henny-Penny* (example 15) can be rewritten, following Rumelhart, as Story − Setting + Episode or, following Labov, that both can be described as having the element Orientation does not do justice to the structuring of the two tales. Introducing characters in frames is not the same thing as introducing them in Placement.

Although the account of the realization of the nursery tale's structure is incomplete, I hope that the preceding discussion has shown that the line of approach suggested here might be a fruitful one. Not only does it permit a statement of the possible tale structures, but coupled with a model of language description in which the relationship between meaning and wording is treated in a systematic, non-*ad hoc* manner, the approach presented here might permit more accurate, more revealing statements than have been possible hitherto. In point of fact, the description of the structure of the nursery tale is simply a modest beginning; the much more challenging question is that of the basis for evaluative judgements of the tales. And this enterprise will require attention to variation in realizational strategies. At that time, we shall have to begin to scrutinize the depth of what Longacre – and many other linguists – refer to as surface structure. For meanings and wording, even though we dissociate them for purposes of analysis, are a unity. The more exciting challenges for linguistics are yet to come, when having abandoned the dissociated approach of deep and surface structure, we enquire into the linguistic bases for understanding inferences and implications. The study of the comprehension of texts, in which the role of language is constitutive, pushes us inevitably in that direction.

Note

1   This is an edited version of the original which was published in *Nottingham Linguistic Circular*, 13, pp. 71–102, 1984.

References

Butt, D. G. (1984) *To Be Without a Description of to Be*. Unpublished PhD thesis. Sydney: Macquarie University.
Coulthard, M. and Montgomery, M. (1981) *Studies in Discourse Analysis*. London: Routledge & Kegan Paul.
Eagleton, T. (1983) *Literary Theory*. London: Basil Blackwell.
Ellis, J. O. (1966) 'On contextual meaning'. In C. E. Bazell, J. C. Catford, M. A. K. Halliday and H. R. Robins (eds) *In Memory of J. R. Firth*. London: Longman.
Goffman, E. (1981) *Forms of Talk*. Philadelphia: University of Pennsylvania Press.
Halliday, M. A. K. (1977) 'Text as a semantic choice in social contexts'. In T. van Dijk and J. S. Petofi (eds) *Grammars and Descriptions*. Berlin: de Gruyter.
Halliday, M. A. K. (1981) 'Text semantics and clause grammar: some patterns of realization'. In J. E. Copeland and P. Davis (eds) *The Seventh LACUS Forum*. Columbia, S.C.: Hornbeam Press.
Halliday, M. A. K. (1994) *An Introduction to Functional Grammar*. 2nd edition. London: Edward Arnold.
Halliday, M. A. K. and Hasan, R. (1976) *Cohesion in English*. London: Longman.
Halliday, M. A. K. and Hasan, R. (1980) *Text and Context: Aspects of Language in a Social-Semiotic Perspective*. Sophia Linguistica VI. Tokyo: Sophia University Press. Revised and reprinted as *Language, Text and Context*. Deakin University Press (1985); Oxford University Press (1989).
Hasan, Ruqaiya (1976) 'The place of stylistics in the study of verbal art'. In H. Ringbom (ed.) *Style and Text*. Stockholm: Skriptor Press.
Hasan, Ruqaiya (1978) 'Text in the systemic-functional model'. In W. U. Dressler (ed.) *Current Trends in Textlinguistics*. Berlin: de Gruyter.
Hasan, Ruqaiya (1979) 'On the notion of text'. In J. Petofi (ed.) *Text versus Sentence: Basic Questions of Textlinguistics*. Hamburg: Helmut Buske, pp. 369–390.

Hasan, Ruqaiya (1980) *Language in the Study of Literature.* Report on *Working Conference on Language in Education,* Sydney University Extension Programme and Department of Linguistics. Sydney: University of Sydney.

Hasan, Ruqaiya (1981) 'What's going on?: A dynamic view of context'. In J. E. Copeland and P. Davis (eds) *The Seventh LACUS Forum.* Columbia: Hornbeam Press.

Hasan, Ruqaiya (ed.) (1984a) *Discourse on Discourse.* Report on Macquarie Discourse Analysis Workshop. Wollongong: Applied Linguistics Association of Australia.

Hasan, Ruqaiya (1984b) 'The structure of the nursery tale: an essay in text typology'. In L. Coveri (ed.) *Linguistica Testuale.* Rome: Bulzoni.

Hasan, Ruqaiya (1985a) 'The structure of a text'. Chapter 5 in M. A. K. Halliday and R. Hasan *Language, Text and Context.* Victoria: Deakin University Press (1985); Oxford: Oxford University Press (1989).

Hasan, Ruqaiya (1985b) 'The identity of a text'. Chapter 6 in M. A. K. Halliday and R. Hasan *Language, Text and Context.* Victoria: Deakin University Press (1985); Oxford: Oxford University Press (1989).

Hasan, Ruqaiya (1985c) *Linguistics, Language and Verbal Art.* Victoria: Deakin University Press.

Kress, G. (1982) *Learning to Write.* London: Routledge and Kegan Paul.

Labov, W. (1972) 'The transformation of experience in narrative syntax'. *Language in the Inner City: Studies in Black English Vernacular.* Philadelphia: University of Pennsylvania Press.

Longacre, R. E. (1974) 'Narrative versus other discourse genre'. In R. M. Brend (ed.) *Advances in Tagmemics.* Amsterdam: North-Holland.

Longacre, R. E. (1977) 'A taxonomic deep and surface structure analysis'. In T. van Dijk and J. S. Petofi (eds) *Grammars and Descriptions.* Berlin: de Gruyter.

Mandler, J. M. and Johnson, N. S. (1977) 'Remembrance of things parsed'. *Cognitive Psychology,* 9, 111–151.

Michaelis, A. (1983) *When is a Story Not a Story: A Study of the TV News Item.* Unpublished BA (Hons) thesis. Sydney: Macquarie University.

O'Toole, M. and Butt, D. G. (1984) 'The analysis of a short story'. In Ruqaiya Hasan (ed.) *Discourse on Discourse.* Report on Macquarie Discourse Analysis Workshop. Wollongong: Applied Linguistics Association of Australia.

Rumelhart, O. E. (1975) 'Notes on a schema for stories'. In *Representation and Understanding: Studies in Cognitive Science.* New York: Academic Press.

Sinclair, J. McH. and Coulthard, M. (1975) *Towards an Analysis of Discourse: The English Used by Teacher and Pupils.* London: Oxford University Press.

Vygotsky, L. S. (1971) *The Psychology of Art.* Cambridge, Mass.: MIT Press.

Nursery tales taken from:

Awdry, Rev. W. (1951) *Troublesome Engines.* The Railway Series No. 5, London: Kaye and Ward.

Gibb, E. (n.d.) *Sammy Meets Father Christmas.* Sammy the Shunter No. 6, Shepperton, Middlesex: Ian Allan.

Hope-Moncrieff, A. R. (n.d.) *The Young Hopeful.* In *Romance and Legends of Chivalry.* London: Gresham Publishing Co.

Jacobs, J. (1967) *English Fairy Tales.* New York: Dover Publications (an unaltered republication of the 3rd edition by G. B. Putnam's Sons and David Nutt, 1898).

Milne, A. A. (1926) *Winnie-the-Pooh.* London: Methuen.

Opie, I. and Opie, P. (1940) *The Puffin Book of Nursery Rhymes.* Harmondsworth: Penguin.

Part Two: Tools

4 The grammarian's dream: lexis as most delicate grammar[1]

1. The lexicogrammatical stratum

It was over two decades ago that Halliday remarked: 'The grammarian's dream is ... to turn the whole of linguistic form into grammar, hoping to show that lexis can be defined as "most delicate grammar" ' (Halliday 1961, 267). This paper briefly explores the reality of that dream by examining two questions: (1) is the project feasible? and (2) what would be the implications of 'turning the whole of linguistic form into grammar'? This formulation, by implication, rejects the views that (a) lexis is not form, and (b) that its relation to semantics IS unique.

Drawing upon Halliday (1977), I shall make the following assumptions:

(1) Language consists of three strata: semantics, lexicogrammar and phonology.
(2) These strata are related by 'realization': meanings are coded as wordings, wordings are coded as sound patterns.
(3) Each stratum is describable as a network of options; the description is therefore paradigmatic, with environments for options also being defined paradigmatically.
(4) The semantic stratum is organized into four metafunctional components: experiential, logical, interpersonal and textual.
(5) Each metafunction specifies a particular (set of) option network(s) as its output at the lexicogrammatical stratum.
(6) Each act of choice – the selection of each option – contributes to the formation of a structure.
(7) A unified structure in its totality is the output of selections from four distinct (sets of) lexicogrammatical networks, specified by the four metafunctions.
(8) 'It is the function of the lexico-grammatical stratum to map these structures one on to another so as to form a single integrated structure that represents [the output of (R. H.)] all [meta-functional (R. H.)] components simultaneously' (Halliday 1977).

Assumption (6) is immediately relevant. Grammars have traditionally been concerned with describing the formation of syntagms, using the syntagm itself as the starting-point for explaining the syntagm-formation phenomena. The Systemic Functional model has abandoned this approach in favour of one foreshadowed by Saussure (1916), Hjelmslev (1961) and Firth (1951), where the grammar of a language is viewed as a network of paradigmatic relations. If 'systemic options contribute to the formation of structure', and if the description of structure-formation is what characterizes grammar, then such system networks ARE the grammar. The question of feasibility can, then, be paraphrased as: 'Is it possible to extend a lexicogrammatical network in delicacy so as to turn it into a device for the description and generation of units of form called "lexical item"?' If so, then we shall have shown that lexis is delicate grammar.

This argument shifts attention to mechanisms whereby the paradigm and the syntagm – the option network and the structure – are brought into relation. (Henceforth the 'options' and 'networks' referred to are lexicogrammatical ones, unless otherwise stated.) An option can be viewed as instruction(s) to operate in a certain way; a specific structure is the outcome of following these operations. The technical term for such instructions is 'realization statement'. So realization statement is a mechanism mediating between networks and structures.

Six categories of realization statement will be used here:

(1) *insert* structural function x;
(2) *conflate* two/more functions into one element;
(3) *order* elements a and b (and ... n) *vis-à-vis* each other;
(4) *subcategorize* some function or feature;
(5) *pre-select* some feature as a concomitant of some insertion/sub-categorization;
(6) *outclassify* some function/feature as incompatible with some insertion/sub-categorization.

This view implies that options have consequences: they are justified by what they 'do'. And, since the doing takes cognizance of relations within the language, an option's justification is intra-linguistic. Simplifying greatly, the options for the description and generation of *enquire* and *ask* might differ in some respects; if so, the justification would not arise from the two activities differing physically, psychologically or socially, but from the differential lexicogrammatical patternings of the two lexical verbs. So ultimately, a delicate network is an enquiry into what Whorf (1956) called 'reactance'.

The network examined here is a minute part of the experiential metafunction's output, known as TRANSITIVITY, whose entry condition is [major] clause. (The technical terms in what follows are used as in Halliday (1985); features are shown in square brackets except in the networks themselves.) Figure 4.1 places TRANSITIVITY in relation to other systems applicable to [major] clause. Systems concurrent with TRANSITIVITY, e.g.

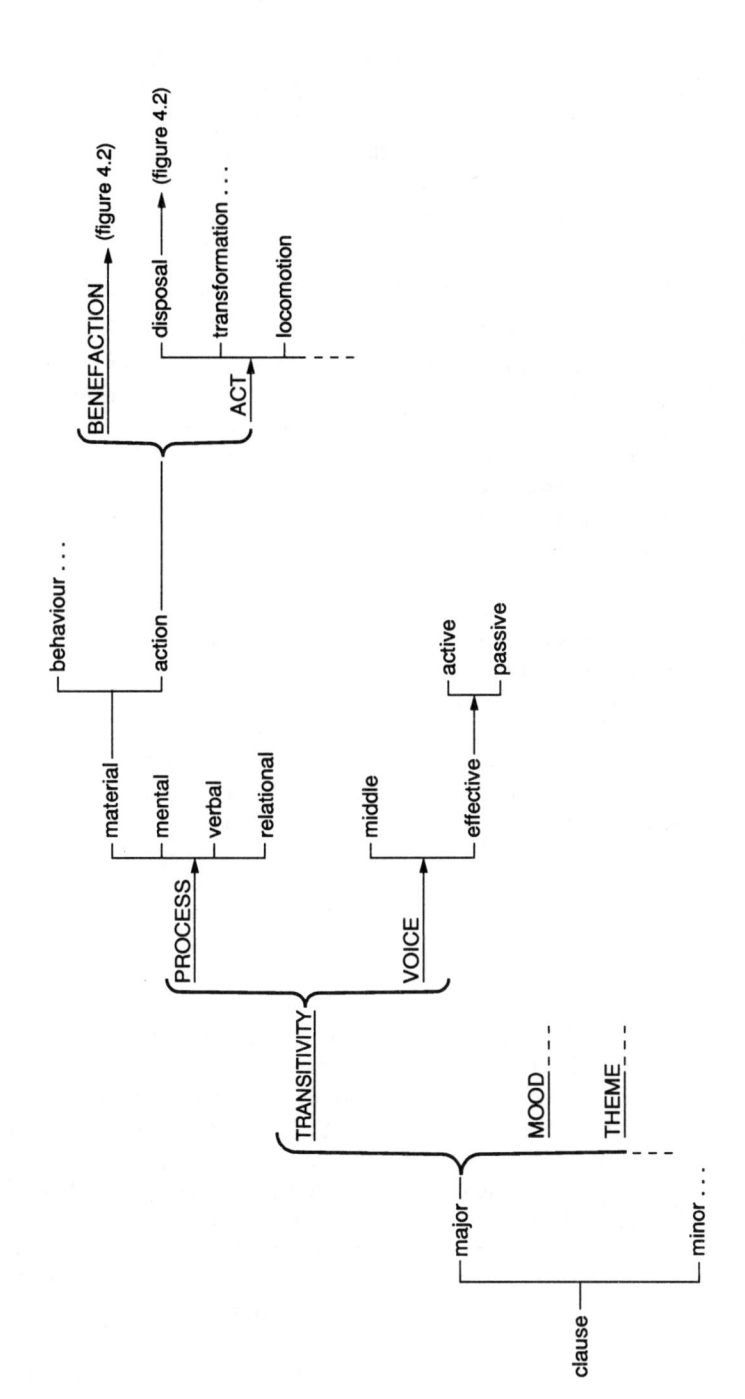

Figure 4.1 The entry condition for transitivity

MOOD, THEME, etc. will be ignored. Within TRANSITIVITY itself, VOICE options will be constantly assumed as [effective: active]. The portion of the network discussed belongs to PROCESS, and it has [disposal] as its entry condition. It is part of the lexicogrammar which constructs the semantic area that can be informally described as 'activities whose completion results in gain/loss of access to things'.

2. The lexicogrammar of acquisition: gather, collect, accumulate

[disposal] entails the options [material:action], which are built into its history, with the implication that the contribution they have made to the formation of the structure remains a constant wherever [disposal] itself is selected. No part of this contribution can be negated by any instruction attached to [disposal] or options dependent upon it. This principle operates across the system, irrespective of the degree of delicacy. Part of the contribution made by [effective:active] VOICE in conjunction with [material:action] PROCESS is:

A: 1. The functions Process, Medium and Agent are inserted
    2. Process pre-selects Event
    3. Medium and Agent each pre-select Thing
    4. Event is subcategorized as /material action/

By virtue of having to follow a particular systemic path, the selection of [disposal] inherits the bundle specified in A1–4. This I shall call PI, for 'systematic path inheritance', to keep it distinct from SI (semantic inheritance) (Brachman 1979; Collins and Quillian 1972) and 'conceptual dependency' (Schank 1972; 1975; Schank and Abelson 1977) in the AI literature. PI differs from both, in that it is not item-centred and is more rigorously defined. To see how PI works, imagine a network with options 1 through 7 as in Figure 4.1a. If (a, b) are the contribution of [1], (c, d) of [2], and (e, f) of [3], then the PI for [2] and [3] is (a, b); for [4] and [5], (a, b, c, d), and for [6] and [7] it is (a, b, e, f). Each progressive step in the network specifies both identity and uniqueness between classes of structures. When the network reaches a point where further uniqueness cannot be postulated, this is the logical endpoint; and the total selection expression – i.e. path specification – will, among other things, specify some formal structure(s) known as 'lexical item(s)'. The uniqueness of each lexical item is widely recognized (Berry 1977; Fawcett 1980; Fillmore 1977; Leech 1974; Lyons 1977). In this chapter I begin by concentrating on the identities of, for example, *give, share, collect, lose*, etc. and work toward their uniqueness.

The realization statements attached to [disposal] are:

B: 1. subcategorize Event as /(material action) of disposal involving change in location of Medium/
    2. subcategorize Medium Thing as /alienable object/

LEXIS AS MOST DELICATE GRAMMAR

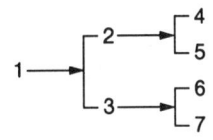

```
         ┌─ 2 ──→ ┌─ 4
1 ──────┤        └─ 5
         └─ 3 ──→ ┌─ 6
                  └─ 7
```

Figure 4.1a A simple system network

      3. subcategorize Agent Thing as /human, person(s) or institutions/

For lack of precise formal information, subcategorization is expressed informally. It should not be confused with Chomsky's selection restriction rules (1965): the latter operate on items; possess directionality, e.g. assign 'features of the Subject and Object to the Verb'; (1965, 92); and their non-observance leads to linguistic malaise. None of these is necessarily true of subcategorization. However, if B1–3 are not followed, the semantics of the resultant clause would be distinct from that of a clause whose underlying selection expression contains [disposal]. Consider:

(1a) Susan collected a lot of leaves.
(1b) The roof collected a lot of leaves.
(1c) She collected her thoughts.

(1a) is in keeping with B1–3; most speakers will 'read' it as Susan gaining access to a lot of leaves when the collecting is done; Susan is the 'doer', and the leaves are 'done-to'. In (1b), instruction B3 is not followed; the Agent is not human. Note that the roof is no longer 'doer', but 'location'. (1b) contains a grammatical metaphor (Halliday 1985), whose congruent pair would be *A lot of leaves collected on the roof*. The non-following of B3 will not always produce the semantic value of 'location' for the Agent (compare *These pipes distribute steam into the system* or *Her room carries the most amazing trash*); it will, however, produce a metaphorical effect. In (1c), B2 is not followed: the Medium is not an object, but rather a concept/abstraction. The clause is a good example of Whorf's 'objectification' (1956), where something itself not an object is treated as such. In English, a standard objectifying device is to use an abstract noun as the Medium of a Process, which normally requires a concrete noun as Medium. But this Medium-like thing, e.g. *her thoughts* in (1c), is not the Medium, as it would fail most of the heuristic tests applicable to that function. (Consider *What is she doing to her thoughts? – Collecting them* and *It is your thoughts you need to collect.*) (1c) is an instance of a complex metaphor, where the entire expression *collect + ... thoughts* must be seen as a unit, since in another such occurrence *collect* may bear little or no resemblance to *collect* in (1c). (Consider *She collected a good deal of kudos from that.*) This discussion, incidentally, justifies the validity of B1–3.

The system of BENEFACTION applies concurrently with that of ACT and is developed in Figure 4.2 below, where the systems dependent on [disposal] are also presented. This device will ensure that all systemic options relevant to [disposal] can be seen at one glance. The selection of [disposal] will demand the selection of one path from each of the three systems developed in Figure 4.2; while the systems of ACCESS and CHARACTER are directly dependent on [disposal], that of BENEFACTION is entailed by virtue of the dependence of [disposal] on [action].

ACCESS options are concerned with the result of the activity. The selection of [acquisition] implies the Agent's gain of access to the Medium, unless otherwise indicated. [deprivation] implies the reverse – the Agent loses access to the Medium. Indicating PI within brackets as before, the instructions for these options are:

C: 1. [acquisition]
   a. subcategorize Event as /(material action of disposal involving change in location of Medium) leading to Agent's gain of access to Medium/
   2. [deprivation]
   a. subcategorize Event as /(material action of disposal involving change in location of Medium) leading to Agent's loss of access to Medium/

CHARACTER options are concerned with the nature of the activity. The selection of [iterative] implies an inherently repetitive activity, in which the Agent–Medium configuration inherently remains identical; [non-iterative] implies an activity that is not inherently repetitive. The instructions are:

D: 1. [iterative]
   a. subcategorize Event as /(material action of disposal involving change in location of Medium) inherently repetitive/
   b. subcategorize Medium Thing as /(alienable object) divisible.
   2. [non-iterative]
   a. subcategorize Event as /(material action of disposal involving change in location) NOT inherently repetitive/

BENEFACTION options are concerned with specifying the benefit of the activity. [beneficile] implies that the activity is capable of permitting the indication of some benefiting party; [non-beneficile] implies that the activity is not capable of permitting such indication. On [beneficile] depend the options [inherent] or [potential]. [inherent] implies that the benefiting party MUST be specified; [potential] that the benefiting party MAY be specified: the resource is there; it may or may not be taken up.

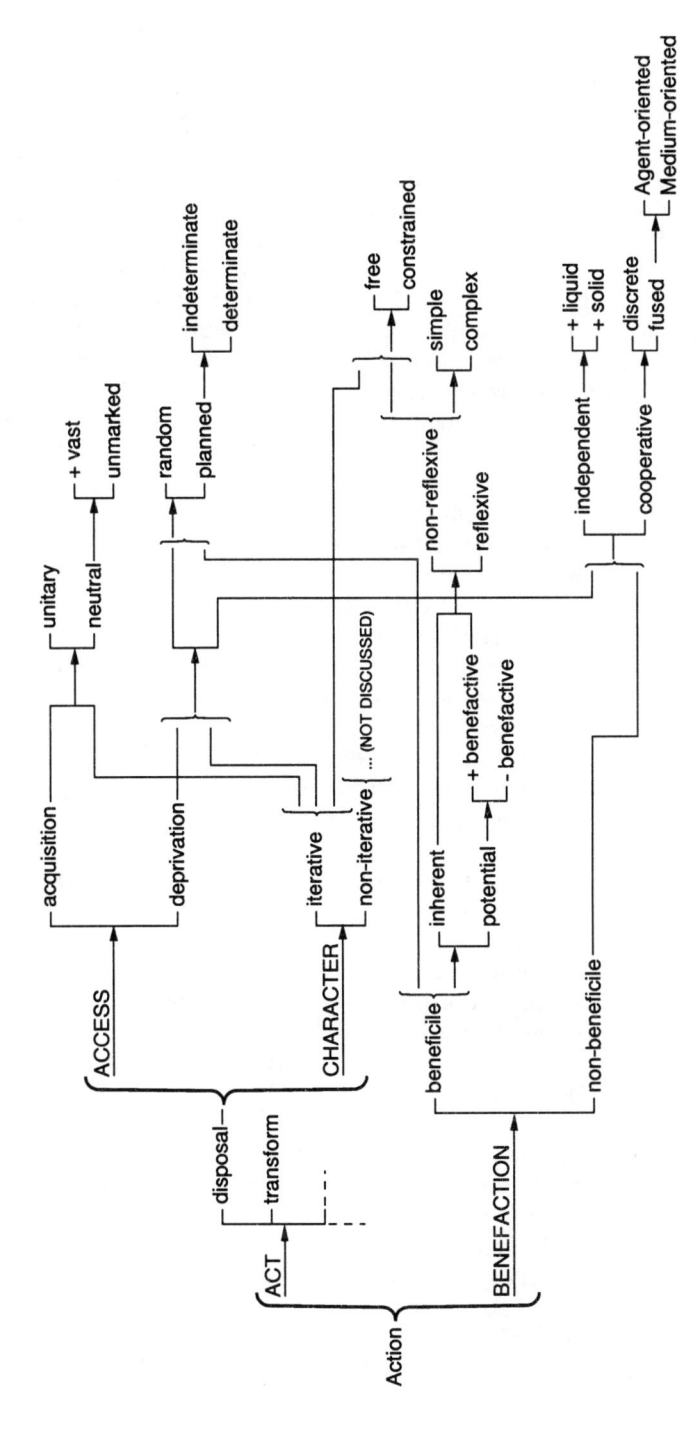

Figure 4.2 The process type [disposal:iterative]

[+benefactive] implies that the resource is to be positively deployed, and a benefiting party is to be specified. [−benefactive] implies that the resource has been passed up, and so no benefiting party is to be specified. When the benefiting party is specified – as entailed by the selection of either [inherent] or [+benefactive] – the option between [reflexive] and [non-reflexive] operates. It is concerned with the specification of the benefiting party's identity. [reflexive] implies that the Agent and the benefiting party are one and the same; [non-reflexive], that they are not the same. The selection of the latter permits the selection between [simple] and [complex] – both being concerned with providing further details about the benefiting party. [simple] implies that only one benefiting party is to be specified; [complex], that two discrete benefiting parties are to be specified. The remaining two options – [free] and [constrained] – will be discussed later. Here I provide the instructions attached to the BENEFACTION options presented so far:

E: 1. [non-beneficial]
     a. subcategorize Event as /(material action) INCAPABLE; of requiring function Benefiter/
     b. outclassify function Benefiter
    2. [beneficile]
     a. subcategorize Event as /(material action) CAPABLE of requiring function Benefiter(s)/
    3. [inherent]
     a. insert function Benefiter-1
     b. subcategorize Benefiter-1 as Recipient
     c. Benefiter pre-selects nominal group with Thing animate
     d. subcategorize Event as /(material action) NECESSARILY requiring Benefiter/
    4. [potential]
     a. subcategorize Event as /(material action) NOT NECESSARILY requiring Benefiter/
    5. [+benefactive]
     a. subcategorize Event as /(material action) requiring Benefiter/
     b. insert function Benefiter-1
     c. subcategorize Benefiter-1 as Client
     d. Benefiter pre-selects nominal group with Thing animate
    6. [−benefactive]
     a. subcategorize Events as /(material action) not needing Benefiter/
    7. [reflexive]
     a. Benefiter pre-selects (nominal group with Thing animate) and co-referential with Agent

8. [non-reflexive]
    a. Benefiter pre-selects (nominal group with Thing animate NOT co-referential with Agent)
9. [simple]
    a. outclassify Benefiter-2
10. [complex]
    a. insert Benefiter-2
    b. Benefiter-2 pre-selects (nominal group with Thing animate NOT co-referential with Agent)
    c. subcategorize Benefiter-2 as Ultimate Client
    d. Ultimate Client pre-selects prepositional group with preposition *for*
    e. conflate functions Ultimate Client and Prepositional Complement
    f. order Prepositional Complement to follow *for*

The notion 'benefiting party' or Benefiter is not self-evident. As Halliday (1985, 135) points out, the Benefiter does not necessarily benefit in the everyday sense of the word as shown by *Jocasta gave Claudius a dose of poison*. Again, in *John drove to the office*, from a common-sense point of view, John could be said to benefit from his driving. So it is important to point out that not only is the function Benefiter at the 'receiving end', but also it is recognized only if there is a dissociation between it and the Agent. The limiting case of the Benefiter is with the option [reflexive], where the benefiting party is co-referential with the Agent (see E7a above). But even here the meaning of Agent^Process^Medium is not the same as Agent^Process^Benefiter^Medium. Consider:

(2a)   Susan bought a dress (Agent^Process^Medium)
(2b)   Susan bought herself a dress (Agent^Process^Benefiter^Medium)

Although in the absence of Good Reason, (2a) would be interpreted as Susan buying the dress for herself, the possibility is always open that this may not be the case; with (2b) this indeterminacy does not exist. Compare:

(3)   Susan couldn't find a better present for Pam,
    (a) So she bought a dress.
    (b) So she bought herself a dress.

Because Susan's buying a dress does not have to be interpreted as Susan buying it for herself, so (3a) in this context can be 'read' as 'she bought a dress as a present for Pam'. (3b) does not permit this reading and will remain odd unless further appropriate speech work is done. The impossibility of conflating the Agent and Benefiter roles is important, as we shall see later. The differences between [beneficile:inherent] and [beneficile:potential:+benefactive] are also important. Consider:

(4) I gave John a book. [beneficile:inherent]
(5) I bought John a book. [beneficile:potential:+benefactive]

In (4), the function Benefiter is entailed (E3a and d, [i.e. E3 [inherent]: a. insert function Benefiter-1; d. subcategorize Event as /(material action) NECESSARILY requiring Benefiter/) -eds]; in (5) Benefiter is simply permitted. *I gave a book* implies an implicit Benefiter (Hasan 1984, for implied vs. implicit); *I bought a book* does not. This aspect of the meaning of *buy* is captured by assuming that the BENEFACTION options underlying this item are [beneficile:potential]. Note the difference in the Benefiter roles inserted in response to [inherent] (E3b) and [+benefactive] (E5c) respectively [i.e. E3b. subcategorize Benefiter-1 as Recipient; E5c. subcategorize Benefiter-1 as Client -eds]. When combined with the option [simple], the Benefiter role for the former (i.e. [inherent]) is more specifically Recipient, for the latter (i.e. [+benefactor]), Client. If the selection expression contains both the option [non-iterative] and [simple], then under certain specifiable conditions, the Recipient and Client-roles can be mapped on to Circumstance. If so, Circumstance will pre-select a prepositional group, which in the former case (i.e. [inherent]) will pre-select the preposition *to* and, in the latter (i.e. [+benefactor]), *for*, with the Benefiter nominal group as its Complement. The result in the case of (4) and (5) would be:

(4a) I gave a book to John. [non-iterative; ... :inherent:simple ...]
(5a) I bought a book for John. [non-iterative; ... :+benefactive:simple ...]

The difference between [inherent] and [+benefactive] is displayed even more sharply if, instead of [simple], the option [complex] is selected. This option inserts the function Ultimate Client (E10c), which can only pre-select a prepositional group, initiated by *for*, with the Benefiter nominal group as Complement. (4) and (5) would then be:

(4b) I gave John a book for Iona. [non-iterative; ... inherent:complex]
(5b) I bought John a book for Iona. [non-iterative; ... +benefactive:complex]

Again, under certain specifiable conditions (4b) – but not (5b) – can take the following forms:

(4c) I gave a book to John for Iona.
(4d) I gave a book for Iona to John.

Parallel to the above we do not have:

(5c) I bought a book to/for John for Iona.
(5d) I bought a book for Iona to/for John.

LEXIS AS MOST DELICATE GRAMMAR

A related observation is that while underlying (4e) would be [complex] (with Recipient implied and implicit), (5e) can only be read as [simple]:

(4e)   I gave a book for Iona.
(5e)   I bought a book for Iona.

The distinction between Recipient and Client as well as that between Client and Ultimate Client appears motivated. Note that when Ultimate Client is inserted, this creates a point of identity in the semantic value of Recipient and Client: both are a means whereby the Medium is passed to the Client. Many interesting questions arising from these details must be shelved, as this much will suffice for the discussion of the [iterative] processes, which is the main focus here. But two generalizations appear appropriate: first, a function inserted by two distinct options – e.g. Benefiter-1 inserted by [inherent] or by [+benefactive] – is not identical in ALL respects; and second, the semantic value of an option – the meanings that it constructs – depends on the environment of that option.

Returning to systems of ACCESS and CHARACTER, the combination of [iterative] and [acquisition] is the entry condition for choice between [unitary] and [neutral]. The combined PI of [iterative;acquisition] is the conjunction of C1 and D1a–b. The instructions for the [unitary] and [neutral] options are:

F: 1.   [unitary]
         a.   Medium pre-selects nominal group with Thing/ (alienable, divisible) and plural/
     2.   [neutral]
         a.   Medium pre-selects nominal group with Thing/ (alienable, divisible) and plural OR non-count/

Ignoring BENEFACTION, the selection expressions of PROCESS up to this point are:
i   [material:action:disposal:acquisition;iterative:unitary]
ii   [material:action:disposal:acquisition;iterative:neutral]

Note that [unitary] is the endpoint of one path in Figure 4.2. Does it specify any unit of form that may be a recognizable lexical item? I claim that the linguistic unit capable of realizing the Event in selection expression (i) must refer to an activity which is concrete, involves change in the location of the Medium, is inherently repetitive, leads to the Agent's gain of access to the Medium, and is such that the Medium is constrained to be 'plural'. In English the only linguistic form that can meet all these requirements is *gather*. The formulation of the realization statement (C1;D1a–b;F1a), while permitting (6c), throws light on the source of the oddity of (6a–b):

(6a)   Leonie gathered the water/meat in the bowl.
(6b)   Leonie gathered one book from her shelf.

(6c)   Leonie gathered some roses from the garden.

[Realization statements C1;D1a–b;F1a are repeated below -eds]

C1.	[acquisition]	a.	subcategorize Event as /(material action of disposal involving change in location of Medium) leading to Agent's gain of access to Medium/
D1.	[iterative]	a.	subcategorize Event as /(material action of disposal involving change in location of Medium) inherently repetitive/
		b.	subcategorize Medium Thing as /(alienable object) divisible
F1.	[unitary]	a.	Medium pre-selects nominal group with Thing/ (alienable, divisible) and plural/)

Selection expression (ii) does not represent the endpoint of a path; dependent upon [neutral] are the options [+vast] and [unmarked]. Nevertheless, taking the selection expression as it stands, it can be said confidently that a form capable of functioning as Event here must differ from *gather* at least in one respect: it should be capable of 'taking' a Medium in which the Thing may be either [plural] or [non-count]. Ignoring the archaic *amass* altogether, in English there appear to be only two lexical items suiting these requirements: *collect* and *accumulate*.

I believe we need to recognize that the orthographic word *collect* is the expression for two distinct – even if related – lexical items: *collect-1*, which is an antonym of *deposit*, and *collect-2*, which is an antonym of *scatter/strew*. Only the latter *collect* is [iterative] and thus subject to the requirement D1b. You can deposit one book or collect it from the library, but you cannot scatter/strew one book or collect it in the sense of *collect-2*. Again, *collect-1* appears to be [non-beneficile]; this is not true of *collect-2* (compare *I collected Iona her son from the school*, which is odd, with *I collected Iona some flowers*, which is quite unremarkable). Given F2, [i.e. [neutral] Medium pre-selects nominal group with Thing/ (alienable, divisible) and plural OR non-count/ -eds] the following are perfectly ordinary English clauses:

(7a)   Susan collected the water in the bowl.
(7b)   Susan collected some leaves from the garden.

But what about *accumulate*? It is at this point that the final option between [+vast] and [unmarked] is needed. Compare:

(8a)   Susan collected some solution.
(8b)   Susan accumulated some solution.
(8c)   Susan accumulated gallons of solution.
(9a)   Leonie collected two dollars.
(9b)   Leonic accumulated two dollars.
(9c)   Leonie accumulated thousands of dollars.

Of these triplets, only the member (b) appears odd, and traditionally it would be described as 'stylistically infelicitous'. But style is not independent of grammar; a delicate grammar can point to the source of stylistic infelicity, as in this case. The instructions for [+vast] and [unmarked] are:

G: 1.   [+vast]
   a.   Medium pre-selects nominal group with Thing /(alienable, divisible, plural or non-count) NECESSARILY indicating high degree of extent/
   2.   [unmarked]
   a.   Medium pre-selects nominal group with Thing/ (alienable, divisible, plural or non-count) indicating any degree of vastness/

These instructions provide a basis for explaining why, side by side with (8a), (8c) and (9a), (9c), we may also have:

(8d)   Susan collected gallons of the solution.
(9d)   Leonie collected thousands of dollars.

and why of (8a–d) and (9a–d) only the (b) member appears stylistically infelicitous. Note also that of the three lexical items yielded by the network so far, *collect* is the most 'versatile', by virtue of the options [neutral: unmarked] (see F2a/G2a [i.e. F2 [neutral] a. Medium pre-selects nominal group with Thing/ (alienable, divisible) and plural OR non-count/; G2a above -eds]). I would suggest that of the three [acquisition;iterative] processes, *collect* would be the most frequently used and *accumulate* the least. If this hypothesis is empirically substantiated, this would imply that a delicate grammar can point to a non-random relationship between the frequency of a particular linguistic unit and its selection expression.

[disposal] options are concurrent with the BENEFACTION ones. Thus although the unique identity of three lexical items has been already established, more can and must be said about them. In the environment of [disposal] BENEFACTION options carry implications for ACCESS. The combination of [acquisition] and [beneficile] implies that the Agent's gain of access to the Medium can be passed over to some Benefiter(s). Interestingly, [acquisition] combines most frequently with [beneficile:potential], though some exceptions can be found, e.g. *snatch, grab* or *inherit*. The combination of [deprivation] and [beneficile] implies that the Agent's loss of access to the Medium is some Benefiter's gain of access to that Medium. [deprivation] combines readily either with [beneficile:inherent] or with [non-beneficile]; it is rare for it to combine with [beneficile:potential], though, again, exceptions can be found, e.g. *scatter* or *throw*.

Assuming that the systemic paths originating at the conjunction of [acquisition;iterative] lead to the selection of Event which can only be expressed as *gather, collect* or *accumulate* as shown above, we may claim that the conjunction of options [acquisition;iterative] carries an instruction:

C1a–D1a: [acquisition;iterative]
   a.   Process pre-selects options [beneficile:potential]

This is tantamount to claiming that there is no process in English whose selection expression contains [acquisition;iterative], but not [beneficile:potential]. If this is true, then *gather, collect* and *accumulate* should each be capable of 'taking' the function Benefiter; and this is indeed the case. In the examples of these lexical items above, the BENEFACTION selection has been [beneficile:potential:–benefactive]; but the selection [beneficile:potential: +benefactive] is also possible. But at this point some delicate distinctions between *accumulate* and the other two lexical items come to light. Consider:

(10a)   I gathered Jenny some flowers.
(10b)   I gathered some flowers for Jenny.
(11a)   I collected the kids some water in the bowl.
(11b)   I collected some water in the bowl for the kids.
(12a)   ? Leonie accumulated John great wealth.
(12b)   Leonie accumulated great wealth for John.

To use traditional terminology, of the three items, *accumulate* alone cannot 'take a direct beneficiary'. There are at least three possible ways of interpreting this difference: First, underlying *accumulate* is the option [non-beneficile] instead of [beneficile:potential]. If so, we imply that *for John* (12b) has a radically different function from *for Jenny* (10b) and *for the kids* (11b), but this is dubious. Second, *for John* is the Ultimate Client because this Benefiter function is always realized only prepositionally (see E10c–d) where the prepositional group takes the form *for* +Benefiter. Against this solution, I would draw attention to (4e)–(5e), [i.e. (4e) *I gave a book for Iona*; (5e) *I bought a book for Iona*. -eds] and the fact that according to E10c, Ultimate Client is a more specific label for Benefiter-2. Unlike *gather* and *collect*, *accumulate* cannot take a Benefiter-2:

(10c)   I gathered Jenny some flowers for her mother.
(11c)   I collected the kids some water in a bowl for their dog.
(12c)   ? Leonie accumulated John great wealth for his children.

To treat *for John* as an Ultimate Client in (12b) would contradict the generalization that this function is inserted only if the function Recipient/Client is systemically 'present' as in (4b) and (5b) [i.e. (4b) *I gave John a book for Iona*. (5b) *I bought John a book for Iona*. -eds]. Third, in the final interpretation, *for John* (12b) is a Client, implying that its function is similar to *for Jenny* (10b) or *for the kids* (11b). Each has the role Benefiter-1 (= Client); however, to (10) and (11) apply certain systemic options from INFORMATION, to which (12) is not susceptible. If the option [beneficile:potential: +benefactive] combines with [(acquisition; iterative): neutral: +vast], then the item capable of acting as Event – i.e. *accumulate* – cannot take a direct

LEXIS AS MOST DELICATE GRAMMAR

Benefiter; it is constrained to take a Benefactive Circumstance, as in (12b) but not in (10) or (11). In this respect, then, *for John* (12b) differs from *for Jenny* (10b) and *for the kids* (11b). I take the last solution as the most acceptable, largely because cases comparable to (12b) will be found at least in the environment of the option [iterative].

This insight is built into the network by indicating that, concurrent with the option [simple] vs. [complex], another systematic choice operates open to any clause whose selection expression contains both [iterative] and [... non-reflexive]. The terms are [free] and [constrained]. The instructions for [constrained] are:

H. 1. [constrained]
     a. Client pre-selects prepositional group with preposition *for*
     b. Recipient pre-selects prepositional group with preposition *to/between/amongst*
     c. conflate Benefiter-1 with Prepositional Complement
     d. order Prepositional Complement to follow preposition

Option [constrained], then, acts upon function Benefiter-1 alone, irrespective of whether it combines with [simple] or [complex]. The two important aspects of the option are (a) that Client/Recipient are constrained as specified above (H1a–d), and (b) that certain specific INFORMATION options do not apply to it. In passing, note that characteristic (b), but not (a), is common also to clauses whose selection expression contains [potential: +benefactive:non-reflexive:complex]; but if characteristic (a) is lacking, they would not be said to contain option [constrained]. The point of similarity between the [constrained] and [potential:+benefactive:non-reflexive:complex:free], is exemplified by (5b), (10c) and (11c):

(5b)   I bought John a book for Iona.
(10c) I gathered Jenny some flowers for her mother.
(11c) I collected the kids some water in a bowl for their dog.

and can be indicated by a realization statement which would demand preselection of some specific INFORMATION option(s).

To summarize the discussion so far, the following array of selection expressions will require that the Event be expressed either by *gather* or *collect* or *accumulate*. Common to each member of the array are the following options:

[material:action:disposal:acquisition;iterative;beneficile:potential]

These options are not repeated but assumed present in each member of the array below:

I: [: UNITARY;–BENEFACTIVE]

EVENT = *gather* e.g.
(6c) Leonie gathered some roses from the garden.
II: [: unitary; +benefactive: non-reflexive: simple; free]
Event = *gather* e.g.
(10a) I gathered Jenny some flowers.
(10b) I gathered some flowers for Jenny.
III: [: unitary; +benefactive: non-reflexive: complex; free]
Event = *gather* e.g.
(10c) I gathered Jenny some flowers for her mother.
IV: [: neutral: +vast; −benefactive]
Event = *accumulate* e.g.
(8c) Susan accumulated gallons of solution.
(9c) Leonie accumulated thousands of dollars.
V: [: neutral: +vast; +benefactive: non-reflexive: simple; constrained]
Event = *accumulate* e.g.
(12b) Leonie accumulated great wealth for John.
VI: [: neutral: unmarked; −benefactive]
Event = *collect* e.g.
(7a) Susan collected the water in the bowl.
(7b) Susan collected some leaves from the garden.
VII: [: neutral: unmarked; +benefactive: non-reflexive: simple; free]
Event = *collect* e.g.
(11a) I collected the kids some water in the bowl.
(11b) I collected some water in the bowl for the kids.
VIII: [: neutral: unmarked; +benefactive: non-reflexive: complex; free]
Event = *collect* e.g.
(11c) I collected the kids some water in a bowl for their dog.

3. The lexicogrammar of deprivation 1: scatter, divide, distribute

Turning now to the options permitted by the combination of [deprivation] and [iterative], the BENEFACTION options have to be taken into account from the very start. This implies that the basis of distinction between the various [deprivation] processes lies not only in whether they are [iterative] or not but also whether they are [beneficile] or not. When [deprivation; iterative; beneficile] combine, this presents a complex entry condition for a choice between [random] vs. [planned]. The former implies that there is no particular design to the disposition of the Medium, while the latter implies an activity in which the disposition of the Medium follows a more or less equitable design. Note the PI for these options is a combination of C2, D1ab, E2a; and the instructions attached to them are:

J: 1. [random]
   a. co-select option [potential]
   b. sub-categorize Medium Thing as /(alienable, divisible) plural or non-count, solid/

LEXIS AS MOST DELICATE GRAMMAR

2. [planned]
   a. co-select option [inherent]
   b. subcategorize Benefiter-1 as /(animate) non-singular/

As [random] represents the endpoint of one systemic path, the selection expression containing the option can be stated as follows:

(iii) [material:action:disposal:deprivation;iterative;beneficile:potential]

In English, the only lexical item capable of functioning as the Event in a clause with the above selection expression is *scatter*. Although the item *strew* resembles it in certain respects, it will not suit the requirements of [beneficile: potential], for this implies that a clause of this kind can 'take' the function Benefiter. With *strew* this possibility is not open (consider: *she strewed the pigeons some breadcrumbs*). Given J1 a–b, (13a–b) are normal clauses of English; (13c) is not:

(13a) she scattered her clothes all over the place.
(13b) she scattered the toys on the floor.
(13c) she scattered juice on the table.

Given the presence of [potential] in (iii), the option between [−benefactive] and [+benefactive] applies. (13a–b) present examples of the former option, while underlying (14) is the option [+benefactive]:

(14) she scattered the pigeons some breadcrumbs.

The selection of [+benefactive] has a somewhat interesting by-product: it creates an impression of intentionality, which is absent from (13a–b). This may not be just an accidental feature of this particular lexical item; so compare *she broke a stick* vs. *she broke them a stick* and *she found a sixpence* vs. *she found them a sixpence*. When the options [random] and [+benefactive] combine, this seems to bear a consequence for the nominal group preselected by the Benefiter: not only does the Thing have to be animate, but there is a very strong probability of it being non-human. Compare (14) with (15):

(15) she scattered the children some bread.

(15) conjures up a picture of a nasty female – perhaps the traditional stepmother in a fairy-tale. Again, [+benefactive: non-reflexive] allows either the selection of [simple] or of [complex], though with [random] the probability of the selection of [simple] is much higher than that of [complex]. We would rarely find clauses such as (16):

(16) She scattered the pigeons breadcrumbs for their chicks.

Although (15) and (16) may be less frequent than (13a) or (14), neither is odd, unlike (13c). So while (13c) would be attributed to a mistake, (15) will be seen as playing upon that part of the meaning of *scatter*, constructed by [random], while the rarity of (16) might arise from a combination of [random] and [+benefactive: non-reflexive: complex]. The former implies that the Medium is being disposed of without any particular design, whereas the selection of the option [+benefactive] raises the possibility of the Agent having a particular design for the disposal of the Medium. Specifically, the selection of the Ultimate Client (which is inserted in response to [complex]; see E10a–f) goes against the lack of a particular design for the disposal of the Medium. So it would appear that all these important facts about *scatter* can be stated without adding any more options to the network in Figure 4.2. The array of selection expressions which would require that the Event be expressed as *scatter* are now described.

Common to each member of the array are the following options, which will be assumed present in IX–XI:

[material: action: disposal: deprivation; iterative; beneficile: potential]

IX: [: random; −benefactive]
Event = *scatter* e.g. (13a, 13b)
(13a) she scattered her clothes all over the place.
(13b) she scattered the toys on the floor.
X: [: random; +benefactive: non-reflexive: complex: free]
Event = *scatter* e.g. (16)
(16) She scattered the pigeons breadcrumbs for their chicks.
XI: [: random; +benefactive: non-reflexive: simple: free]
Event = *scatter* e.g.
(14) she scattered the pigeons some breadcrumbs.

There may be one problem with the description of *scatter* presented here. I have implied that if option [free] is present, then with the selection of certain options from the INFORMATION system, the function Client would be realized as a Benefactive Circumstance. More specifically, the prepositional group would take the form *for* +*Benefiter*-1 nominal group. The proportion between (14) and (14a) is the same as that between (10a) and (10b):

(14a) she scattered some breadcrumbs for the pigeons.

But is (14b) also an equally normal clause?

(14b) She scattered some breadcrumbs to the pigeons.

If so, then *scatter* would appear to allow a Benefactive Circumstance, which is allowed to occur only if the Benefiter-1 role is subcategorized as Recipient; and I have argued that this role only occurs if the option [inherent] is selected (see, e.g. 4b–4e [repeated below -eds]:

(4b) I gave John a book for Iona.

(4c) I gave a book to John for Iona.
(4d) I gave a book for Iona to John.
(4e) I gave a book for Iona.

If *scatter* is neutral as between taking Recipient or Client, then the instruction J1a is incorrect [i.e. J1 [random]: a. co-select option [potential] [-eds]; and the network is misleading. However, while I am certain that (14a) is a perfectly normal clause, I am not certain about the status of (14b). So I shall leave the discussion of *scatter* with this query.

[planned] permits a choice between [indeterminate] and [determinate]. The instructions are as follows:

K: 1.   [indeterminate]
          a. subcategorize Medium Thing as /(alienable, divisible) singular, plural or non-count/
          b. co-select options [inherent] and [constrained]
    2.   [determinate]
          a. subcategorize Medium Thing as /(alienable, divisible) plural or non-count (i.e. outclassify singular)
          b. co-select options [inherent] and [free]

The implication is that if the option [indeterminate] is selected, then any item capable of acting as the Event can take a singular/plural/non-count noun as Thing in the Medium; the activity must imply a Recipient (as for *give*, cf. e.g. (4a–4e)); and the Recipient can only take the form of a Benefactive Circumstance, where the prepositional group begins with *to/ between/among*. The only lexical item in English capable of meeting these requirements is *divide*. Like *collect*, *divide* expresses two distinct lexical items: *divide*-1 which is roughly synonymous with *cut*, and is an antonym of *join*; the closest in meaning to *divide*-2 is the item *distribute*, or the archaic *apportion*; its closest antonym is the iterative *collect*, and possibly *hoard*. I am concerned only with *divide*-2 here. Together with the PI of [indeterminate] K1a–b explicitly allow for the following:

(17a) she divided the apple between John and Jenny.
(17b) she divided the sweets amongst the children.
(17c) the Head of School divided the money between the two research directors for their assistants.

Note how (17a) differs from (18a–b):

(18a) she divided John and Jenny an apple.
(18b) she divided an apple for John and Jenny.

The *divide* in (18a–b) is *divide*-1, not a material action of disposal but of transformation. This *divide* does not have [inherent] BENEFACTION; so it is also possible to say (18c) without implying a Benefiter role:

(18c) she divided an apple (in half).

How right Whorf was in maintaining that 'we are all mistaken in our belief that any word has an "exact meaning" ... the reference of the words is at the mercy of the sentences and the grammatical patterns in which they occur.' (Whorf 1956, 258–9). It is only by constructing delicate grammars that we can show which grammatical patterns determine what reference for some linguistic form. The description of *divide* as of *collect* perhaps shows clearly that it is more important to devise ways of making explicit 're-actances' between units of linguistic form than to concentrate on ways of segmenting given strings, and reordering and labelling the products of the segmentation.

The combination of [deprivation;iterative;beneficile:inherent] has another consequence, captured in J2b: the nominal group pre-selected by the Benefiter must have the feature plural. Note the difference between (17a) [(17a) *she divided the apple between John and Jenny* -eds] and (18d–e):

(18d) she divided John an apple.
(18e) she divided an apple for John.

The [iterative] *divide* is said to have the option [constrained] precisely because Benefiter-1 can never occur as a direct beneficiary. The option [inherent] is said to be pre-selected because Benefiter-1 will always be interpreted as a Recipient (as with *give, sell, lend*). These features, together with the option [planned], might explain why the Benefactive circumstance can be realized only by a prepositional group with *between* or *amongst*. But I believe that another aspect of [planned] processes is important here. Just as the selection of [+benefactive] with [random] (*scatter*) creates the impression of intentionality, so also the combination of [inherent] and [planned] is capable of creating an impression of 'exhaustivity'. (17b), for example, [*she divided the sweets amongst the children* -eds] creates the impression that after the dividing is done 'the sweets' are exhausted, though this impression can be overridden by indicating otherwise (e.g. *she divided some of the sweets amongst the children*). Note, however, the difference between:

(19a) she distributed some medicine to the refugees.
(19b) she distributed some medicine amongst the refugees.

I feel that only (19b) creates the impression that 'some medicine' was exhausted after the distributing was done. If this is so, this may provide a better explanation for the selection of *between/amongst* with *divide*, which may be said to carry the connotation of exhaustivity, unless otherwise indicated. Note that further detail will be needed to differentiate between the selection of *between* and *amongst*, but perhaps the lines along which this may be done are clear enough not to need discussion.

The array of selection expressions requiring that the Event be expressed as *divide* are entered below (XII–XIII). Common to each are the following selections, which are not repeated in the individual arrays:

[material: action: disposal: deprivation; iterative; beneficile: inherent: non-reflexive]

XII: [:indeterminate; simple; constrained]
Event = *divide* e.g.
(17a) she divided the apple between John and Jenny.
(17b) she divided the sweets amongst the children.

XIII: [:indeterminate; complex; free]
Event = *divide* e.g.
(17c) the Head of School divided the money between the two research directors for their assistants.

If the option [determinate] applies, the implication is that any item capable of acting as the Event cannot take a singular noun as Thing in the Medium; the activity must imply a Recipient (this is, of course, in addition to all the characteristics inherited through the PI up to this point). The lexical item that will meet all of the requirements is *distribute*. Compare (17a) and (20a):

(20a) she distributed an apple to the children.

Again, if we have *they distributed some medicine*, a Recipient is implied in the same way as it is in *I'm giving a book* (as a present). I am treating *distribute* as having the option [free] (see K2b [co-select options [inherent] and [free] -eds]). This implies that it can take a direct Benefiter-1, as in:

(20b) the government distributed the peasants a new high-yielding variety of wheat seeds.

The option between [simple] and [complex] also applies:

(20c) to celebrate the event, they distributed everyone bags of sweets.
(20d) on Mother's Day, we distributed the children presents for their mums.

Note that the non-singularity of the Benefiter can be indicated in different ways, and it is likely that the subcategorization statements in K1a [subcategorize Medium Thing as /(alienable) -eds] and K2a [subcategorize Medium Thing as /(alienable, divisible) plural or non-count (i.e. outclassify singular) -eds] will need to be formulated more carefully. Consider:

(21a) she distributed pamphlets to the students.
(21b) she distributed a pamphlet to each student.

(21c) ?she distributed pamphlets/a pamphlet to a student.

The array of selection expressions requiring that the event be expressed as *distribute* are entered below (XIV–XV). Common to each are the same selections, shown above for XII–XIII, and these are not repeated:

XIV: [:determinate; simple; free]
Event = *distribute* e.g.
(20a) she distributed an apple to the children.
(20b) the government distributed the peasants a new high-yielding variety of wheat seeds.
(20c) to celebrate the event, they distributed everyone bags of sweets.

XV: [:determinate; complex; free]
Event = *distribute* e.g.
(20d) on Mother's Day, we distributed the children presents for their mums.

4. The lexicogrammar of deprivation 2: strew, spill, share

The above section concludes the description of processes which combine [deprivation; iterative; beneficile]. When [deprivation; iterative] combine with [non-beneficile], this acts as a multiple entry condition for the options [independent] vs. [cooperative]. The option [cooperative] implies that the activity cannot be carried out without a 'co-doer'. So that just as a Recipient is always 'present' in a clause with the option [inherent], so a function I shall call Cooperant is always 'present' in a clause with [cooperative] as in (*Eric is so sweet*) *he always shares his toys*. When the option is [independent], the function Cooperant is not permitted; in this sense, then, I am making a distinction between 'joint' doing as in *Eric and Jim played with the toys*, and cooperancy as in *Eric shared his toys with Jim*. The instructions for the two are:

L: 1. [independent]
    a. subcategorize Event as /(material action inherently repetitive, leading to Agent's loss of access to Medium, incapable of requiring Benefiter) and NOT INHERENTLY REQUIRING a co-doer/
    2. [cooperative]
    a. subcategorize Event as /(material action inherently repetitive, leading to Agent's loss of access to Medium, incapable of requiring Benefiter) and INHERENTLY REQUIRING function Cooperant/

[independent] is the entry condition to two options, which are so obvious they do not need much discussion. They lead to the subcategorization of the Medium as follows:

M. 1.   [+solid]
      a.   subcategorize Medium Thing as (alienable, divisible) plural or count, solid/
    2.   [+liquid]
      a.   subcategorize Medium Thing as (alienable, divisible) liquid

The options [independent:+solid] require that the Event be realized by *strew* while the options [independent:+liquid] require that it be realized by *spill*. It may be argued that *scatter* is a possibility for the former; but note that *scatter* has also the options [beneficile:potential]. When this combines with [... :–benefactive], there would appear to be some interchangeability between *strew* and *scatter*. So we can have:

(22a)   she had scattered everything on the floor.
(22b)   he had strewn everything on the floor.

But, as lexical items, *scatter* and *strew* cannot be said to be exactly alike. There are no such clauses as:

(23a)   she strewed the pigeons some breadcrumbs.
(23b)   she strewed some breadcrumbs for the pigeons.

Another question may be raised: why should option [independent] be recognized in the case of *strew* but not in that of *scatter*? This is because it is only in the environment of [deprivation; iterative; non-beneficile] that the contrast carries any significance, since all other [disposal] processes are uniformly like *strew* in not being able to require the function Cooperant. As a lexical item, *strew* appears far less frequently than *scatter*, and this may be because *scatter* can do everything that *strew* can and also some more things which *strew* cannot do, e.g. take a Benefiter. *Spill* differs from *strew* only in that its Medium must 'be' liquid. Note the metaphoric nature of *spill the beans* and *spill his guts*. Here is an example of *spill* comparable to (22b):

(22c)   the waiter spilt soup on her dress.

Turning to the option [cooperative], it is best first to develop the notion of the function Cooperant. A Cooperant differs both from a Benefiter and from the informal notion 'joint doer'. A Benefiter, I have argued above, is not only always at the receiving end but must also be dissociated from an Agent. This is not true of Cooperant. Consider:

(24)   they shared the sweets.

This clause would be interpreted as *they shared the sweets between/amongst themselves*. But if so, this is because the functions Agent and Cooperant are both systemically present and realized by *they*. Compare (24) with:

(24a)   he shared the sweets.

Here the Cooperant is both implied and implicit; notwithstanding the absence of explicit mention of a Cooperant, the assumption is that the function is essential, since in the absence of the Cooperant the activity of sharing cannot be undertaken. So, unlike a Benefiter, a Cooperant is neither at the receiving end nor does it necessarily have to be dissociated from the Agent, though it can be as in:

(24b)   John shared the sweets with Jenny.

In (24b) the function Cooperant is realized by *with Jenny*, that of the Agent by *John*. Cooperant is also different from 'joint doer'. In

(25a)   they walked together to the station.
(25b)   Eric walked to the station with Jim.

there is no cooperant function. In the first place, the activity of walking can be carried out without two or more persons' involvement; secondly, no matter how many persons function as the Agent, each is responsible for his/her own action. Not so with *share*. Sharing cannot be done without involvement of at least two persons; and the action of one is a condition for that of the other. There are certain non-disposal-type processes that resemble *share* in this respect, e.g. *marry, fight, meet, agree*. But of the disposal processes *share* alone has this characteristic. And although *sell, lend* might appear to be like *share*, there is an important difference. In

(26)   John sold/lent Melanie a car.

although John and Melanie are involved in the same exchange, their roles *vis-à-vis* the Event are not the same. If John shared sweets with Jenny, then it follows that Jenny shared sweets with John; but if John sold Melanie a car, it does not follow that Melanie sold John a car. But if the relationship of the Cooperant and the Agent to the activity is the same, then why should two separate functions of Agent and Cooperant be recognized? The simple answer is because the functions can be separated from each other. We would not need to dissociate the functions Subject and Actor and Theme, if, under certain specifiable conditions, each could not be realized by a different constituent of the clause. Moreover, there is a meaningful distinction between (24b) [*John shared the sweets with Jenny* -eds] and (24c):

(24c)   John and Jenny shared the sweets.

In (24b), John is likely to be seen as the one who had prior access to the sweets; (24c) is neutral about the prior ownership of the sweets. Moreover, (24b) leaves no room for indeterminacy; (24c) does, as comparison with (24d) shows:

(24d) John and Jenny shared the sweets with Benny.

It is important, then, to recognize a distinction between [discrete] and [fused] – the two options shown to depend on [cooperation]. The option [discrete] would carry the following instructions:

N: 1.   [discrete]
    a. insert function Cooperant
    b. Cooperant pre-selects prepositional group with preposition *with*
    c. conflate Cooperant with Prepositional Complement
    d. Prepositional Complement pre-selects nominal group animate nor co-referential with Agent
    e. order Prepositional Complement to follow preposition *with*

Underlying (24b) then would be the options [:cooperative:discrete], while underlying (24c) would be [:cooperative:fused]. The only instructions for [fused] are:

N. 2.   [fused]
    a. insert function Cooperant
    b. Cooperant pre-selects nominal group animate

This option is the entry condition for a further systemic choice between [Agent-oriented] and [Medium-oriented]. (24c) [*John and Jenny shared the sweets* -eds] exemplifies the former; an example of the latter would be:

(24e) John shared Jenny's sweets.

I suggest that in the absence of a Good Reason, (24e) would be interpreted as 'John and Jenny shared the sweets and the sweets were Jenny's'. This is one reason why it is possible to clinch the matter by saying:

(24f) John shared Jenny's sweets with her.

The instructions for the last pair of options are as follows:

P: 1.   [Agent-oriented]
    a. pre-select nominal group complex
    b. pre-select additive complexing conjunction *and*
    c. order Agent to precede *and*
    d. order Cooperant to follow *and*
    2.   [Medium-oriented]
    a. Cooperant pre-selects possessive – *'s*
    b. conflate Cooperant with Possessive Modifier in Medium

The difference between (24d) and (24f) is important. In the former, *with Benny* is Cooperant, while *John and Jenny* are (joint) Agent. In (24f), the function of *with her is* different; it is a kind of 'marking' and I am assuming that the option(s) that govern its appearance do not belong to TRANSITIVITY, but to options from some other system network which is the output of the textual metafunction. Such marking can also occur with [Agent-oriented] as in:

(24g)   John and Jenny shared the sweets with each other.

Note that the prepositional groups here are constrained to be co-referential with the Cooperant; thus if (24f) had been *John shared Ben's sweets*, then the prepositional group would have been *with him*. I shall not pursue this any further here, but conclude with the comment that the only lexical item capable of acting as the Event in a clause with options [deprivation;iterative;non-beneficile;cooperative] is *share*.

The array of selection expressions requiring that the Event be expressed as *strew* or *spill* or *share* is presented below (XVI–XX). The selections common to each and so not repeated are:

[material:action:disposal;iterative;non-beneficile]

XVI: [: independent:+solid]
         Event = *strew* e.g.
         (22b) she had strewn everything on the floor.
XVII: [: independent:+liquid]
         Event = *spilt* e.g.
         (22c) the waiter spilt soup on her dress.
XVIII: [: cooperative:discrete]
         Event = *share* e.g.
         (24b) John shared the sweets with Jenny.
         (24d) John and Jenny shared the sweets with Benny.
XIX: [: cooperative:fused:Agent-oriented]
         Event = *share* e.g.
         (24c) John and Jenny shared the sweets.
         (24g) John and Jenny shared the sweets with each other.
XX: [: cooperative:fused:Medium-oriented]
         Event = *share* e.g.
         (24e) John shared Jenny's sweets.
         (24f) John shared Jenny's sweets with her.

5. The continuity of grammar and lexis

The above discussion has, hopefully, established nine distinct lexical items:

gather	scatter	strew
collect	divide	spill
accumulate	distribute	share

Common to these lexical verbs is the characteristic that they can function as the Event in clauses whose selection expression contains the options [disposal] and [iterative]. There appear to be some seventy-odd [non-iterative] [disposal] processes. It has not been possible to discuss any of these for reasons of space; this is a natural concomitant of attempting to write a delicate grammar. However, I hope that the description will permit the claim that the project of turning the whole of linguistic form into grammar is feasible. In fact I believe that I have demonstrated not only that 'lexis' equals 'delicate grammar' but also that there is [grammar beyond lexis]. So far as *gather, collect* and *accumulate* are concerned, their unique identity vis-à-vis each other can be established by virtue of the options [unitary], [neutral], [+vast] and [unmarked]. To show the combination of these with BENEFACTION options is to do grammar after lexis, which has hopefully led to a better understanding of the identities and differences between members of the paradigm.

It needs to be made quite clear that the description presented here of the nine items is not complete. This follows from assumption (7) in section 1. The account is simply the output of one metafunction – the experiential. In the description of larger linguistic units, e.g. the clause, the validity of assumption (7) has been demonstrated by Martin (1984), Fawcett (1980), Halliday (1969; 1970; 1985), Mann and Matthiessen (1983), Young (1980), and others. It remains to be seen whether the postulate of concurrent multiple structures extends right down the rank scale to the smaller units, e.g. the lexical item. *A priori* there seems no reason to rule out this possibility; rather there is some favourable suggestive evidence. For example, synonymy is a well-recognized concept, though a troublesome one (Leech 1974; Lyons 1977). If pairs such as *ask, enquire/buy, purchase/smile, grin/cry, bawl* are examined closely, we are likely to find that while their experientially motivated grammatical structure is the same, their interpersonally motivated structure differs. A similar phenomenon is evident in *day, today* and *two, both*: both members of each pair are likely to have the same experientially motivated structure, though they most probably differ in their textually motivated structure. Unlike larger structures, the lexical item is unsegmentable; but if we accept that, in principle, different functions can be conflated on to the same segment, there would appear to be no reason for denying that a lexical item could be the expression of two or more conflated grammatical functions. These remarks are speculative, and are intended as an invitation to closer examination.

One may ask: What exactly is the basis of these options? Where do they come from? And isn't there some circularity? Is one simply pretending to start from the network as if it were *sui generis*, while in fact the options appear to be postulated precisely because certain lexical items are known to exist?

I would answer this by saying that no matter what aspect of the lexico-grammar we describe, we are in the last analysis describing the possibilities of only that which is known to us, and this knowledge is based upon our experience of language. The options of the networks are not 'universals', 'primitives' or God-given truths: they are schematic pointers to man-made meanings which can be expressed verbally. The options are presented in certain relations to each other because this is how I understand English ways of meaning; they are not there because the making of any other kind of relation is impossible. For example, in Urdu, while there seems to be a close parallel to the options [unitary] vs. [neutral] (cf. tʃunna and dʒʌmə kʌrnə), the distinction I needed to recognize by [+vast] vs. [unmarked] does not appear necessary. The networks *represent* a language; they do not *invent* it. Moreover, I doubt that any grammar can invent a language, though it can make an effort to distort other people's meanings to make them appear as replicas of, say, English meanings (cf. Hasan 1984).

Lack of space does not permit a detailed discussion of the implications of turning the whole of linguistic form into grammar, but if the account of the nine lexical items presented above has appeared valid, then it certainly upholds the systemic functional view of an uninterrupted continuity between grammar and lexis. It rejects the approach wherein the bricks of lexis are joined together by the mortar of grammar. The notion of the lexicon as an inventory of items, each having its own meaning in itself, stands refuted, and the insights of Saussure (1916), Firth (1935), Hjelmslev (1961), Whorf (1956) and Halliday (1961) are confirmed. The complex relation between the signification and value of a linguistic sign is also highlighted.

The concept of reference has been a problematical one in semantics (Lyons 1977). The interpretation of the term 'reference' as an onomastic relation to existents is a limiting one, which arbitrarily cuts the sign system into two distinct areas: there are signs such as *tree* 'referring' to TREE, a concrete object, a member of a class 'out there'; and there are signs such as *gather, collect* which lack referents. This leaves the question unanswered: how is it that such signs make any contact with the world of action/state, which is the only reason for their existence? Why is it that where it will do to say *the book is in that bag*, it will not do to say *the book is on that bag*?

The description offered here implies that the ways in which the reference of *book* or *bag* is achieved is essentially the same as that for *is, in, on, that* and *the*. Saussure created an unnecessary enigma in his account of value and signification. In part this was due to the cleavage between *langue* and *parole*. Any viable account of reference will have to take *parole* into account, and this not just so that we know that the name *John* and *the man in blue jeans* may point to the same person. But *parole* dissociated from contexts of human living is an anomaly. The reason Malinowski (1923; 1935) was able to turn Saussure's relation of value and signification upside down (Hasan 1985) was that ways of saying – *parole* within contexts – is creative of the *langue*. This is how I understand Hjelmslev's comment that process determines system; a phenomenon cannot achieve the status of a process without systematicity. Value and signification are indeed two sides of the same coin. Looked at from the point of view of the system – the *langue* – we may claim that signification depends on value; looked at from the point of view of process – the *parole* – our claim would be that value depends upon what the speakers have consistently signified by sign – how it has meshed in with their structures of action and thought. Looking for meaning in use (Wittgenstein 1958) implies looking at both kinds of use – how a sign combines or contrasts with other signs in a string or a paradigm and how (some part of) the string applies to the world.

This line of argument needs further exploration. In most linguistic writing today, there is an uneasy amalgamation of two irreconcilable views: language as the representation of meanings that exist *sui generis*, and language as the construction of meanings, whose existence is beholden to the existence of that network of relations which, for short, we call 'language'. From the latter point of view, what is called 'world knowledge' or 'knowledge structure' is largely constructed by language itself; from the former, it is divorced from language, so that 'knowledge of the world' and 'knowledge of language' are seen as two distinct concepts. Such a view can be criticized at least on two counts: in practice it presents the advanced Western peoples' knowledge of the world as *the* knowledge of the world; if to them the shape of that world appears eminently reasonable, it is only because they are not at the receiving end of being brainwashed into someone else's ideology. Secondly, current postulates of world knowledge fail to address the fascinating question of how the information constructed by the various semiotic systems is integrated into some kind of working whole. When interest in this question arises, a delicate grammar of the type presented here would be an essential prerequisite to the enquiry. The notion of PI explicitly points out that the implicational shadows of signs are very long indeed. Such grammar has the potential of making explicit the concepts of 'semantic inheritance' (Brachman 1979) and 'conceptual dependency' (Schank 1975). At the same time, it seems likely that it will be of considerable use in explaining much of what Wilkes's preferential semantics is based on (Wilkes 1978).

The Systemic Functional model has always rejected the absurd postulate that transformations are meaning preserving – a view that can be upheld only if semantics equals the experiential metafunction and certain parts of the interpersonal metafunction selected on an *ad hoc* basis. It has also rejected the view that the only valid form a grammar can take is to trace the genealogical relationship between transformationally related strings. Once these two presuppositions are removed, transformations are transformed into the relation of agnation; and the rationale for the existence of certain transformational possibilities can be made explicit on the basis of a grammar of the type presented here (Hasan 1971).

When the grammarian's dream comes true, it will in all likelihood enable us to throw better light on the notions of synonymy, antonymy and hyponymy. It will force us to make more explicit the basis of the distinction between 'grammatical item' and 'lexical item'. Also, I believe, it will help in making more precise Firth's view of collocation (Firth 1951a). Meanwhile, in order to translate the dream into reality much work is needed. The beginning made here represents no more than an iota of the total potential of English language for constructing meanings.

Note
1 In this paper, the editors have taken the liberty of repeating some realization statements and examples where these have been referred to at some distance from their original location in the text.

References

Berry, Margaret (1977) *An Introduction to Systemic Linguistics, 2: Levels and Links.* London: Batsford.
Bobrow, D. and Collins, A. (eds) (1975) *Representation and Understanding: Studies in Cognitive Psychology.* New York: Academic Press.
Brachman, R. J. (1979) 'On the epistemological status of semantic networks'. In N.V. Findler (ed.) *Associative Networks: Representation and Use of Knowledge by Computers.* New York: Academic Press, 1979.
Chomsky, N. (1965) *Aspects of the Theory of Syntax.* Cambridge, Mass.: MIT Press.
Collins, A. M. and Quillian, M. R. (1972) 'Experiments on semantic memory and language comprehension'. In L. W. Gregg (ed.) *Cognition in Learning and Memory.* New York: Wiley, 1972.
Fawcett, R. P. (1980) *Cognitive Linguistics and Social Interaction.* Exeter: Julius Groos Verlag and Exeter University.
Fillmore, C. J. (1977) 'Topics in lexical semantics'. In *Current Issues in Linguistic Theory*, Cole, R. W. (ed.). Bloomington: Indiana University Press.
Firth, J. R. (1935) 'The technique of semantics'. *Transactions of the Philological Society.* Reprinted in J.R. Firth *Papers in Linguistics 1935–1951.* London: Oxford University Press, 1957.
Firth, J. R. (1951) 'General linguistics and descriptive grammar'. *Transactions of the Philological Society.* Reprinted in J.R. Firth *Papers in Linguistics 1935–1951.* London: Oxford University Press, 1957.
Firth, J. R. (1951a) 'Modes of meaning', in *Essays and Studies*, The English Association, reprinted in J.R. Firth *Papers in Linguistics 1935–1951.* London: Oxford University Press, 1957.
Halliday, M. A. K. (1961) 'Categories of the theory of grammar', *Word*, 17, No. 3.
Halliday, M. A. K. (1969) 'Options and functions in the English clause', *Brno Studies in English*, 8, reprinted in M.A.K. Halliday and J.R. Martin (eds) *Readings in Systemic Linguistics.* London: Batsford, 1981.
Halliday, M. A. K. (1970) 'Language structure and language function'. In J. Lyons (ed.) *New Horizons in Linguistics.* Harmondsworth: Penguin, 1970.
Halliday, M. A. K. (1977) 'Text as semantic choice in social contexts'. In T.A. van Dijk and J. S. Petofi (eds) *Grammars and Descriptions.* Berlin: de Gruyter, 1977.
Halliday, M. A. K. (1985) *An Introduction to Functional Grammar.* London: Edward Arnold.

Hasan, R. (1971) 'Syntax and semantics'. In J. Morton (ed.) *Biological and Social Factors in Psycholinguistics*. London: Logos, 1971.
Hasan, R. (1984) 'Ways of saying, ways of meaning'. In R.P. Fawcett, M.A.K. Halliday, S.M. Lamb and A. Makkai (eds) *The Semiotics of Culture and Language*, Vol. I: *Language as Social Semiotic*. London: Pinter, 1985. (Chapter 8 of this book).
Hasan, R. (1985) 'Meaning, text and context: fifty years after Malinowski'. In J.D. Benson and W.S. Greaves (eds) *Systemic Perspectives in Discourse*, Vol. I: *Selected Theoretical Papers from the Ninth International Systemic Workshop*. Norwood, N.J.: Ablex, 1985.
Hjelmslev, L. (1961) *Prolegomena to a Theory of Language* (trans. J. Whitfield). Madison: University of Wisconsin Press.
Leech, G. N. (1974) *Semantics*. Harmondsworth: Penguin.
Lyons, J. (1977) *Semantics*, Vols I and II. Cambridge: Cambridge University Press.
Malinowski, B. (1923) 'The problem of meaning in primitive languages', Supplement I to C.K. Ogden and I.A. Richards *The Meaning of Meaning*. London: Kegan Paul, 1923.
Malinowski, B. (1935) 'An ethnographic theory of language'. In *Coral Gardens and their Magic*, Vol. II. London: Allen and Unwin.
Mann, W. and Matthiessen, C. M. I. M. (1983) 'Nigel: A systemic grammar for text generation (Chapter 2), Information Sciences Institute Research Report 83–105.
Martin, J. R. (1984) 'On the analysis of exposition'. In *Discourse on Discourse*, Hasan, R. (ed.). Sydney: Applied Linguistics Association of Australia, Publication No. 7.
Saussure, F. de (1916/74) *A Course in General Linguistics*, English edn. (trans. W. Baskin). London: Fontana.
Schank, R. (1972) 'Conceptual dependency'. *Cognitive Psychology*, 3.
Schank, R. (1975) 'The structure of episodes in memory'. In Bobrow and Collins (eds) (1975).
Schank, R. and Abelson, R. (1977) *Scripts, Plans, Goals and Understanding*. Hillsdale: Lawrence Erlbaum Associates.
Whorf, B. L. (1956) *Language, Thought and Reality* (Carroll, J. B. (ed.)). Cambridge, Mass.: MIT Press.
Wilkes, Y. (1978) 'Making preferences more active'. *Artificial Intelligence*, 11.
Wittgenstein, L. (1958) *Philosophical Investigations*, 2nd edition. London: Basil Blackwell.
Young, D. J. (1980) *The Structure of English Clauses*. London: Hutchinson.

5 Semantic networks: a tool for the analysis of meaning

1 Introduction

Some 25 years ago, Mary Douglas wrote a paper called 'Do dogs laugh' (Douglas 1971). In reflecting on semantic networks, I have sometimes wondered: *Do dogs have ideology?* The question is not raised flippantly. If ideology has anything to do with language – and today the consensus seems to be that the linguistic sign system is entirely ideological – then the nature of linguistic meaning – i.e. semantics – must play a crucial role in making it so. I say this because the ideological impact of language is primarily in the meanings people mean and the meanings others hear them as meaning: it is not immaterial that in speaking ideological dissonance takes the form of semantic dissonance[1] (Hasan 1987), which could itself be viewed as an extreme case of semantic variation[2] (Hasan 1989; 1992a; 1992b; Hasan and Cloran 1990; Cloran 1994; Williams 1995). This, on the one hand, throws in doubt that idealization of reflexivity whereby the relations of meaning-wording have been supposed by some linguists to be identical for all members of a speech community; and, on the other hand, it emphasizes the possibility of systematic differences in the speaking subjects' perspectives whereby the 'same' context presents itself as an occasion for saying not necessarily the 'same' things: the subject's different social positioning leads to different linguistic coding orientations (Bernstein 1990) – different linguistic *habitus* (Bourdieu 1990), which lies between the total meaning potential of language and the habitual ways of saying and meaning that characterize a subject's use of language. It would seem then that what makes it possible for human languages to be ideologically saturated is the plasticity of relations between the levels of content and expression, which in its turn has implications for the conceptualization of the level of semantics. Notably, this plasticity of relation appears impossible where meaning is simply a function of 'correspondence' between a signifier and some 'bit' of extra-linguistic reality as, for example, in the infants' protolanguage. The human infant's protolinguistic system and the systems of animal communication are alike in one respect: both bypass internal organization (Halliday 1973a;

1975), their elements corresponding directly to bits of extra-linguistic situation, be they concrete phenomena or abstract ones such as the system user's internal states. This would suggest that both the human infant at least up to its protolinguistic stage as also the animal must remain innocent of ideology. To be complicit in the creation and maintenance of ideology as the system of language is, it must on the one hand have some resource for construing meanings, and, on the other hand, the meanings construed by language must relate to an extra-linguistic reality which is capable of being contested in some respect or other. In other words, there has to exist the possibility of variation in how people use the lexicogrammatical resources of their language to construe meanings and there has to exist the possibility of variation in using the semantic potential of language to construe contexts.

If this observation is true, then it argues for a model of language description such as presented in Figure 5.1, which postulates the internal structure of language as tristratal consisting of semantics, lexicogrammar and phonology, and shows this tristratally structured language to be anchored as a whole into the reality of its users by being ineluctably related to their ways of living their life – i.e. to their context of culture and situation.[3]

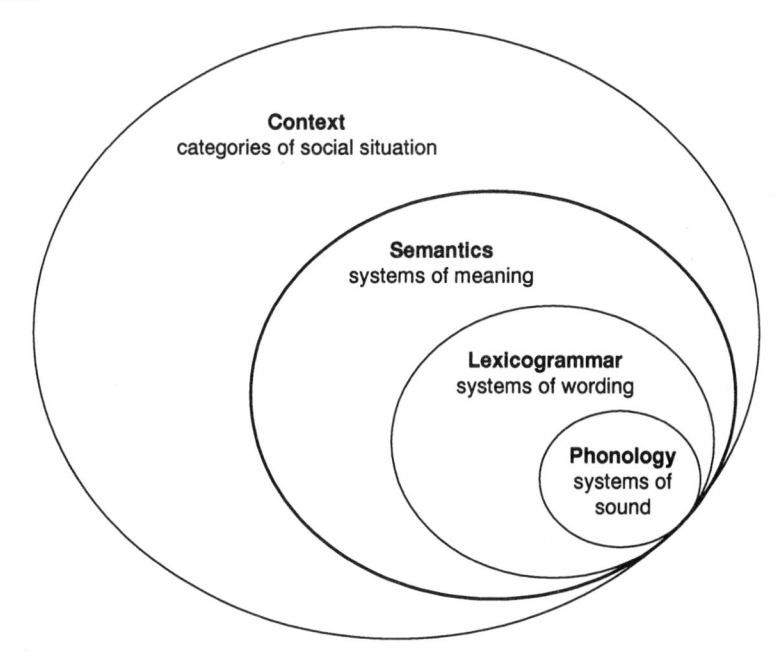

Figure 5.1 Strata for linguistic description

Since much has already been written about relations across the strata, it is not necessary to repeat those details here[4]; it is sufficient to note that the relation of realization between context, semantics and lexicogrammar is a dialectical one. The claim is, then, that the warrant for analysing a linguistic meaning as such and so resides in the perceived relations of semantics to context on the one hand, and to lexicogrammar, on the other. Context is implicated as the activator of a speaker's choices[5] in meaning; lexicogrammar enters into the picture as the resource for construing those semantic choices in that specific language. Conversely, it is also the case that contexts – the relevant aspects of extra-linguistic situation – are unknowable without reference to meaning: it is the semantic choices which construe much of the context for the listener; and a similar dialectic obtains between semantics and lexicogrammar (for further discussion, see section 2.2 below). This suggests that a tool for the analysis of linguistic meaning has better chances of being effective if, together with the ability for describing the meaning potential of language, it is also able to take systematic account of context and lexicogrammar in relation to the choices in meaning. This is what I believe a semantic network does. In this paper I will outline briefly certain general concepts that are also relevant to systemic representation of semantic facts (section 2). This will, as it were, determine the identity and value of the terms *context, semantics, lexicogrammar* within the descriptive system known as systemic functional linguistics (SFL). In section 3, concepts that are specifically relevant to semantic system networks will be discussed. The paper will close with an appraisal of semantic system networks as a tool for the analysis of meaning.

2 Language description and system networks

First, however, a word on the very notion of *system network*,[6] familiar to most systemic linguists and somewhat unhelpfully and superficially discussed by Hudson (1986). A system network is a form of representation for the description a systemic linguist assigns to some (part of a) linguistic stratum. It is thus a hypothesis regarding relations that according to that linguist obtain in some specific area of linguistic description; the system network is essentially a mode of presentation for a hypothesis about the value and identity of some linguistic unit(s) at some stratum postulated in the linguistic model. The concepts fundamental to system networks thus logically relate to two areas: (i) the formalism for representing the details of the hypothesis systemically, and (ii) the basis for validating them. These concepts apply to description at each stratum, including that of semantics, so a brief discussion of both is appropriate here.[7]

2.1 *Systemic representation: formalism*

Four basic concepts are relevant to the representation of hypotheses in the form of a system network: *environment, choice, and* and *or*.[8] The last two, i.e. *and/or*, are relations which operate on the first two – i.e. environments and choices. The environment is that which is under description; that is to say the hypotheses embodied in the system describe this environment in terms of the possibilities it offers at that point of the analytic process. So the assumption is that it is the environment that furnishes the frame within which what the speakers can 'do' – what they can mean, what they can say – has any significance. The choices (or, interchangeably, *features*, *options*) represent this potential. Thus, suppose for English *clause* is taken as the environment, the description at the primary degree of delicacy (on delicacy see Halliday 1961; 1988; 1992) is exhausted by saying that at this point in the description the clause may *either* have the feature [major] *or* the feature [minor], as shown in Figure 5.2a.

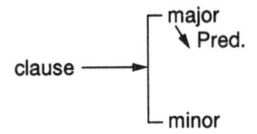

```
                  ┌─ major
                  │   ↘ Pred.
clause ──────────▶│
                  │
                  └─ minor
```

Figure 5.2a   Clause as point of origin

It is this possibility of choice in a given environment that is the essence of a paradigmatic orientation for linguistic description, and the form of the system network[9] is designed to capture this orientation. In most traditional, including formal, grammars, the clause is described as a combination of constituents – a 'string' – and it is in terms of 'constraints' on these combinations that the clause has to be described. This is a syntagmatic orientation, familiar to us since the days of the ancient Greek. However, in models with paradigmatic orientation, as for example in systemic functional linguistics, the explicitly recognized foundation for the description of the clause is not in terms of the combination of its constituents but in terms of its potential, any one combinatory shape of the clause being simply a specific instance of some systemic choice(s). This, *contra* McGregor (1995), does not imply that the syntagm has been abandoned or underplayed in systemic functional linguistics; rather, the syntagm is seen as related to the paradigm via instantiation and realization (more on these terms in section 2.2). As theoretical constructs, the terms *paradigm/syntagm* are not immanent categories (cf. Firth 1957), having a reality outside a descriptive framework. They are simply two different perspectives on the same phenomena: the system of features, i.e. the paradigm, specifies the potential; a specific syntagm represents one actual (deemed possible in light of the potential). In describing language, the act of linguistic analysis intervenes between the potential and any actual(s), which is to say that underlying all descriptions which start with a syntagm there are **unuttered hypotheses** of the potential. On the basis of one clause (type) the linguist has no ground whatever for saying that it consists of a noun phrase and a verb phrase or of a subject and a predicate.

In Figure 5.2a, clause is an example of a specific kind of environment – the initial environment for a systemic description. The initial environment is what is known as the *point of origin* for a system network. This contrasts with the subsequent environment known as the *entry point*. Subsequent environments – entry points – are constituted when a systemic feature in its turn is taken as the environment for a more delicate systemic option. For example, the feature [major] is the entry point for several system networks,[10] including those of MOOD, MODALITY, TRANSITIVITY, and THEME as shown in Figure 5.2b.

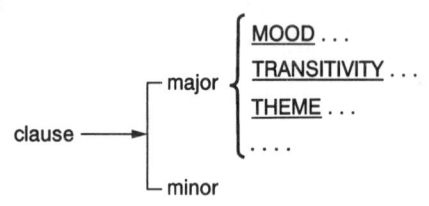

```
                    ┌  MOOD ...
                    │  TRANSITIVITY ...
          ┌─ major ─┤  THEME ...
clause ───┤         └  ....
          └─ minor
```

Figure 5.2b   [major] as entry condition to multiple systems

An entry point is often *simple*, constituted by a single feature, as is the case for example with [major]. However, two or more features in either the relation *and* or the relation *or* may constitute an entry point. When, of two or more features, *either* one *or* another can act as the entry point to a specific system of options, the entry is said to be *disjunct*. An example is furnished by the system with the features [tagged] or [non-tagged] in Figure 5.3 below; in most dialects of British English, the entry point for this system is *either* the feature [declarative] *or* [imperative]. By contrast when two or more features together constitute the entry point for some system, this is known as a *conjunct entry point*. For example *both* the features [declarative] *and* [tagged] *together* constitute the entry point to the system [reversed] or [constant]. Irrespective of whether the entry point is disjunct or conjunct, it might itself function as either an environment for just one or more than one system of features. For example the features [declarative] and [tagged] constitute the conjunct entry point for two *concurrent* systems: [tagpositive] v. [tagnegative] *and also* another system [reversed] v. [constant]. Figure 5.3 – a simplified version of the MOOD system network with clause as the point of origin and [major] as the entry point – presents the systemic environment of the features used above for exemplification.

Note that the *or* relation is indicated by square brackets, the *and* by a brace; when the *and/or* relations operate on a system of features, the brackets and braces face right; when they operate on the environment – with disjunct/conjunct entry point – the brackets/braces face left. Note also that each time a systemic feature functions as an entry point for a new system, this constitutes a further move in *delicacy*. Whatever the degree of delicacy, the entire description provided can be presented in terms of 'choice paths'. The choice path is known as *selection expression* (SE), and a system network must allow at least two selection expressions, consisting of no less than two features. The SEs [indicative:interrogative:polar] and

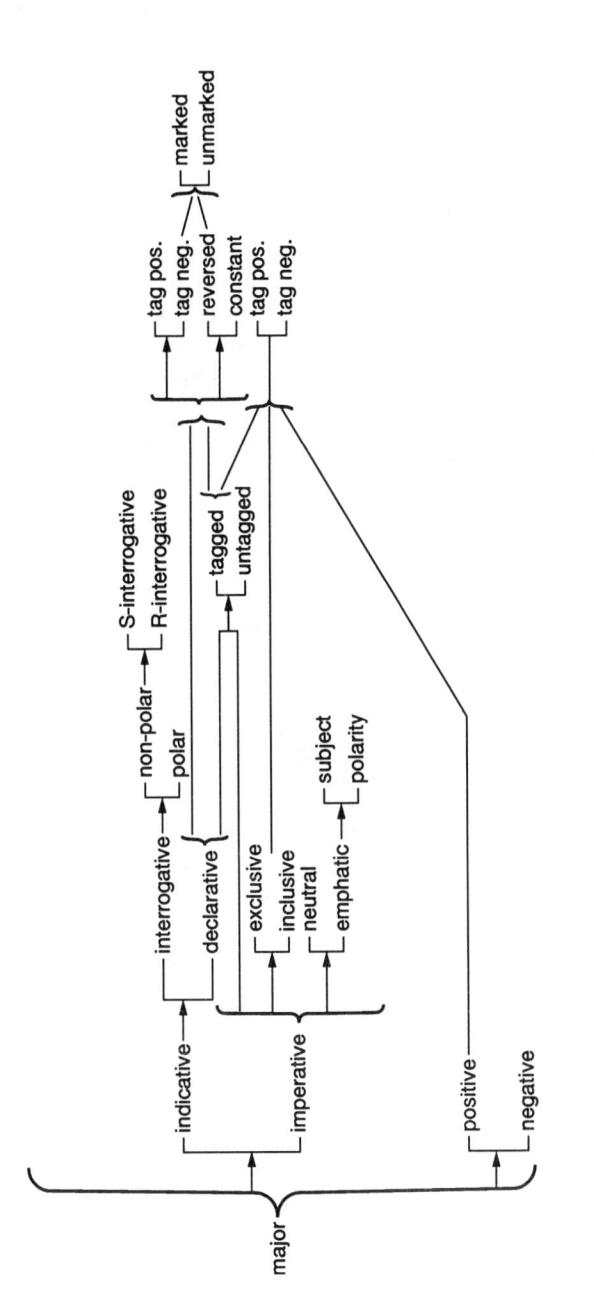

Figure 5.2b A simplified fragment of the system of MOOD

[indicative:declarative:untagged] are just two of the actualizations of the potential represented in Figure 5.3. Each such SE is the hypothesized description of some linguistic unit at a certain point in delicacy. The four basic concepts and others derived from them, which I have introduced in this subsection by reference to lexicogrammar, apply also to the level of semantics.

2.2 Concepts relevant to validating a system network

If the system network embodies hypotheses about the description of some linguistic unit, there has to be some way of deciding whether the hypothesis is valid. In SFL both for the level of semantics and of lexicogrammar, the criteria for validating hypotheses have a triple focus – what Halliday (in press, a) has called a trinocular perspective. Taking semantic networks as an example, the validity of the postulated semantic features would be confirmed IF (i) they construe some recognizable contextual feature, AND IF (ii) there exist identifiable lexicogrammatical features which function systematically as the expression of the postulated semantic features, AND IF (iii) a postulated semantic feature is systematically related to other semantic features, without internal contradiction or duplication. The first of these parameters is a focus from 'above' (i.e. here from the stratum of context), the second is from 'below' (i.e. from the stratum of lexicogrammar), and the last from 'around' (the same stratum, i.e. here semantics, at which the system network is located)[11] (see Halliday 1973b for discussion).

This trinocular perspective underlies three crucial concepts relevant to validation in SFL: first, *realization*, second, *instantiation*, and third, *agnation*. Of these, realization is perhaps the most complex and has been discussed in some detail (Halliday 1992; Hasan 1995; Lemke 1984; Matthiessen 1996; Martin 1992; Fawcett 1988; Cloran 1994; Berry 1977; Williams 1995). One reason for this complexity lies in the fact that realization is both multifocal and bidirectional. The bidirectionality of realization is perhaps already obvious from the discussion of the trinocular perspective: realization involves also the dual perspective of *construal* and *activation*. Thus semantic features *construe* contextual feature(s), and they are themselves construed by lexicogrammatical feature(s). *At the same time*, semantic features are *activated* by the contextual ones; and, in their turn, they themselves activate lexicogrammatical features. The activation aspect of realization is operative in speakers' language use: that is to say, speakers don't just mean *in vacuo*; they do so apropos some context, and they do not produce formal patterns simply because they are *homo grammaticus* but because they are *homo semioticus*: grammaticality and sensicality are two sides of the same coin. In the context of semantic networks, this dialectic is significant: it implies that to be recognized as valid in the SF model, semantic features (by themselves or in company with other semantic features) must display contextual significance and that at the same time they must be formally 'ratified' (for a discussion of the meaning and scope of 'formal criteria' see Hasan and Fries 1995;

Matthiessen and Nesbitt in press). This is an interpretation of Halliday's claim about the 'natural', 'nonarbitrary' relation between lexicogrammar and semantics: whatever is a linguistic meaning is lexicogrammatically construed; the form of language is a resource for meaning. Thus the term *functional* in *systemic functional* is not in mutual exclusion from *formal* as it tends to be in much of pragmatics or critical linguistics. The recognition of the semantic level as distinct from the level of context is a crucial step in the denial of the speaker's intention as the determining factor in the listener's interpretation; at the level of semantics, there are no intentions, just as there are no coconuts in the mind, only representations (Bateson 1972). And the separation of semantics and lexicogrammar is an essential ingredient in showing the power of grammar as a resource for meaning: to hear something as inappropriate, aggressive, persuasive is to relate grammar, meaning and context.

Let me now briefly explain what I mean by the multifocal nature of realization. It is multifocal in that it relates facts of different order at the same stratum: i.e. it refers to intra-stratal relations; it also relates facts pertaining to distinct metafunctions: i.e. it 'calibrates' metafunctions; and further, it relates the facts of one stratum to those of another: i.e. the term refers to inter-stratal relations. The majority of realization statements pertain to intra-stratal relations, as will be seen from a consideration of Table 5.1, where for the most part options from Figure 5.3 are used as examples:

Table 5.1: Types of realizational statement (Hasan 1992a, 243)

i	structuring	(a)	insert element Mood
		(b)	expand Mood as Subject Finite
		(c)	order S F as S^F
ii	layering		conflate two/more functions, e.g. Subject/Actor
iii	pre-selecting	(a)	from another rank within the same stratum
		(b)	from another stratum

All *structuring* realization statements are intra-stratal. i(a–b) realize the feature [indicative]; i(c) [declarative]. All of these pertain to the lexicogrammatical stratum, as do the elements Subject and Finite. The second category *layering* calibrates concepts pertaining to distinct metafunctions. Thus Subject is an interpersonal function realizing some feature from the system of MOOD, and Actor an experiential one, realizing some feature from TRANSITIVITY; they are conflated through layering as a realization of [active] VOICE. The third category *pre-selecting* operates both intra-stratally, as in iii(a), and inter-stratally as in iii(b). An example of the former is the following: with the SE [imperative:exclusive;neutral;negative] the verbal operator *do* will be pre-selected with polarity features [negation:weak] *n't*, as in *don't tease me*. An example of iii(b) – inter-stratal realization – would be as follows: with semantic SE [**demand;information:confirm:enquire:ask**][12] (see Figure 5.4), the following MOOD SE is pre-selected [indicative:interrogative:polar], an example of which will be a clause such as *do they eat people?*

Inter-stratal realization relation appears to be limited to pre-selection, while intra-stratal realization relations of the types discussed above are characteristic of the lexicogrammatical stratum: there are, thus, no semantic SEs that are not realized as some specific linguistic form. In other words, lexicogrammar is both systemic and structural, paradigmatic and syntagmatic. Implicit in this discussion is the claim that the formation of syntagma is 'part of the process of realisation'. To quote (Halliday 1981, 15):

> A structural expression is the product of the realisation of some selection expression, some set of features from the network of systemic options. It is in this sense that structure is said to be 'derived'.

The term *instantiation* refers to what in my understanding Firth (1957) meant by his axiom of 'renewal of connection with data'. So far as the validity of the description embodied in the system network is concerned, the claim is that there is no valid SE such that it cannot be instantiated. Instantiation is not necessarily something that has already been 'said/uttered'; it is the 'sayable' – what could be taken as an instance of the category in question.[13] So without the relation of instantiation, the notion of observational adequacy is meaningless: the observed in the process of analysis is not the 'sensed'; it is that which can be systematically related to some description. Instantiation is not stratally limited: for example the semantic SE [**demand;information:confirm:enquire:ask**] could be instantiated by *do they eat people?*, and as pointed out above the same clause could also instantiate the lexicogrammatical SE [indicative:interrogative:polar].

We owe the term *agnation* to Gleason, though the idea underlying the concept was already entailed in Hjelmslev's and Firth's systemic orientation. Two or more instances are agnates if underlying them are some systemic features in common. Items in agnation relation are the 'same' in respect of some systemic features at some point in delicacy; they can clearly never be 'identical' in all systemic respects, given the postulate of lexis as delicate grammar. The relation of agnation is variable, the variability resulting from what is treated as the defining characteristic of the paradigm under focus, i.e. what systemic features are required to be in common. Thus such clauses as *the robber shot Liz* and *Liz wasn't shot by the robber* could be treated as agnates if the criterion is simply the feature [declarative]; but equally, it is possible to set up a much tighter, i.e. more delicately defined criteria, by for example incorporating the feature [negative] POLARITY for the system of MOOD and also [active] VOICE from a different system altogether as criterial to the definition of this paradigm, as with Huddleston's 'basic clause' and early Chomsky's 'kernel sentence'. In that case, the two clauses just cited would not be treated as agnates, and the first but not the second would qualify as basic/kernel. These points are obvious enough; what I want to emphasize is the fact that agnation is not *sui generis*; it is not *pre-analytic*, but *given only post-analytically*. There is thus no foundation for considering any unit as basic without offering an explanation of basic-ness.

3 Semantic system networks

The idea of semantic networks is not new in the systemic functional model, as they were already in use in the late 1960s. The impetus for devising an intersubjectively objective analysis of meaning in discourse arose from the sociolinguistic research being carried out under Basil Bernstein's direction in the Sociolinguistic Re   arch Unit at the University of London Institute of Education. The earliest published examples of semantic networks are those by Halliday (1973b) and Turner (1973). The context in which these semantic networks were produced as an analytic tool had some important consequences for how the details of the semantic network were conceptualized. A decade later, in 1983, I constructed a semantic system network with the aim of establishing semantic variation as a valid sociolinguistic category (on semantic variation see especially Hasan 1989; 1992a). It is not the aim of this paper to present the details of this semantic network. I will begin with a review of Halliday 1973b, with the aim of drawing attention to the ways in which the concept of semantic network has undergone some significant changes in my work (Hasan 1988; 1989; 1991; 1992a; 1992b; Hasan and Cloran 1990) and that of my colleagues (Butt in press; Cloran 1989; 1994; Williams 1995). By this approach I hope to be able to address certain basic issues relevant to the place of my semantic networks in the general framework of SFL. I will be concerned with the relation of semantic network to context (section 3.1), the question of conceptualizing points of origin for semantic networks (section 3.2), the relation of semantic network to metafunctions (section 3.3), and to lexicogrammar (3.4). The actual network representation will be dictated by the needs of the argument; in other words, the fragments do not present the full range postulated in Hasan (1983), and touch only incidentally upon modifications suggested by Cloran (1994) and Williams (1995). The concluding section will draw attention to some uses of a semantic network of the type presented here.

3.1 Semantic networks and context

Halliday (1973b, 76)[14] introduced his semantic networks as follows:

> A semantic network is a hypothesis about patterns of meaning, and in order to be valid it must satisfy three requirements. It has to account for the range of alternatives at the semantic stratum itself; and it has to relate these both 'upwards', in this instance to categories of some general social theory or theory of behaviour, and 'downwards', to the categories of linguistic form at the stratum of grammar.

This, if you like, is an early formulation of the relevance of the trinocular perspective in validating systemic description (cf. section 2.2). At this early stage of its development the point of origin for semantic networks is not very obvious. As to the nature of the meanings to be represented, the idea of potential is clearly articulated. A semantic network is what the speaker 'can do' in a specific environment, where doing is to be interpreted as the acts of meaning and saying: 'we are making a hypothesis about what the speaker can do, linguistically, *in a given context*: about what meanings are accessible to him' (p. 76; emphasis mine). Halliday's semantic network is, thus, not an attempt to represent the meaning potential of a language in general terms; the meanings represented there may be described as crucial to a specific register; they are thus meanings that I have referred to as 'register specific meaning potential' (Hasan 1985). The rationale for choosing a particular context – that of control – was found in Bernstein's sociological theory, which considered the context of control as critical to socialization and thus to coding orientation. A rationale for context specific networks is given in the following terms (p. 79; emphasis mine):

> The behavioural options are specific to the social context, which determines their meaning; for example, *'threat' in a mother–child control context has a different significance from 'threat' in another context, such as the operation of a gang.*

There is also a sense that attempts to represent the meaning potential of the language without linking it to some specific context would be profitless. This situation gives rise to a paradox: 'The input to the semantic network is *sociological* and *specific*; their output is linguistic and general' (p. 80). I will review both the assumption that semantic networks are context specific and that the nature of context is sociological, since the semantic network I have formulated may neither be said to be context specific nor to take a sociologically defined context as its point of departure, though it was designed specifically to examine a sociolinguistic problem.

Turning first to the specificity of the semantic network, four observations appear pertinent. First, it is obvious that (a) on Halliday's 'infinite system, finite text' (1993) principle, no one speaker will ever use the entire meaning potential of a language, say, English; and (b) the constraints on the privilege of using certain meanings rather than others would always be contextual. However, in principle, this situation is not very different from that of the lexicogrammatical potential. Today with advances in register studies, we recognize that specific lexicogrammatical choices are at risk in specific types of language use (Halliday in press, b). This has, in my opinion rightly, not been interpreted as a reason for making lexicogrammatical networks context specific.

My second observation concerns the nature of context and the process of language. In the process of language – that is, from its instantial perspective – the 'actualized' semantic choices will always construe some, one unique context, quite irrespective of whether the semantic network is context specific or not. By contrast what the semantic system network is *capable of generating* even where it represents the semantic potential relevant to some one specific context is not just one unique context; instead, it is capable of creating a multiplicity of agnate contexts. So even with the context specific network of control if the instantiated choices are [**threat:punishment**] as opposed to [**appeal:person-oriented**], we already have two systemically related cases of the context of control. This *within context* variation illustrates Bernstein's claim that the recognition and performance criteria for contexts differ depending on the speaker's social positioning. It would seem then that the notion of delicacy applies to context; its specificity is variable: what the system, being a representation of the potential is capable of generating will become unique and specific only in the instantiation, only in the use. In fact, the issue of semantic variation turns on the assumption that two or more actual contexts can be seen as delicate variants of the same primary context: the primary context for control 'is' more delicately a context for control by threat *or* by appeals to 'logical' reasons (Hasan 1992a; 1992b), and so on. This makes the idea of context specific semantic networks somewhat problematic.

Thirdly, the problem is further exacerbated by the fact that the meanings relevant to two primary contexts, for example those of control and of pedagogic instruction, bear a non-accidental relationship to each other (cf. Bernstein's theory of the structuring of the pedagogic discourse). This necessitates 'bringing together' the semantic system specific to control and that specific to instruction within the pedagogic context. In principle, then, as the semantic description develops it would be found that the contextually specific semantic systems are permeable just as contexts themselves are permeable (Hasan 1973; 1995).

Finally, to say as we do in SFL that a specific context is construed by a specific range of semantic features argues that even if we do not begin with a context specific semantic network, even if the network is (ambitiously) a representation of the meaning potential of English, the choice paths in it, if it is a valid representation, will construe a range of unique contexts – agnates, in fact (Hasan 1995) – recognizable to the acculturated members of a community as at once the same and not the same. These arguments suggest a *contextually open* semantic system network rather than a contextually constrained one as the goal of semantic description,[15] just as a grammar is semantically open, not constrained by the recognition of specific semantic areas.

Turn now to the emphasis on the need for a sociologically informed notion of context: 'The input to the semantic network is *sociological* and *specific*; their output is linguistic and general' (p. 80; emphasis mine). Appeal to sociological criteria seems necessary most probably because there is no intrinsic reason for taking, say, the primary context of control as criterial. Making a distinction between *social* and *sociological*, I would suggest that in SFL now the social nature of linguistic meanings is adequately captured through Halliday's metafunctional hypotheses (see Halliday 1977;

1979 for further discussion). If the semantic network represents the *interpersonal, experiential, logical,* and *textual* meaning potential of a language, it is by implication representing the sociality of meanings. When, however, we turn to the sociological significance of the activation of a specific set of semantic features such as have been discussed in the work on semantic variation, then we do need an informed sociological theory. And it is in the light of that theory that we might be able to explain why the features [**prefaced**], [**elaborated**] and [**non-assumptive**] are habitually selected by middle-class mothers. For example, I explained the actual pattern of instantiations in my data by reference to Bernstein's theoretical framework which relates ideological perspectives to social positioning, and social positioning to macro-sociological phenomena. However, the selection patterns have both a linguistic and a sociological character. As linguistic units, these semantic features have a default value, a typical significance, and their co-occurrence is not random. I have argued (Hasan 1989; 1991) that there is a semantic prehension between these categories such that it would be somewhat contradictory for the same speaker to be habitually oriented to, say, the features [**prefaced**] and [**assumptive**], just as it would be contradictory to claim that something is white all over and also black all over. The question why speakers in a specific social position prefer *this* conjunction of semantic features or *that* cannot, however, be answered from within the inner structure of language, nor even through the metafunctional hypothesis. For this we need a theory of context which combines both Halliday's insights and those of Bernstein, whereby social relation is seen from multiple perspectives, including that of the social positioning of the interactants (Hasan forthcoming). A mother's threat to the child differs from a gangster's but this is precisely what should be explained by a powerful theory of context which would specify the extra-linguistic features relevant to the context of discourse. These arguments encourage me to propose that contextually open semantic networks will be a more powerful tool for the analysis of meaning in discourse. The semantic network I formulated in 1983 is one tentative step in the vast enterprise of modelling the meaning potential of English.

The material to be analysed semantically in my research[16] occurred naturally in contexts which had some features in common up to a certain point in delicacy: for example in Phase I of the research, *mothers* were *chatting* with *children* (see Hasan and Cloran 1990 for details). But perhaps only one parameter – that of *mode* – was largely constant (for a fuller discussion of this parameter see Cloran 1994), while, within this general uniformity, the more delicate attributes of tenor and field varied significantly. In Phase II, *teachers* and *pupils* were co-engaged in some pedagogic activity, while recordings were also made of *children's peer group* interaction while 'at play'. With minor modifications, Hasan's 1983 semantic network proved adequate for the semantic analysis of this varied range of discourses. Though the data itself was dialogic, the features in the network allowed the analysis of both dialogic and monologic discourse. Cloran

(1994) extended the network in a way that enabled her to analyse, albeit from a restricted perspective, the language of a small extract from written academic discourse. It is also significant that Williams (1995), whose data matched mine in most respects but was more specific than mine with regard to field being concerned with the activity of book reading at home and in school, was still able to use the same network with minor modifications. Maley and Fahey (1991) used the network – again with minor modifications – for the analysis of courtroom interaction. In addition Cloran (1989) utilized the same network for a study of the ontogenesis of gender-based discourse. The claim is not that this network represents the entire semantic potential of English – far from it; the claim is simply that it is not specific to a particular context, and that the features in it are not sociologically determined. However, through the semantic analysis of the data it was possible to construe certain context types, e.g. for Phase I data, the contexts of control, information exchange, reasoning, and instruction. The speaker's habitual selections 'are' Whorf's 'fashions of speaking' – ways of saying: ways of meaning.

3.2 *Semantic networks: point of origin*

As a system network, the semantic systems too must have some justifiable point of origin (see discussion in section 2.1). For Halliday 1973b, the frame for the semantic network was a socially significant human activity; the meanings represented as the accessible ones in the network mediated behaviour in that specific context. The question of the point of origin is not raised because what is being described is not a linguistic unit as such, but the linguistic correlates of a social activity. In a semantic network realizationally related to context in general this solution was not available.

Hasan (1983) used the semantic unit *message* as the point of origin for the network which thus presents hypotheses about the value and identity of message types. Message is a linguistic unit at the semantic level. Seen from above, it is the smallest significant semiotic action that an interactant might take in the context of an interaction so as to affect its character. As an indication of this I suggested in various writings (see also Cloran 1994) that the message is the smallest semantic unit which is capable of realizing an element of the structure of a text. Research by Cloran (1994) on the notion of *rhetorical units* (RUs) has since suggested an intermediate unit between text and message, such that it can be claimed that texts consist of one or more than one RU, and the latter consist of one or more than one message. This suggests a hierarchy of units at the semantic level. In fact, Cloran (1994) suggests a further rank to which she refers as *message component*. This is, if you like, in the nature of a *text radical*, and just as clauses typically do not consist of morphemes, so also it seems very likely that text radicals (or Cloran's message components) will not enter into the structure of the text directly. On the basis of these enquiries, I would propose a four-unit rank scale at the semantic level; moving from the largest to the smallest these are:

text, rhetorical unit, message and text radical. Some of the specific types of text radical are *entity, event, quality*. Message types is what my semantic network set out to specify through the systemic options open to speakers in that environment. Rhetorical units have been discussed in detail (Cloran 1994): they cut across the monologic/dialogic distinction, identifying certain types of textual strategies which are at risk at certain points in the structuring of a discourse. In light of these developments Martin's (1992, and elsewhere) label for the semantic level as *discourse semantics* appears appropriate, though it is hard to see what else semantics could be within a functional model of the SFL variety.

The contextual and semantic characterization of message can be taken as specifying its definition. Its recognition criteria are furnished by the lexicogrammar: a message is typically realized by pre-selection as a ranking clause, except where the clause is a projecting one. For example *did you know that they're going to leave?* has two ranking clauses: *did you know*, a projecting clause, and *(that) they're going to leave*, a projected one. They are, however, treated as one message with the feature [**prefaced**], where *did you know* prefaces *(that) they're going to leave*: note that without phoric presupposition the first part of such a message, realized by a projecting clause, cannot function as one element of text structure. (For further discussion of the discursive and ideological significance of this message type, see Cloran, forthcoming.) The hypotheses to be represented in the network about the range of semantic features – about the meanings that are accessible in producing a message – constitute the description of message up to a certain point in delicacy.

3.3 Semantic network and the metafunctional hypothesis

The primary system applicable to message is [**punctuative**] v. [**progressive**].[17] The former is realized by [minor] clause, the latter by [major]. The feature [**punctuative**] construes what I would like to describe as 'locutionary and/or expressive guidance'. The appropriateness of the term 'locutionary guidance' can be appreciated by a consideration of examples such as *hi!, good morning, John!, you know what?, what?, that's it., that's all., o.k., right!, rightio!, just a sec., well, come again!, pardon?* . . . To paraphrase these in general terms, messages such as these say one of the following things: 'pay attention!'; 'engage with me'; 'go ahead/continue'; 'you/I (have to) stop/conclude (this part of) interaction now'; 'I'm not ready yet for interaction'; or 'repeat that'. Contextually these and other such messages guide the flow of interaction, often punctuating its stages. It is phenomena of this kind that Ventola (1979) referred to as 'conversation management devices'. Then there are meanings of the general type 'I have an affect toward something/someone', providing expressive guidance to the listener, as in *bless you/him/my soul, great!, thanks, oh shit!, hell!, blast that idiot!, God help you* . . .

In SF descriptions, [minor] clause is usually said to be realized by the absence of the element Predicator; typically it tends to be a nominal expression. Looking at this lexicogrammatical feature from semantics, it seems reasonable to suggest that [minor] should be treated as an entry point to a system with terms [predicated] v. [unpredicated], since strictly speaking quite a few of the above examples have a Predicator element in them. The difference between these and [major] clause is, however, clear: the pattern in [minor] clause is 'formulaic', i.e. it has few if any structural agnates, only semantic ones. For example, *how do you do?* is not in a paradigm with *how will you do, how did you do.* In other words, the lexicogrammatical systemic options open to clauses [minor:predicated] are different from those available to [major] clause. This confirm's Halliday's insight that such messages are like the protolinguistic utterances of a child – a simple content-expression pair, without any systematic organization at the semantic and lexicogrammatical strata. Let me here draw attention to a general point: because this semantic network describes a linguistic unit – i.e. message – the description sheds light on hypotheses about the lexicogrammatical units realizationally related to it – i.e. clause – just as at the level of lexicogrammar ambiguity, for example, cannot be handled without an (overt/covert) appeal to meaning, no matter how 'formal' the grammar. In practice, this is an example of lexicogrammar being validated from 'above': protests by formalists notwithstanding, grammar without meaning is impossible, if the goal is descriptive and/or explanatory adequacy. The choice is whether this relation between meaning and grammar will be left implicit or made explicit. Formal grammarians choose the former solution.

The characterization of the [**punctuative**] message reveals that its orientation is predominantly interpersonal, being concerned with speech role allocation management and the expression of internal states, be that surprise, joy or disgust. And while there is a clear experiential difference between *bless you* and *blast you*, as also between *good morning* and *good evening*, it would, in fact, be quite wasteful to postulate any system of options concerned with 'state of affairs' in the environment of this feature, since the experiential differences are not systematic. A [**punctuative**] message neither varies systemically by attributes of performer of activity (i.e. who does to whom/what; grammatically Actor Goal, etc.) nor by the attributes of activity (i.e. where, when, how ... ; grammatically Circumstance). It has a simple metafunctional identity, i.e. interpersonal, but no experiential, logical or textual identity. By contrast, the description of messages with the feature [**progressive**] must take into account a multiple metafunctional perspective. This makes a contextually open network such as Hasan 1983 'big' (cf. Halliday in press, b). And while this network is far from an exhaustive account of the meanings of English,[18] even so, the range of the options is wide enough so that the presentation of all the meanings captured by it[19] requires extensive documentation. I will present snippets from it selected to suit the aims of this paper (see section 3.3). Figure 5.4 presents the primary options.

In this network the slanted arrow ↘ precedes the lexicogrammatical feature which realizes the semantic feature under focus. Thus ↘ *minor* is

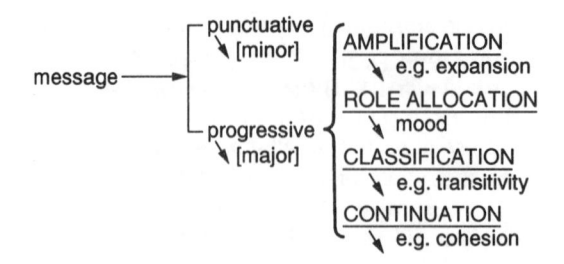

```
                    ┌─ punctuative      ┌ AMPLIFICATION
                    │   ↘ [minor]       │    ↘ e.g. expansion
   message ──────   │                   │ ROLE ALLOCATION
                    │                   │    ↘ mood
                    └─ progressive  ────┤
                        ↘ [major]       │ CLASSIFICATION
                                        │    ↘ e.g. transitivity
                                        │ CONTINUATION
                                        └    ↘ e.g. cohesion
```

Figure 5.4 Primary systems in a context open semantic network

the realization of [**punctuative**]. The feature [major] realizes [**progressive**] which in turn acts as the entry point for a number of systems, where CLASSIFICATION is experiential, AMPLIFICATION is logical, ROLE ALLOCATION is interpersonal, and CONTINUATION is textual.

The incorporation of the four Hallidayan metafunctions in the network is significant. It is doubtful that a context specific semantic network could successfully make this case; by contrast, on the basis of the 1983 network it can be justifiably argued that the level of semantics is metafunctionally organized just as the levels of context and lexicogrammar are. The fractal organization of language (Butt 1988; Matthiessen 1995) from context right through to lexicogrammar is a strong indication of the viability of the metafunctional hypothesis. The systems in message semantics are indeed (a) simultaneous, arguing for the equal status of the four metafunctions; and (b) they are at the primary degree of delicacy also relatively independent of each other, arguing for the individual integrity of each metafunction. This important issue, unfortunately, cannot be developed within the scope of this paper as the evidence for these claims must involve (i) presentation of at least all primary systems; and (ii) their lexicogrammatical realization. Some indication supporting these arguments may be found in Cloran (1994) and Williams (1995).

3.4 Semantic networks: the relations of semantics and grammar

Although the semantic features are realized by pre-selecting certain lexicogrammatical choices, this does not mean that they are isomorphic, with a one-to-one relation. Realization relation is not a correspondence relation; the prehension between the specific features of one stratum and the next is neither random, nor absolute: it has to be simply well above chance level in order to make the postulate of two distinct levels a useful descriptive device (Hasan 1995). Let me look a little more closely into this claim by focusing on a fragment of the system of ROLE ALLOCATION, which is presented in Figure 5.5. I choose this particular fragment because it is one which I and others have discussed elsewhere (Hasan 1989; 1991; Hasan and Cloran 1990; see also Cloran 1994; Williams 1995), which hopefully permits discussion without needing to present detailed information about the realization of each and every feature in the network. A full list of realization statements can be found in Cloran (1994).

Using Halliday 1994, the network postulates two concurrent systems, with features [**give**] v. [**demand**] and [**information**] v. [**goods&services**] (= [**g-s**]). The features in this network are realized by those in the system of MOOD, though not in a one-to-one relation. Certainly there is regularity of realizational relation between semantic options and lexicogrammar. Thus [**apprize**] is realized as [..interrogative:non-polar]; however, the feature [**confirm**] is realized either by [..interrogative:polar] or by [..declarative:non-tagged]. These distinct realizational possibilities represent distinct choice points in the semantic network. Suppose we were to revise the network as in Figure 5.5a so as to favour the grammatical system: This has the advantage that the realization[20] of [**verify**]* can now be said to pre-select the feature [..declarative] while [**ask**]* would be realized as [..interrogative:polar]. This regularization of realization appears simple from the grammatical perspective. However, it distorts relations at the level of semantics. To see this, we need to focus on the system [**assumptive**] v. [**non-assumptive**].

The critical considerations here are that according to Figure 5.5 (i) these systemic options have a disjunct entry point: either [**enquire**] or [**explain**]; (ii) in the former environment, the options are concurrent with the systemic option [**check**] v. [**ask**]; and finally (iii) the feature [**assumptive**] is lexicogrammatically realized by pre-selecting the polarity feature [negative]. By placing the semantic system [**assumptive**] v. [**non-assumptive**] here in the network, I am claiming that the lexicogrammatical feature [negative] construes different meanings in (1–3i) from those it construes in the others:

1:	didn't you see me?
2:	why don't you love Rosemary?
3i:	you didn't eat it?
3ii:	you ate it didn't you?
4:	who hasn't finished yet?
5:	they didn't see me.
6:	don't leave the books there.

Notably, it is only in (1–2 and 3i) that the feature [**assumptive**] can be said to be present. From above, looking at the option contextually, it implies that the speaker has definite views on what the state of affairs ought to be. Thus when Karen's response to (1) is *no*, her mother tells her *you must be blind*, implying clearly *you should have seen me*, since in fact Karen is not blind. Julian, after reassuring his mother that he does love Rosemary, asks *who else do you want me to love*, again implying *your question shows that you know whom I should/shouldn't love*. The feature [**assumptive**], then, construes a specific attitude on the part of the speaker, such that the attitude itself remains 'unuttered'. This is important. Consider the difference between (3ii) and

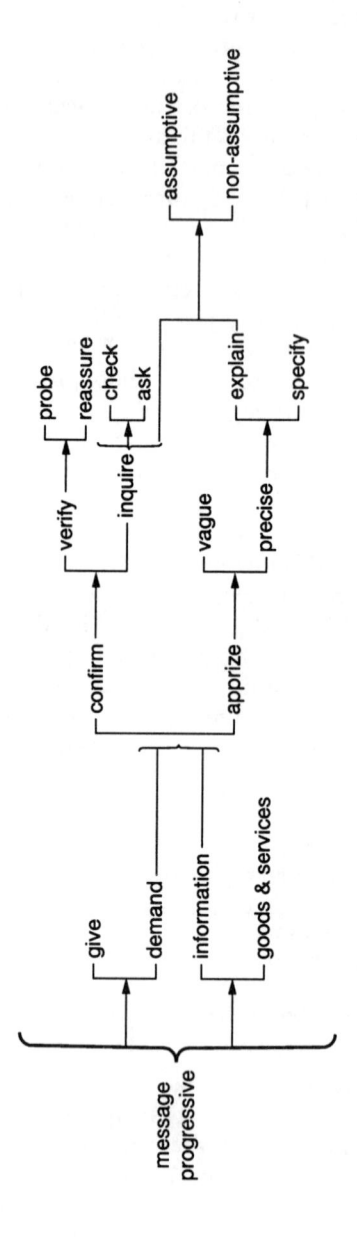

Figure 5.5 A fragment of ROLE ALLOCATION system

SEMANTIC NETWORKS

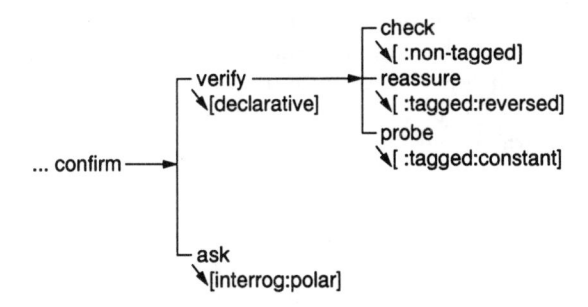

```
                           ┌─ check
                           │  ↘[ :non-tagged]
              ┌─ verify ───┼─ reassure
              │  ↘[declarative] │  ↘[ :tagged:reversed]
              │            └─ probe
... confirm ──┤               ↘[ :tagged:constant]
              │
              │
              └─ ask
                 ↘[interrog:polar]
```

Figure 5.5a Revised semantic network favouring the grammatical system

(3i) *you didn't eat it?*; in (3ii) there is no 'unuttered' assumption – in fact the assumption is already stated in the main part of the clause; all that is needed is a confirmation that the uttered assumption is correct. In (3i) the reverse is true as with (1–2). Thus, from the point of view of context and semantics, the representation in Figure 5.5 appears preferable to that in Figure 5.5a, because the former is both semantically and contextually consistent. We are forced then to accept 'asymmetry' between semantics and lexicogrammar.

Consider now (4), which has the features [..**apprize:precise:specify:actant**]. Here there appears to be no definite assumption of what the state of affairs should be. This is at variance from the situation in the case of [..**apprize:precise:explain**]. In other words the meanings of [negative] vary subtly depending on the environment in which it is selected. In point of fact, the negative tag in the environment of [**demand;g-s**] construes meanings which are remarkably different from those we find in the environment of [**demand;info**]. In one sense, being the marked term of the system, negation could invite explanation. For example *they didn't see me because I was behind the door*, or *don't leave the books there because I need them right now*. However, in (3ii and 4–6) negation does not construe an **unuttered** attitude of the speaker, that is to say it is not [**assumptive**], substantiating the claim that the relationship between grammatical systemic features and semantic ones cannot be thought of as one to one. This lack of exact fit between the two strata is noticeable in every system. For example, from the system of AMPLIFICATION, the feature [**supplementing**] is not necessarily realized by a hypotactic or paratactic clause, though this is often the case; the feature [**prefaced**] is not always realized by a projecting clause complex, since clauses such as *it was good that you helped mummy* and *it's not that I mind you playing with the marbles* are not projecting clause complexes. These examples could be multiplied. The moral of this seems to be that we need both the lexicogrammatical descriptions and the semantic ones: while the systemic functional grammar is pushed in the direction of semantics, it still remains true that the one cannot officiate for the other.

One aspect of the lexicogrammatical construal of the semantic features needs brief mention. As remarked earlier, the lexicogrammatical realization forms the recognition criteria for any semantic feature(s). I have also pointed out that inter-stratal realization typically takes the form of preselecting. In principle, to say that, for example, the feature [**ask**] is realized as [interrogative:polar] is sufficient as recognition criterion; but in actual practice, the recognition criteria for the grammatical features themselves are found in their intra-stratal realization, which brings in the crucial properties of the clause as a structure.

4 Conclusion: the uses of a semantic network

The subtitle of this chapter is 'A tool for the analysis of meaning'. It may be objected that the paper does not give sufficient indication of how meaning is to be analysed, particularly in language in process. This is true enough in one respect: I have not used an exchange structure or segment of mother–child talk to present its exhaustive analysis in terms of the semantic network. But such an analysis would have been just as incomprehensible as the detailed SF grammatical analysis of any passage would be in the absence of the large scholarship that supports it. Such support is as yet not a reality for semantic descriptions of the type I have introduced here. It may none the less be relevant to close this paper by drawing attention to the major strength of a contextually open semantic network such as exemplified by Hasan 1983 and others based on it.

A little reflection will show that a contextually open semantic system is the specification of meaning potential from the point of view of an absentee receiver of discourse – a distant addressee or even an outsider to the interaction. Much play has been made of the synoptic quality of descriptive frameworks which use such 'products' as their starting-point (Martin 1985; 1992; Ravelli 1995; O'Donnell 1990). However, the understanding of products such as these puts the listener under pressure: there are often no other modalities of meaning exchange compresent with the product in such cases. What permits the interpretation? Surely there could be past experience of interaction with the other whose discourse might be being accessed, though in today's world this is by no means to be taken for granted. Whatever the case, the receiver's linguistic ability to make sense, to construe meanings, from such displaced texts is put to much harder work than in those cases which are often cited as the ultimate instances of the dynamic. A system which is to be put to hard work cannot be modelled on the assumption of some specific context. This is what requires that the different metafunctional meanings should be modelled in such a network, and that these meanings should be represented as features, not as packaged bundles, which is what terms such as *questions, answers, statement, command* are. For packaged bundles are prefabricated, and in this prefabrication their variant characteristics become invisible. The contextually open semantic system is, in principle, a device to 'address' any social context. Being a potential it is in this sense dynamic: it is equal to any situation. For example, we know that not all questions are answered. An exchange structure must postulate some sort of response: to say that there is an exchange structure is to say that at least the elements initiate and respond are present. I shall ignore the fact that exchange structure analyses fail to tell us what counts as initiate and what as its response, i.e. how are these realized in language. This is a shortcoming they share with speech act analysis, which is not surprising since they are distantly derived from a speech-act-based description (Sinclair and Coulthard 1975; Berry 1981). With message semantics, curiously, in view of the declared synoptic nature of system networks (Ventola 1987; Ravelli 1995), there is a greater possibility for accommodating dynamic moves. Thus in the 1983 network, there is no 'necessity' for a message with feature [**demand;information**] to be followed by a response or even what I refer to as [**response:facilitative**], roughly equivalent to Goffman's side-sequences. In the process, the response may never come, as often happens in my mother–child talk. Or the response may be an [**evasion**] or if it comes it may be [**inadequate**], i.e. fail to address the query point of the question, again a behaviour noted in my data. It is only a synoptic network of **the meaning potential** of language that can, it seems, handle the dynamic nature of the process. The scope of this paper does not permit exploration of this interesting paradox.

The ideological nature of human discourse is the focus of much attention today. The usefulness of the contextually open semantic network in identifying ideological perspectives has been demonstrated in all the studies that have made use of it. Of course, it is always possible to talk about ideology without specifying on what basis one attributes a specific ideological perspective to this or that speaker. This is the privilege of the native speakers of a language, since they are already socialized into making meanings with their mother tongue. But just as knowledge of the mother tongue does not guarantee the ability to teach it, in the same way this familiarity with meaning making does not enable the analyst truly to analyse: at most it permits a labelling. And at any time labelling is a far less illuminating exercise than helping to understand, and this I hope is what the contextually open semantic network enables one to do.

Notes

1   This is not to say the origin of ideological dissonance lies in speaking alone. Rather, ideology is a function of social positioning (Bernstein 1990), and as such it 'identifies' what is possible, what is relevant, and their opposites in every field of human existence and action. It is the underlying principle in the evaluation of self or others.
2   I do not wish to give the impression that a community-wide ideology is an impossibility. In fact the level at which Whorf (1956) was examining the ideology construing power of language is different from that which is the concern of scholars such as Volosinov (1973), Bernstein, Bourdieu and many others. As Whorf maintained, common-sense conceptions of time and space tend to be shared throughout a community; in my opinion this is so irrespective of the various forms of social hegemony. An ideology centuries long and

communities wide is the conception of the place of women *vis-à-vis* men in society to which, despite local variations in manifestation, not very many alternatives were found in any known society until quite recently (Hasan 1986).

3   Elsewhere, e.g. Hasan (1989) I have postulated a linguistic model with five strata by dividing context into the stratum of context of culture and a separate stratum of context of situation. I believe this view has some severe problems. For a discussion of the relation between these see Halliday (1991) and also Hasan (1995).

4   The reader might wish to consult Halliday (1992); Hasan (1995); Lemke (1984); Matthiessen (1996) for some discussion of the relations between strata in a model of the type presented here.

5   The term *choice* does not necessarily imply *conscious choosing* in the context of this discussion any more than intentionality in speech production necessarily implies that someone deliberately intends, for in order to intend deliberately there would have to be a representation of the intention – a recipe for infinite regress! See the discussion of systemic choice in section 2.1.

6   I wish to acknowledge my debt to M. A. K. Halliday, Carmel Cloran, Geoff Williams, and especially to David Butt. with whom I have discussed the concept of network over a long period of time. I alone am responsible for the views presented here.

7   For further discussion of system networks, see Halliday (1973a; 1973b); Fawcett (1988); Martin (1987; 1991); Cloran (1994); Williams (1995); Butt (in press); Matthiessen (1994; 1996)

8   I have not included the widely recognized *if/then* relations in my account, since it seems to me that the general principle of choice having significance only in some given environment already contains the *if/then* relation. The ambiguity of *then* as a temporal is a good reason for avoiding these terms, unless their exclusion makes the account of system network formalism impossible. This I do not believe to be the case.

9   I shall not comment on the controversy amongst some systemic linguists on whether or not the validity of descriptions is compromised if hypotheses about linguistic units are not represented in the form of system networks. It seems to me that a distinction must be made between a paradigmatic orientation and systemic representation: paradigmatic orientation is an essential condition for systemic representation; the reverse is not true. I would argue though that a systemic representation is economical; a discursive presentation of the same hypotheses occupies much more time and space – one of the reasons why detailed realizational statements and discussions of the validity of the hypotheses embodied in the network are not frequent. By the same token, a discursive account runs greater risk of overlooking certain relations which may be criterial to the identity and value of the unit under description, since a complex unrepresented space is much more difficult to monitor.

10 In ordinary writing, systemic features are enclosed in square brackets. Dots in system networks indicate continuity of description. In principle, the system is open-ended, i.e. no description is deemed complete.

11 For obvious reasons, both context and phonology are immune to this principle, as there is no descriptive stratum above context and none below phonology, or perhaps one should say that in both these cases the validating focus lies in the

primary, subjective experience – for context, from the familiar sensible world, and for phonology, from the sensible acoustic waves.

12 Systemic features are typically shown in brackets. In this paper, features pertaining to the semantic stratum are shown in bold in order to distinguish them from those belonging to the lexicogrammatical stratum.

13 It has been suggested (Martin 1987; Hudson 1987; Fawcett 1988) that the notion of validity for systemic features demands that each and every feature of the system network should have a specific realizational consequence. I now believe that this is an arbitrary requirement; further I believe that the interpretation of the expression 'realizational consequence' is itself contestable. To say the least, it should not be equated with 'structural reflex', especially if by structure we mean a sequence of elements *in praesentia*. For lack of time and space I postpone this discussion.

14 From now on all page references in parentheses refer to Halliday (1973b), unless otherwise indicated.

15 Sometimes I have used the terms *context-independent* and *context-dependent* for what I am describing here as *contextually open* and *contextually constrained*. I prefer *contextually open* to *context-independent* since in a functional model such as SFL, descriptions at the levels of semantics and lexicogrammar cannot, in the last resort, be context-independent since through the workings of the metafunctions context permeates these strata, as they in their turn permeate context.

16 The research project was descriptively called 'The role of everyday talk between mothers and children in establishing ways of learning'; it, and its offshoots, were funded by the Australian Research Grant Scheme and the Australian Research Council during 1983–1988 and intermittently by the Macquarie University Research Grant Scheme over 1983–1994. The valuable contribution of Carmel Cloran to this research is gratefully acknowledged.

17 Nothing hangs on the names given to features; the important issue is what does a feature construe, i.e. its contextual content, and what construes it, i.e. its lexicogrammatical expression.

18 Just as all grammars, not excepting the monumental Quirk *et al.*, which have of course received far more concerted attention than the newly introduced semantic network, are still very far from an exhaustive account of the forms of English.

19 As a research instrument, the options of the network carried their lexicogrammatical realizations with remarks where necessary regarding their additional recognition criteria. This was sufficient to ensure the consistency of the analysis, especially since there were regular consultations between myself and Carmel Cloran who did most of the analysis.

20 In this discussion I have placed an asterisk on the semantic features taken from Figure 5.5a to distinguish them from those with the same label from Figure 5.5.

References

Bateson, G. (1972) *Steps to an Ecology of Mind*. Ballantine: New York.
Bernstein, B. (1990) *The Structuring of Pedagogic Discourse: Class, Codes and Control*, Vol. IV. London: Routledge.

Berry, M. (1977) *Introduction to Systemic Linguistics*, Volume II: *Levels and Links*. London: Batsford.

Berry, M. (1981) 'Systemic linguistics and discourse analysis: a multi-layered approach to exchange structure'. In M. Coulthard and M. Montgomery (eds) *Studies in Discourse Analysis*. London: Routledge & Kegan Paul, pp. 120–145.

Bourdieu, Pierre (1990) *Language and Symbolic Power*. Edited by John B. Thompson; translated by G. Raymond and M. Adamson. London: Polity Press.

Butt, David G. (1988) 'Randomnness, order and the latent patterning of text'. In *Functions of Style*, edited by David Birch and Michael O'Toole. London: Pinter.

Butt, David G. (in press) 'Critical abstractions and rhetoric: the latent order of pedagogic discourse'. In *Essays on Language Offered to J. M. Sinclair* edited by A. Pakir. Singapore: National University of Singapore.

Cloran, Carmel (1989) In *Language Development: Learning Language, Learning Culture: Meaning and Choice in Language: Studies for Micahel Halliday*, edited by Ruqaiya Hasan and J. R. Martin. Norwood, N. J.: Ablex.

Cloran, Carmel (1994) *Rhetorical Units and Decontextualization: An Enquiry into some Relations of Context, Meaning and Grammar*. Monographs in Systemic Linguistics, No. 6. Nottingham: School of English Studies, Nottingham University.

Cloran, Carmel (forthcoming) 'Constructing point of view'. Revised version of paper presented at the XXI International Systemic Functional Congress, Gent, Belgium, August 1994.

Douglas, Mary (1971) 'Do dogs laugh?' *Journal of Psychosomatic Research*, 15. Reprinted in *Implicit Meanings*, edited by Mary Douglas (1975). London: Routledge & Kegan Paul.

Fawcett, R. P. (1988) 'What makes a "good" system network good? – four pairs of concepts for such evaluation'. In J. D. Benson and W. S. Greaves (eds) *Systemic Functional Approaches to Discourse*. Norwood, N. J.: Ablex

Firth, J. R. (1957) *Papers in Linguistics 1934–1951*. London: Blackwell.

Halliday, M. A. K. (1961) 'Categories of the theory of grammar'. *Word*, 17.3.

Halliday, M. A. K. (1973a) 'The functional basis of language'. In *Explorations in the Functions of Language*. London: Edward Arnold.

Halliday, M. A. K. (1973b) 'Towards a sociological semantics'. In *Explorations in the Functions of Language*. London: Edward Arnold.

Halliday, M. A. K. (1975) *Learning How to Mean: Explorations in the Development of Language*. London: Edward Arnold.

Halliday, M. A. K. (1977) 'Text as semantic choice in social contexts'. In *Grammars and Descriptions*, edited by Teun A. van Dijk and Janos S. Petofi. Berlin: Mouton de Gruyter.

Halliday, M. A. K. (1979) 'Modes of meaning and modes of expression: types of grammatical structure and their determination by different semantic functions'. In *Functions and Contexts in Linguistic Analysis: A Festschrift for William Haas*, edited by D. J. Allerton, E. Carney and D. Holdcroft. Cambridge: Cambridge University Press

Halliday, M. A. K. (1981) 'Introduction'. In M. A. K. Halliday and J. R. Martin (eds) *Readings in Systemic Linguistics*. London: Batsford Academic and Educational Ltd.

Halliday, M. A. K. (1988) 'On the ineffability of grammatical categories'. In *Linguistics in a Systemic Perspective*, edited by James D. Benson, Michael J. Cummings and William S. Greaves. Amsterdam: John Benjamin.

Halliday, M. A. K. (1991) 'The notion of "context" in language education'. In *Language Education: Interaction and Development*, edited by T. Le and M. McCausland. Launceston: University of Tasmania.

Halliday, M. A. K. (1992) 'How do you mean?' In *Recent Advances in Systemic Linguistics: Theory and practice*, edited by Martin Davies and Louise Ravelli. London: Pinter.

Halliday, M. A. K. (1993) 'The act of meaning'. In *Language, Communication and Social Meaning*, Georgetown University Round Table on Languages and Linguistics 1992, edited by James E. Alatis. Georgetown, DC: Georgetown University Press.

Halliday, M. A. K. (1994) *Introduction to Functional Grammar*. 2nd edition. London: Edward Arnold.

Halliday, M. A. K. (in press, a) 'On grammar and grammatics'. In *Functional Descriptions: Theory in Practice*, edited by Ruqaiya Hasan, Carmel Cloran and David G. Butt. Amsterdam: John Benjamins.

Halliday, M. A. K. (in press, b) 'Language in relation to the evolution of human consciousness'. In *Of Thoughts and Words: Proceedings of Nobel Symposium 92 'The Relation between Language and Mind'*, edited by Sture Allen. Singapore and London: World Scientific Publishing.

Hasan, Ruqaiya (1973) 'Code, register and social dialect'. In *Class, Codes and Control*, Vol. II: *Applied studies towards a sociology of language*, edited by B. Bernstein. London: Routledge & Kegan Paul.

Hasan, Ruqaiya (1983) *A Semantic Network for the Analysis of Messages in Everyday Talk between Mothers and Their Children*. (Mimeo, Sydney: Macquarie University.)

Hasan, Ruqaiya (1985) 'The identity of a text'. In *Context and Text: Language in a Social-Semiotic perspective*, by M. A. K. Halliday and Ruqaiya Hasan. Geelong, Victoria: Deakin University Press.

Hasan, Ruqaiya (1986) 'The ontogenesis of ideology: an interpretation of mother–child talk'. In *Semiotics, Ideology, Language*. Sydney Studies in Society and Culture, 3, edited by Terry Threadgold, Elizabeth A. Grosz, Gunther Kress and M. A. K. Halliday. Sydney University: Sydney Association for Studies in Society and Culture. (Chapter 6 of this book).

Hasan, Ruqaiya (1987) 'Reading picture reading'. In *Proceedings from the 13th Conference of the Australian Reading Association*. Sydney, July 1987.

Hasan, Ruqaiya (1988) 'Language in the processes of socialization: home and school'. In *Language and Socialization: Home and School*, edited by L. Gerot, J. Oldenburg and T. Van Leeuwen. Proceedings from the Working Conference on Language in Education, November, 1986. Sydney: Macquarie University.

Hasan, Ruqaiya (1989) 'Semantic variation and sociolinguistics'. *Australian Journal of Linguistics*, 9.

Hasan, Ruqaiya (1991) 'Questions as a mode of learning in everyday talk'. In *Language Education: Interaction and Development*, edited by T. Le and M. McCausland. Launceston: University of Tasmania.

Hasan, Ruqaiya (1992a) 'Meaning in sociolinguistic theory'. In *Sociolinguistics Today: International Perspective*, edited by Kingsley Bolton and Helen Kwok. London: Routledge.

Hasan, Ruqaiya (1992b) 'Rationality in everyday talk: from process to system'. In *Directions in Corpus Linguistics: Proceedings of Nobel Symposium 82, Stockholm, 4–8 August 1991*, edited by Jan Svartvik. Berlin: Mouton de Gruyter.

Hasan, Ruqaiya (1995). 'The conception of context in text'. In *Discourse in Society*, edited by Peter H. Fries and Michael Gregory. Norwood, N. J.: Ablex.

Hasan, Ruqaiya (forthcoming) 'Context from the perspective of discourse'. Plenary paper presented at the XXII International Systemic Functional Congress, Beijing, China, August 1995.

Hasan, Ruqaiya and Cloran, Carmel (1990) 'A sociolinguistic study of everyday talk between mothers and children'. In M. A. K. Halliday, John Gibbons and Howard Nicholas (eds) *Learning, Keeping and Using Language*, Vol. I. Selected Papers from the 8th World Congress of Applied Linguistics, Sydney, August 1987. Amsterdam: John Benjamins.

Hasan, Ruqaiya and Fries, Peter (1995) 'Introduction'. In Ruqaiya Hasan and Peter H. Fries (eds) *On Subject and Theme: From a Discourse Functional Perspective*. Amsterdam: John Benjamins.

Hudson, Richard (1986) '*Systemic grammar (review of Halliday* 1985 and Butler 1985)'. *Linguistics* 24, 791–815.

Hudson, Richard (1987) 'Daughter dependency theory and systemic grammar'. In M. A. K. Halliday and R. P. Fawcett (eds) *New Developments in Systemic Linguistics*, Vol. I: *Theory and Description*. London: Pinter.

Leech, Geoffrey N. (1983) *Principles of Pragmatics*. London: Longman.

Lemke, J. L. (1984) *Semiotics and Education*. Toronto, Canada: Toronto Semiotic Circle Monograph No. 2.

Lemke, J. L. (1995) *Textual Politics: Discourse and Social Dynamics*. London: Taylor and Francis.

McGregor, William (1995) 'The English "tag question": a new analysis, is(n't) it?' In *On Subject and Theme: From a Discourse Functional Perspective*, edited by Ruqaiya Hasan and Peter H. Fries. Amsterdam: John Benjamins.

Maley, Y. and Fahey, R. (1991) 'Presenting the evidence: construction of reality in court'. *International Journal for the Semiotics of Law*, 4.10, 3–17.

Martin, J. R. (1985) 'Process and text: two aspects of human semiosis'. In *Systemic Perspectives on Discourse*, Vol. I, edited by James D. Benson and William S. Greaves. Norwood: Ablex.

Martin, J. R. (1987) 'The meaning of features in systemic linguistics.' In M. A. K. Halliday and R. P. Fawcett (eds) *New Developments in Systemic Linguistics*, Vol. I: *Theory and Description*. London: Pinter.

Martin, J. R. (1991) 'Intrinsic functionality: implications for contextual theory'. *Social Semiotics*, 1.1, 99–162.

Martin, J. R. (1992) *English Text: System and Structure*. Amsterdam: John Benjamins.

Matthiessen, Christian (1994) 'Paradigmatic organization: thirty years of system networks – today's potential'. Plenary paper presented at the XXI International Systemic Functional Congress, Gent, Belgium, August 1994.

Matthiessen, Christian (1995) 'Fractal principles in language: expansion and projection'. Plenary paper presented at the XXII International Systemic Functional Congress, Beijing, China, August 1995.

Matthiessen, Christian (1996) *Lexicogrammatical Cartography: English Systems*. Tokyo: International Language Sciences Publisher.

Matthiessen, Christian and Nesbitt, Chris. (1996) 'On theory-neutral descriptions'. In *Functional Descriptions: Theory in Practice*, edited by Ruqaiya Hasan, Carmel Cloran and David G. Butt. Amsterdam: John Benjamins.

O'Donnell, Michael (1990) 'A dynamic model of exchange'. *Word*, 41.3.

Ravelli, Louise (1995) 'A dynamic perspective: implications for metafunctional interaction and an understanding of Theme.' In *On Subject and Theme: From a Discourse Functional Perspective*, edited by Ruqaiya Hasan and Peter H. Fries. Amsterdam: John Benjamins.

Sinclair, J. and Coulthard, M. (1975) *Towards and Analysis of Discourse: The English Used by Teachers and Pupils*. London: Oxford University Press.

Turner, Geoffrey J. (1973) 'Social class and children's language of control at age five and age seven'. In *Class, Codes and Control*, Vol. II: *Applied Studies Toward a Sociology of Language*, edited by Basil Bernstein. London: Routledge & Kegan Paul.

Ventola, Eija, M. (1979) 'The structure of casual conversation in English'. *Journal of Pragmatics*, 3, 267–298.

Ventola, Eija, M. (1987) *The Structure of Social Interaction: A Systemic Approach to the Semiotics of Service Encounter Interaction*. London: Pinter.

Volosinov, V. N. (1973) *Marxism and the Philosophy of Language*. Trans. L. Matejka and I. Titunik. Cambridge, Mass.: Harvard University Press.

Whorf, Benjamin Lee (1956) *Language, Thought and Reality*, edited by John B. Carroll. Cambridge, Mass.: MIT Press.

Williams, Geoffrey (1995) *Joint Book-Reading and Literacy Pedagogy: A Socio-Semantic Interpretation*. Unpublished PhD dissertation. Sydney: School of English, Linguistics and Media, Macquarie University.

Part Three: Language and Society

6 The ontogenesis of ideology: an interpretation of mother–child talk

In their introduction to Karl Marx, Bottomore and Rubel comment that Marx used the term ideology in 'different senses'; and in one of these senses, ideology for Marx is a 'deliberately misleading system of ideas'. (1963, 21). The sense in which I wish to use this word will differ from the former, by expunging the modifiers 'deliberately misleading'. This is not to deny that the construction of ideology is non-accidental to the extent that it arises from sustained social practices; nor is it to deny that ideologies can be nurtured deliberately in the sense of receiving a coherent seeming philosophico-logical rationale in the un-common-sense reflections of a community. Elshtain (1981) shows how the ideology of womanhood has been so nurtured in the Western traditions; and Wearing's empirical study (1984) confirms the power of that ideology, which controls women's perceptions of their role(s) in society to this day. However, ideologies live through the common everyday actions – both verbal and non-verbal – of a host of social actors who are far from thinking consciously about it. In fact, if ideology is a misleading system of ideas, then conscious deliberation, once it becomes accessible, is likely to lead to exposure, and could conceivably become instrumental in introducing change. Looked at from this perspective, the most important attribute for the maintenance of ideology appears to be its socially constructed inevitability. Again, a system of ideas can definitely be misleading even while it is being supported by an overarching, most clear-sighted-seeming analysis of social phenomena; but the very description of some analysis as 'over-arching' or 'most clear-sighted' implies a point of view. One misleading system of ideas can be replaced by another ideology, which may in its turn be revealed as a misleading system of ideas. There is no intention to make a play on words here, but in one sense, at least, ideology cannot be misleading since it leads us to the essential principles governing the social structure in which the ideology is embedded and for which it provides support. Thus it becomes diagnostic of the values that (some section of) a community lives by. For these reasons, I prefer to think of ideology as a socially constructed system of ideas which appears as if inevitable.

I shall be concerned here with the ideology of woman's work – that is to say the system of ideas that surrounds the work women do in the privacy of their homes. Of course, the ideology of woman's work can be viewed from many angles; my own focus is limited – I am interested not in how the ideology came to be constructed – i.e. what is its historical genesis in the West – but in how the constructed ideology is transmitted. And my answer to even this limited question is not a complete one, since it is based on an interpretation of mother–child talk, which is neither supplemented by father–child talk nor a firsthand observation of patterns of daily living.

The conversations which form the basis of my answer were collected from 24 mother–child dyads in and around Sydney. All mothers were born and brought up in Australia; the average age of the children at the time of recording was approximately 3 years 8 months. The breakdown of the population is presented in Table 6.1.

Table 6.1 The apprentices to ideology

Child	(A) Low education, manual occupation		(R) High education, specialized job	
	Cell 1	Cell 2	Cell 1	Cell 2
Female	3	3	3	3
Male	3	3	3	3
	6	6	6	6

It does not appear necessary to explain the table further, since for the present discussion, the subclassification of the population is not highly relevant. The data consists of natural conversation between the child and the mother and was collected for an ARGS project to examine the role of mother's talk in establishing ways of learning. Working on this project, with me, were Carmel Cloran and David Butt, though I alone am responsible for the views presented here. The recordings were made by the mothers themselves in their home environment. The mothers were requested to turn on the tape recorder whenever they felt that they were engaged in a chat with the child in question; no other requirements were made. On average each dyad took about six weeks to complete six hours of recording time, which, on average, yielded four hours of recorded tape.

I should like to draw attention to the suitability of such conversation as a means of understanding adult preconceptions. To a large extent, all casual conversation is revealing about the shared assumptions of a community, precisely because of its unselfconscious, casual nature which masks its deeper social purposes and gives it the air of an activity that is directed toward nothing but the achievement of talk itself. But casual conversation

THE ONTOGENESIS OF IDEOLOGY

between a close adult and a very young child is especially revealing in that often the very basic assumptions necessary for the continuity of talk have to be spelt out. With such young children, the comfort of sharing the same language does not go so far as to produce the assurance that the other 'understands' the sayings as the adult-speaker does. Garfinkle (1967) provides several examples of the break-down of conversation in which an experimenting student deliberately displayed inability to understand another's 'perfectly ordinary utterances'. Example 1 is taken from his book to illustrate the point:

Example 1
(S) Hi, Ray. How is your girlfriend feeling?
(E) What do you mean, 'How is she feeling'?
    Do you mean physical or mental?
(S) I mean how is she feeling? What's the matter with you?
    (He looked peeved.)
(E) Nothing. Just explain a little clearer what do you mean.
(S) Skip it. How are your Med School applications coming?
(E) What do you mean, 'How are they'?
(S) You know what I mean.
(E) I really don't.
(S) What's the matter with you? Are you sick?

(Garfinkle 1967, 42)

But this posture of 'you know what I mean' cannot always be adopted in regard to very young children's questions. In the following extract Kirsty (3; 7) is discussing with her mother the death of a moth whose wings had got steamed when it flew too low over a hot drink. The child is deeply concerned, and on the verge of tears, because she believes '... it wouldn't have wanted to die'. In the midst of this serious discussion, her attention is distracted by her younger sister's behaviour, who is busying herself with tearing some paper. This leads to the exchange below:

Example 2
C: That's [? broken] ... Rebecca teared it.
M: She what?
C: Teared.
M: Oh it's O.K.
C: Why's it O.K.?
M: Pete just brought it home for me to have a look but he didn't need to keep it.
C: Why didn't he?
M: Oh. Oh I don't know. (LAUGHING) I don't think he needed to keep it ... He'd probably read it already.
C: Why he probably read it already?
M: Um I think if he had wanted to keep it and he needed it he would have told me to put it somewhere safe. But he put it there which is the place where we put stuff we don't really care about. That's why I think that he didn't need it. Either he'd already read it or he didn't want it.*

It is only at this point that, presumably satisfied, Kirsty returns to the question of life and death which had preoccupied her earlier. Probings by children, then, produce the near optimal environment for an explanation of those very phenomena which we consider most ordinary, most inevitable and most self-evident.

And there is an important difference between Garfinkle's experimenting students and young children; unlike the students, the children are not being meta-textual: they are actually engaged in constructing the text of their immediate culture. So talk becomes a vehicle of learning the taken-for-granted aspects of lived reality. Of course this is not the only vehicle. The data shows the acuteness of children's observation. When Alison (3; 5) helps mother make coffee, she observes her own actions, performed under the mother's close supervision; so much coffee per cup, so much sugar and then hot water and *then* milk. 'Ah' says Alison 'milk after.' 'Yeah,' says the mother 'You gotta pour milk after.'

With so much listening and talking, so much confirming by observation, the picture of woman's work is constructed for the child through the innumerable small moments of everyday life. I have chosen to talk about this aspect precisely because across the spectrum of my data, this picture emerges with a certain degree of homogeneity – a homogeneity that the data may very well not possess in some other respects. This explains my earlier comment that the subclassification of the population is irrelevant, where the study of the ideology of woman's work from this data is concerned. It does not matter which section of the population the mothers belong to, they share similar views about woman's work. While not every dyad presents each of the features I discuss below, each displays some combination, and none contradicts any of the features. So while the total picture is a synthesis, I believe it respects the mothers' views as displayed in their talk. Let me first spell out the four most outstanding kinds of things that these women with small children, with or without husbands, take in their stride every day of the week, every week of the year.

(i) First, every woman is an *instructor*. Quite irrespective of her place in the social hierarchy, every woman taking care of a small child is exposed to innumerable searching questions. These questions cover an enormous range: who looked after me when you were a baby, why is Johnny fatter than me, why are those clouds grey, why do you put parsley in water, don't birds talk like us and how does the lavatory chain work and do chickens have knees? Now there is no implication at all that the answers are always accurate, or that they are always provided. Sometimes questions get lost in the flow of conversation; sometimes they are answered tautologically, but it can be claimed with confidence that in every mother–child dyad there is evidence of effort to explain. I suspect that the differences will lie in kind of explanations offered and the frequency with which they are offered.

(ii) Every woman is a *labourer*. As I remarked earlier, the setting for these conversations is everyday life. The conversations construct the picture of these women as busy around the house with cooking and washing, getting the kids to bed, getting them ready for school and ministering to their needs. Outside the house, there is the shopping and the garden.

(iii) Every woman provides *emotional support* to the child/children in the house; this can take the form of praise, concern over a physical hurt or the dispensation of justice if it is needed.

(iv) And finally every woman is a *companion* to her child. By companionship I mean that the mothers put time and effort into activities which are primarily for the diversion of the young child, participating in colouring pictures, playing with trains and car sets, joining in the football or the cricket game – whatever is going on.

The nature of my data does not permit me to make any systematic comments on the activities of these women in relation to other members – particularly, the adults of the household. No doubt mothers talk to other members of the family, both adults and other children; no doubt, they have friends and neighbours. And, no doubt, apart from these four aspects listed above, there is more to every woman's work. The reason I restrict myself to just these four aspects lies in the fact that proof of the mother's engaging in these four types of activities can be provided directly from my data; and for the present discussion, I am limiting myself entirely to what is in the data, ignoring other parameters whose relevance I would definitely accept.

Now, if the findings were limited to simply a construction of these four facets of every woman's work, there would be nothing remarkable. It is common knowledge that women do these things; and we, perhaps, need no research project to show that this is how it is. Let me now shift my focus, by raising the question: how do these women present themselves and their work to the children, in the course of their talk?

Let us first look at the instructor role. It is remarkable how consistently mothers underplay this role. There is not one instance in the entire data, where a mother can be found to claim credit for having solved a problem, for having worked out, even cooperatively with the child, an explanation to some phenomenon. On the contrary, there is evidence that, at least some mothers, explicitly emphasize the picture of 'silly mummy'. Here is Helen's mother in Example 3. She is a remarkably capable woman, and the evidence of her ability to think on her toes can be found across her conversations with Helen. Here she is finding out what Helen did at preschool that day.

Example 3
C: Play with the playdough.
M: And what else?
C: And you forgot my painting!
M: Did you do a painting? ... You didn't tell me ...
C: Well you should've looked at the [?] on those cupboards.
M: Oh I know but I'm such a forgetful mother you should know by now you have to tell me you have to remind me about these things because I – my brain doesn't work too well sometimes.
C: Mum.
M: Mm?

C: All you have to do is tell the teachers if you forget.
M: Trouble is I forget to tell the teachers.

This is not an isolated instance; nor is the 'silly mummy' picture limited to one class. Of course, a simple rationale for such behaviour is easy to find: it makes the child feel superior; and, after all, should it not be regarded as simply a 'game', a 'pretence' whose aim is to boost the child's ego? I have no clear-cut answer to this question, but I cannot help wondering if such behaviour is totally unrelated to the popular picture of woman as somewhat lacking in intellect. In reviewing the *Fontana Biographical Companion to Modern Thought* (Bullock and Woodings) for *The Sunday Times* (2 October 1983), John Vincent pointed out how thinking as an intellectual enterprise is seen by the authors to be the preserve of the white male:

> Thinking, it appears, is what white males do. The most numerous peoples, the Indians and Chinese, do not figure. The Japs seem to get along splendidly without thinkers. All three lag behind speakers of Portuguese.
>
> As for women, they are dragged in, as it were, by the hair: Marilyn Monroe, Iris Murdock, and Bessie Smith, Queen of the Blues, for instance. Less than one per cent of modern thought is female. Women are good at writing novels and being entertainers, but then they always were, back to Scheherzade.

Of course, we could shrug off this publication as an example of the author's unthinking bias; but two points appear relevant. First, there is very close relationship between unthinking biases and the maintenance of ideology; and, secondly, centuries and decades of unthinking biases, codified in scholarly tomes do represent that which by and large becomes 'fact'. 'Truth', we have the saying 'will out'. But, whose truth? and seen from what point of view? I do not think that it is fanciful to claim that it is codified 'fact' generated by unthinking biases that speaks every day out of the mouths of the mothers. In my view, this 'fact' does not fall on fallow ground. If language plays any role in the development of consciousness – and I believe that it does – then, it must shape the consciousness of the apprentices to ideology, the mothers' children.

Equally important is the question: Is there anyone else in the house who might say to the child: 'clever mummy'? My data of course provides no answer here. But it does have Julian's mother saying to him:

> I don't know ... you must be clever ... Maybe you got it from your Dad.

where *it* is the child's cleverness. Across the data, irrespective of the family's socio-economic location, with the exception of single-parent families, mothers do build an image of the fathers as the one who should know, as the one who is resourceful in finding practical solutions, as the one who is the *locus* of intellectual authority. Isn't it quite obvious that organizing 14 meals a week, for every week of the year, for a family of three or more requires no practical organization? And who ever heard of the need for 'rational thinking' in answering children's questions? Would you believe that knowing the names of all the herbs and spices is an accomplishment of the same order as knowing the names of all the tools in a carpentry set? Adrian's mother knows about the herbs anyway, but she also reels off the name and function of all but two items from a carpentry tool set. So she tells Adrian: 'Daddy'll know the names of them', which is more or less echoed by the child: 'Yes, he'll know all the names. Daddy'll know.' I would like to draw attention particularly to the near-certainty of the mother's prediction. It may be that Adrian's father, a banker by trade, is also an accomplished handyman, and the near-certainty of her prediction through the use of the auxiliary *will* (in reduced form) is justified. However, the interesting fact remains that in talking thus of their husbands, the mothers do not make use of the modals of lower orders of probability; we find *Daddy'll/will* but, in such environments, we do not find *Dad might/may/could/perhaps be able to*. Let me hasten to add that there is no implication that excellence cannot be shared by both partners; I simply do not have the data to confirm or refute this view. It is, however, remarkable that through thousands of transcribed messages these women's assessment of their own accomplishment is meagre in their own wordings, while, in many cases, their handling of the children's questions is relatively a contradiction of this assessment.

If the mother's presentation of her instructor role is muted, that of her role as labourer carries certain ambiguities which, at the least, are interesting to note. There are various strands to this. First, there is the view that the exertion and toil in the house are not work. Example 4 is a dialogue between Alison and her mother.

Example 4
C: Is Pop home?
M: No ... They're all out. They're all at work.
C: Bob and Mark are working.
M: Yes, Bob's at work. Mark's at work. Everybody's at work.
C: I not at work.
M: No, you're only little.
C: Youse at work?
M: I don't work. I look after you. ...
C: Who's playing with Pammie?
M: Nobody. Who'd look after you if Mummy went to work ... eh?

Not all mothers are as explicit about the non-work nature of their work at home; the view ranges from this to the mother in group B who comments that the child's grandmother does not babysit her anymore because the mother is no longer working. Small wonder, that in the Macquarie Dictionary, there is not one sense of worker that fits woman as a worker in her house. This definition is reproduced as Example 5 below:

Example 5
WORKER (2003)
1. one who or that which works: *he's a good steady worker.*
2. one employed in manual industrial labour.

3. an employee, esp. as contrasted with a capitalist or a manager.
4. one who works in a specified occupation: *office workers, research workers.*
5. (in the USSR) a citizen, excluding the peasants and members of the army or navy.
6. *Entomol.* the sterile or infertile female of bees, wasps, ants, or termites, which does the work of the colony.
7. Also working girl. *Colloq.* a prostitute.

The nearest a woman engaged in woman's work comes to is sense 5, but we are not in the USSR; or to 6, but women with offspring are obviously not sterile or infertile, even though they may be busy as bees! There is then the paradox that when, as David's mother, one employs someone to look after the children, then that person is a worker, but the person whom she replaces is not a worker!! It would be a mistake to take Example 5 as an attack on the Macquarie Dictionary. It is no part of a dictionary to moralize; its business is to record the usage of the community. For the community, in general, woman's work is just not work, as the definition of 'work' in the same dictionary will show. By these 'fashions of speaking' (Whorf 1956) whose motivation ultimately traces itself to the principles of the community's economic organization, a woman working in the privacy of her home is consigned to the grey space between the 'dole-bludger' and the 'honest worker', who brings home a 'decent pay', for his/her physical exertion. She is not even 'self-employed'; she is 'house-wife'. The assumption is not lagging far behind that what a woman works at in her house is her private business, without any more consequence for the life of the community than you or me polishing our shoes, or weeding our own private patch of the garden.

The second strand to which I would draw attention is the presentation of the work as uninteresting. In Example 6 Cameron's mother is decidedly trying to get him off her hands; Cameron is interested in staying back to watch the cartoons, but note how much more is passing between the two interactants:

Example 6
M: [? You'll probably] have to get changed into your work clothes later, because Daddy's going to the tip.
C: What for?
M: Daddy needs a helper.
C: Oh.
M: When he goes to the tip.
C: What?
M: Daddy needs a helper when he goes to the tip.
C: Oh I want to play on my bike. I don't want to go to the tip.
M: You do?
C: I want to stay here [?] . . .
M: You haven't been to the tip [? with your Daddy] for a long time.
M: It'd be much more interesting going to the tip than helping Mummy do the vacuuming.

C: Mm.
M: Because that's a boring job isn't it?
C: I have to stay home to watch my cartoons.

Now it is true that Cameron's mother wants him out of her way; but this is definitely not the whole of the story. For lack of space I have not included the remaining part of this dialogue covering about a page and a half, in which the mother points out to Cameron that he is behaving like Piggie Won't, whose brothers were adventurous, went out into the world and had fun while Piggie Won't, staying at home, missed out on everything worth doing. The same fate, she suggests, awaits Cameron unless he gets out to help Daddy at the tip instead of helping Mum cleaning the house. Kirsty's mother who shows exemplary patience and a sensitive understanding of her own children's needs, tells Kirsty:

> I think that you probably don't play with little kids because they're not very interesting most of the time.

Cameron's mother discusses with him the various professions that he might take up when he's big. The fire brigade, the police force and the construction and building trades are discussed in some detail. Cameron appears to work with a paradigm: If I can't be this, what can I be? As the possibilities of those professions which presently engage his attention are exhausted, he asks at least twice: Mum, what could I be in the home, in the house? Is it at all significant that Cameron's mother does not even 'hear' this question?

The household labour is a fact that impinges upon people in the house all the time – but it impinges upon them as a necessity, not as something that could ever be enjoyed. And this is the third strand.

Pete's mother says:

> I have to take in laundry.

Daniel's mother echoes:

> I just have to go and get the washing in now, I'm afraid.

Sam's mother explains her tired yawn:

> I had to get up twice last night because Johnny kept crying.

And, of course, many of the mothers say at one time or another.

> I have to fix the tea/dinner now.

The modals of necessity and obligation come into full play. This is definitely not the only environment in which they appear; but this is one environment in which they are used with a high frequency.

Finally, woman's work is presented as hard work, but in an oblique manner. It is an interesting aspect of this presentation that such comments on the part of the mother occur unexpectedly and fleetingly in the middle of some other activity, the course of which is hardly disturbed by such admissions. In Example 7 Julie's mother has been bathing her, playing with her daughter's toes and letting the daughter play with her own fingers. Julie is trying to get her mother's fingers soaped and washed, she requests the mother to lay them down flat in the bath.

Example 7
C: 'Cause the water's [? low] now ... you've got strong glue that one.
M: Yes, I have rather, haven't I? Oh, they're beautiful. Thank you.
C: Up.
M: Oh, Mummy's fingers are so tired tonight.
C: You can put them down.
M: They've been very busy fingers, haven't they?

Child and mother continue playfully as if the tired fingers had never been mentioned. There is no point in multiplying such examples, but of the 24 mothers nearly three-quarters mention the fact of tiredness at sometime. Significantly, the mother's tiredness never appears to affect the flow of activity. Whether it is 'work' in the 'true' sense or not, it still 'has to be done'.

Moving now to the third aspect of woman's work in the home – that of providing emotional support, I come to a finding that was completely unexpected. Many of the mothers express the need for such support from their children – it is as if the actual roles were being reversed through these sayings. In Example 8 it is Karen's mother who seeks this support:

Example 8
M: Oh I've got a bad cold.
C: Oh.
M: Are you going to look after me ... eh?
M: Oh ah, sorry. (COUGHING AGAIN)
C: I can't when I have to go to school.
M: But you don't have to go to school for a few days.
C: I know.
M: You going to look after me?
C: Yeah.
M: O.K.

In Example 9, it is Nathan's mother who seeks such support and the child's bewilderment appears quite obvious:

Example 9
M: I have to lie down and put my leg in the air. Will you look after me?
C: No.
M: You won't! (SURPRISED)
C: Why?
M: You won't look after me?
C: Where are you – where are you gonna do it?

M: In the lounge-room [I think]
C: No, do it here.

On the question of companionship, the data presents nothing significant, apart from the fact that mothers are lavish in the expression of appreciation whenever the child helps in the house – this happens more often with girls than with boys. So what conclusions can we draw about the ways that mothers present themselves and their work to their children?

I feel that there is a tension here. The child's active experience of happenings in the house must, in some sense, create the idea that mothers are busy; that their 'non-work' is in some sense 'work'. But the evaluation of that which claims the mother's physical efforts and attention is a different matter. With but a few possible exceptions, most human action is neither inherently good nor bad; it neither inherently merits prestige nor stigma, as Durkheim (1964) suggested; nor is the evaluation rationally commensurate with the benefit that might accrue from human action to (some sections of) the community. There is, thus, an essential arbitrariness about values attached to human actions. I shall comment briefly on this point below. Here let me say simply that while language is not the only means for (re)producing the values attached to human action, it is, none the less, one of the most powerful instruments for the purpose. If this premise is accepted, then, from the examples of mothers' sayings presented here, it would appear inevitable that the very young child, whose primary domain of experience is the home, would imbibe a view of woman's work in which it has the status of a toil imposed by necessity, a physical exertion which is not work, a tiresome enterprise which is inherently uninteresting and definitely lacking in demands on the higher functions of human intellect. As the young children walk out of their homes, where the foundations of their social being are laid, they are more than passively prepared to acquiesce in a confirmation of this early, perhaps not yet well-articulated view, which will be strengthened to a clear certainty, by experiences outside the house. The evidence from my data suggests, then, that the ontogenesis of ideology occurs early if the ideology is to take hold. And the mechanisms for this ontogenesis are the habitual forms of communication, wherein the taken-for-granted nature of the social world is transmitted. A dominant ideology has to receive support at every level of human experience to survive, otherwise the fabric of inevitability is torn and glimpses of an alter-ideology are afforded which have the potential of undermining the credibility of the dominant ideology. Whatever one's reservations against or enthusiasms for the 'feminist' discourse, it certainly has performed the function of rupturing the credibility of one of the most dominant, most universally shared ideologies.

Seen from this point of view, the distinction between deep and surface phenomena, so fashionable in today's academic discussions, appears entirely unconvincing. There is no essential discontinuity between what human beings do, which includes what they say (Halliday 1973; 1978), and the social structure in which they have a *locus*. The social structure comes into being and is continuously enacted through what human beings are doing, have done, and will do. It would, however, be naïve to suppose that the ideology of woman's work can be changed simply by changing the habitual forms of maternal communication. Such an implication is nowhere intended in this paper. Habitual forms of communication spring from a perception of what appears socially relevant. There is thus a logical contradiction in entertaining the belief that the habitual forms of communication can be consistently and successfully changed without other accompanying changes; it is my understanding that this is one of the arguments Bernstein (1971) developed some time ago. Clearly this argument holds not because forms of communication, as many other human acts, display only 'the regularities and complexity perceived on the surface of the social world' (Sharp 1981); rather, it is because ideologies, like other social facts, are orchestrated simultaneously at multiple levels of human existence. For example, the ideology of woman's work reaches out beyond the house into the market-place where labour is sold for wages, and thus turned into 'work'. And no doubt that behaviour, in its turn, reaches out to other areas of socio-economic organization. The values attached to the actions of women in the privacy of their homes appear arbitrary – i.e. unmotivated – only so long as the wider context is ignored: within the four walls of the house, it appears extraordinary to think of woman's work as non-work; but as it makes contact with a wage-based economy, which operates in most societies today, its non-work nature is legitimized. One important reason why woman's work is not work lies in the fact that, of itself, it does not create the kind of economic independence granted to most wage-earners. At this stage of the analysis, the standard dictionaries are not 'misleading'; they are simply recording what we actually do. It seems to me that none of these levels of analysis is just a 'surface' behind which hides the 'ultimate truth'. The examination of ideology – and of social phenomena, in general – requires a spiral model, rather than a box model in which the lid – the surface – is lifted to reveal the content – the ultimate truth. Subscribing to the age-old division of the ultimate cause existing independent of the effect, we tend to be looking for the 'underlying determinants of surface manifestation' (Sharp 1981). I would suggest that Barthes' generalization regarding the relation between 'content' and 'form' in literature can be usefully extended to the study of the social as well, so that a social phenomenon would be like

> an onion, a construction of layers (or levels, or systems) whose body contains finally no heart, no kernel, no secret, no irreducible principle, nothing except the infinity of its own envelopes – which envelop nothing other than the unity of its own surfaces. (Barthes 1971)

Rejecting, then, this dichotomy between the surface and deep, we can turn to language as a form of human action (Malinowski 1923; 1935), which contributes, along with other semiotic systems, to the construction of the social world. A special focus on language is clearly required in the study of the onset of forms of social consciousness. This is because the location of very young children in society is ambiguous. They are not active participants in many of its processes, and at least in the early years of their life, they may be said to enter society, as it were, secondarily through their contacts with adults. In this contact many of the social systems do not impinge upon them directly, but are refracted through the adult's systems of communication, amongst which language undoubtedly has an important place, if only due to the child's early-developed ability to enter into linguistic processes. In talking about the role of maternal linguistic communication in the ontogenesis of a particular ideology, I have borrowed the expression 'fashions of speaking' from Whorf (1956), while the phrase 'habitual forms of communication' is derived from my reading of both Whorf and Bernstein. I believe the full import of these expressions needs to be understood to grasp their relevance to the role of language in the creation and maintenance of ideology.

Even to imply that ideology, through however many layers of the 'onion' of culture can finally be seen as language is at once claiming too much and saying too little. It is claiming too much, because of the simple fact of omission, it ignores the many non-verbal semiotic systems, whose existence side by side with language is not immaterial to the examination of ideology. The claim of a bi-unique connection between ideology and language – even though many-layer-mediated – could be valid only on the assumption that there exists a complete translatability between language and other semiotic systems. I would suggest that this assumption is questionable. To quote Foucault (1970):

> It is not that words are imperfect, or that, when confronted by the visible, they prove insuperably inadequate. Neither can be reduced to the other's terms: it is in vain that we say what we see; what we see never resides in what we say. And it is in vain that we attempt to show, by the use of metaphors, or similes, what we are saying; the space where they achieve their splendour is not deployed by our eyes but that defined by the sequential elements of the syntax.

Vološinov (1973) voices the same position:

> None of the fundamental, specific ideological signs is replaceable wholly by words. It is ultimately impossible to convey a musical composition or pictorial image adequately in words. Words cannot wholly substitute for a religious ritual; nor is there any really adequate verbal substitute for even the simplest gesture in human behaviour. To deny this would lead to the most banal rationalism and simplisticism.

Complete translatability is a myth not only across two languages, but also across the verbal and non-verbal semiotics within the same culture. To the extent that this claim is true, it would be misleading to create the impression that the examination of ideology boils down to an examination of language. Languages may presuppose ideology; but, both for its genesis and its sustenance, ideology needs more than language. The semiotic potential of a culture is not equal to the semantic potential of the languages of a culture (Halliday 1973). It appears, then, that a linguist who would aspire to throw light on the construction and maintenance of ideology, must be prepared, first, to place the verbal semiotic side by side with other semiotic systems. and secondly, to examine the ways in which the various semiotic systems of a culture are calibrated to produce recognizable semiotic styles (Hasan 1978; 1984b) I agree with Vološinov that the various sign systems, operative within a culture, do not 'remain in isolation' from each other; but mutual support is not tantamount to mutual identity.

On the other hand, the claim that language can be shown to be entirely a purveyor of ideology does not say enough; it provides no explicit indication of how the same language can be used in the construction and maintenance of qualitatively distinct ideologies. Granted that the notion of 'same language' is theoretically problematic, still, I believe, we would wish to say that both Halliday and Chomsky use the same language for the exposition of their ideologies about language, which are miles apart from each other. It is true that if two texts by these authors are placed side by side, the lexicogrammatical analysis of the two will show them to be different; but it is equally true that any two texts by any one of these authors will show lexicogrammatical differences. So naturally there arises the question: which differences are significant for their ideologies and which are not? I believe that this question cannot be answered without some such concept(s) as 'orientation to coding' (Bernstein 1971) or 'configurative rapport' and 'fashions or speaking' (Whorf 1956) or 'consistency of foregrounding' (Hasan 1984c) or 'semantic style' (Hasan 1984b) or 'semantic drift' (Butt 1983), without implying that each of these concepts is entirely identical. A brief discussion of at least the Whorfian notions appears necessary.

The belief is widely accepted that 'language is independent of any specific purpose' (Hjelmslev 1961). More explicitly, by virtue of its internal design, every language has the potential of meeting any of the needs of its speakers. This is not because language is an impartial mirror of an immanent reality; rather it is because the speakers' reality is a reality largely created by language (Hasan 1984a). This position implicit in Saussure's work (1966) is made explicit in Hjelmslev (1961), and better elaborated in Whorf's studies, who maintained that:

> the world is presented in a kaleidoscopic flux of impressions which has to be organized by our minds – and this means largely by the linguistic systems in our minds. We cut nature up – organize it into concepts, and ascribe significances as we do, largely because we are parties to an agreement to organize it this way – an agreement that holds throughout our speech community and is codified in the patterns of our language. The agreement is, of course, an implicit and unstated one, *but its terms are absolutely obligatory*; we cannot talk at all except by subscribing to the organization and classification of data which the agreement decrees.

I would draw attention to the latter half of this extract, according to which (a) the codified patterns of a language are universal to all its speakers; and (b) the flouting of these patterns is tantamount to the impossibility of talk. Had Whorf stopped at this point, he could have been accused more justifiably of a simplistic hypothesis about 'mind in the grip of language' (Bolinger 1975). But Whorf also made an important and systematic distinction between common-sense and un-common-sense knowledge, showing how the vicissitudes of the evolution of the latter are related to common-sense knowledge constructed by everyday fashions of speaking wherein the lexicogrammatical patterns of a language assume a background status, making certain concepts of reality appear inevitably real. There is thus a qualitative difference between habitual forms of communication and communications in which one is attempting to be, as it were, meta-semantic, though the latter is still not completely freed from the exigencies of the former (Halliday 1984). The possibility of the evolution of un-common-sense knowledge to the point where in some specific respect it runs counter to everyday reality constructed by language – e.g. the Einsteinian hypothesis – is important to Whorf's argument: it points to the tenuousness of the relationship between 'codified patterns of language' and our pro tem 'dissections of nature'. Such tenuousness would not exist if language were a mirror of reality. At the same time the relationship between the form of language and concepts of reality accounts for the persistence of common-sense knowledge, according to which the speakers of English, for example, still subscribe to a concept of time as independent of space and as an aggregate of discrete, individual moments. For example, this concept of time is validated each time we say 'each time'. Whorf argues that the concepts of reality constructed by everyday habitual forms of communication are accepted at some level of consciousness by all speakers of a language; that this tacit acceptance is essential to the possibility of talk.

If we argue that the reality constructed by the background phenomena of a language – its automatized formal patterns – is a reality specific to that language and not necessarily an account of how-things-really-are, then all speakers of a language may be said to subscribe to the same ideology at some level of consciousness, in the specific sense of seeing something as inevitably so. I would suggest that this kind of general 'agreement' represents an infrastructure whose presence is a *sine qua non* for the construction of more specific ideologies, e.g. that of woman's work. But Whorf showed quite clearly that even at the most general level of analysis the characterization of the ideology cannot be achieved by the examination of isolated lexicogrammatical patterns. He suggested that for such an examination we need the concept of configurative rapport. I believe by this expression Whorf meant the bringing together of those patterns of language which, *in toto*, construct a consistent semantic frame, leading to the 'deep persuasion of a principle behind phenomena'. One outstanding example of configurative rapport provided by Whorf is that which articulates the principle of objectification. Articulating this principle in SAE languages are phenomena – i.e.

patterns of language – which from the point of view of lexicogrammar could only be considered heterogeneous. According to Whorf they include the number system, the tense system, the binomial pattern and the weakening of grammatical distinctions between abstract and concrete nouns. No single category here is by itself sufficient for the articulation of objectification, which can be glossed as the treatment of abstracts as if they were concrete objects with spatial extension and clear boundaries. Together they all point in the same direction. Using similar techniques, I have attempted to show (Hasan 1984b) that in Urdu there exists a configurative rapport between patterns of reference, ellipsis, and a bundle of patterns normally known as 'honorifics'. One principle this configurative rapport articulates is that of the sanctity of boundaries between hierarchies of social roles.

In my view it is this kind of analysis which is capable of indicating which linguistic patterns are relevant to the construction of which ideology; and by so doing, such an analysis can provide a basis for understanding the meaning of lexicogrammatical differences between two or more texts – i.e. whether the differences are ideologically significant or not. I do not think that we can argue that modality or suppressed negation (Kress and Hodge 1979) or subordination (Martin and Peters 1984) are inherently significant ideologically. Nor can we argue that all differences between texts are necessarily constitutive of different ideologies. Each one of the extracts from my data presented above differs from the others in some lexicogrammatical respect(s). But if by presenting this data I have been able to construct a picture of (at least some aspects of) the ideology of woman's work, then this is because there are linguistic patterns present whose constellation articulates a consistent semantic frame. Some of these patterns are (i) a contrast in attributes ascribed to male and female parent, whereby the latter carries the less desirable attribute(s); (ii) the presence of modals of obligation in the environment of material actions (e.g. *cook, wash-up, make, clean*) if the role of actor is realized by an item referring to mother; (iii) the textually ambiguous status of the ascription of physical exhaustion to mother, which ambiguity arises from the lack of cohesive support for such items as *tired, exhausted*, etc.; (iv) the juxtaposition of *work* and behavioural processes, e.g. *look after, take care of,* so that their equation is negated, whether explicitly or implicitly. Although a more meticulous analysis might reveal other relevant patterns, perhaps the above list is sufficient to support the claim that to the articulation of an ideology what is criterial is the constellation of a set of linguistic patterns – a configuration of patterns in rapport with each other.

But wherein does the origin of such constellations lie? If we consider language as a paradigmatic, then the system permits, certainly not all, but many combinations – which is one of the reasons why language can be independent of any specific purpose. For example, the selection of almost any modal feature is possible with material action – not only *have to wash up*, but also *can/might wash up*; contrasting with the attribute *silly* for *mummy*, is also the possibility of the attributes *clever/bright* and so on. The selection of a specific constellation of patterns cannot, then, be seen as dictated by the system of language. If a specific set of options is selected it is there because it is capable of constructing the meanings the occasion is perceived to require. This implies that the patterns in a constellation – the patterns possessing a configurative rapport – display a semantic consistency. If in the context of control, it would be odd to find an utterance such as: *I'd rather you didn't make so much noise, otherwise I'll hit you*, this is because the meanings of the two messages are not consistent with each other; threats are not consistent with the granting of personal discretion. Using Bernstein's terminology we may say that the production of texts – language operating in the context of situation – requires 'coding orientation'. It is probably true that our ideas about the study of meanings have not reached the stage where the kind of semantic consistencies I have drawn attention to can be described in an explicit way. But if linguists are interested in the examination of ideologies and other important matters concerning the relationship between language and society, then such advances in the study of language as a meaning potential will have to be made. And it is my belief that when progress in this area begins, we shall need to bridge the gulf between Saussure's '*langue*' and '*parole*', probably very much along the lines suggested by Hjelmslev (1961), Firth (1957) and Halliday (1977b). If a specific configurative rapport – a constellation of linguistic patterns – is perceived as criterial in the context of some ideology, it is not because the system of language has forced these patterns together; its contribution lies in providing the resources. The configurative rapport comes into existence and acquires a life because of our fashions of speaking as our fashions of speaking are the bearers of our ideology. It is through these fashions of speaking that the prehension between the patterns of a configurative rapport becomes established and we come to recognize that the deployment of such and such lexicogrammatical patterns constructs such and such a grouping of meanings, which finds support through such and such of our doings and thus perpetuates an ideology which we ourselves have created through our sayings and doings. Helen's mother is far from having attempted an analysis of these phenomena, but she appears to subscribe to some such view in the following extract. Helen is helping mother wash up a saucepan lid which appears to need a lot of scrubbing:

C: You have to do it hard, don't you?
M: Mm you do, don't you, yes ...
C: Doesn't matter for you or me to do these.
M: No.
C: Because we can do it the right way, God teaches us.
M: No God doesn't teach you things like that, it's mummy's job to teach you things like that.

Note

* *Transcription conventions:* M = mother; C = child; [?] = unintelligible; [? + item(s)] = item(s) not clearly intelligible, best guess in view of contextual, co-textual and phonological clues; ( ) = encloses contextual comment, not evident from wording alone; large square bracket left open covers overlapping speech by the dyad.

References

Barthes, R. (1971) 'Style and its image'. In *Literary Style: A Symposium*, S. Chatman (ed.). New York: Oxford University Press.
Bernstein, B. (1971) *Class, Codes and Control*, Vol. I. London: Routledge & Kegan Paul.
Bolinger, D. (1975) *Aspects of Language* (2nd edn). New York: Harcourt Brace & Javanovich.
Bottomore, T. B. and Rubel, M. (eds) (1963) *Karl Marx: Selected Writings in Sociology and Social Philosophy*. Harmondsworth: Penguin.
Butt, D. G. (1983) 'Semantic drift in verbal art'. In *Australian Review of Applied Linguistics*, 6.
Durkheim, E. (1964) *The Division of Labour in Society* (G. Simpson, trans.). New York: Free Press.
Elshtain, J. B. (1981) *Public Man, Private Woman*. Oxford: Martin Robertson.
Firth, J. R. (1957) *Papers in Linguistics 1934–1951*. London: Oxford University Press.
Foucault, M. (1970) *The Order of Things*. London: Tavistock Publications.
Garfinkle, H. (1967) *Studies in Ethnomethodology*. Englewood Cliffs: Prentice-Hall.
Halliday, M. A. K. (1973) *Explorations in the Functions of Language*. London: Edward Arnold.
Halliday, M. A. K. (1977a) 'Language as social semiotic: towards a general sociolinguistic theory'. In *Linguistics at the Crossroads*, A. Makkai, V. B. Makkai and L. Heilmann (eds). Illinois: Jupiter Press.
Halliday, M. A. K. (1977b) *Aims and Perspectives in Linguistics*. Applied Linguistics Association of Australia (Occasional Paper No. 1).
Halliday, M. A. K. (1978) *Language as Social Semiotic: The Social Interpretation of Language and Meaning*. London: Edward Arnold.
Halliday, M. A. K. (1984) 'On the ineffability of grammatical categories'. In *The Tenth LACUS Forum*. Columbia: Hornbeam Press.
Hasan, R. (1978) 'The implications of semantic distance for language in education'. Xth International Congress of Anthropological and Ethnological Sciences.
Hasan, R. (1984a) 'What kind of resource is language?' In *Australian Review of Applied Linguistics* (Chapter 1 of this book).
Hasan, R. (1984b) 'Ways of saying: ways of meaning'. Paper presented at Bourg Wartenstein Symposium No. 66, August 1975. To appear in *Semiotics of Language and Culture*, R. Fawcett, M. A. K. Halliday, S. M. Lamb and A. Makkai (eds). London: Frances Pinter (Chapter 8 of this book).
Hasan, R. (1984c) *Linguistics, Language and Verbal Art*. Deakin University Press.
Hjelmslev, L. (1961) *Prolegomena to a Theory of Language* (J. Whitfield, trans.). Madison: The University of Wisconsin Press.

Kress, G. and Hodge, R. (1979) *Language as Ideology*. London: Routledge & Kegan Paul.

Malinowski, B. (1923) 'The problem of meaning in primitive languages'. Supplement 1 in *The Meaning of Meaning*, C. K. Ogden and I. A. Richards. London: Kegan Paul.

Malinowski, B. (1935) *Coral Gardens and Their Magic*, Vol. II. London: Allen & Unwin.

Martin, J. and Peters, P. (1984) 'On the analysis of exposition'. In *Discourse on Discourse*, R. Hasan (ed.) Applied Linguistics Association of Australia (Occasional Paper No. 7).

de Saussure, F. (1916) *A Course in General Linguistics* (W. Baskin, trans.). New York: McGraw-Hill Paperback Edition.

Sharp, R. (1981) *Knowledge, Ideology and the Politics of Schooling*. London: Routledge & Kegan Paul.

Volosinov, V. N. (1973) *Marxism and the Philosophy of Language* (L. Matejka and I. R. Titunik, trans.). New York: Seminar Press.

Wearing, B. (1984) *The Ideology of Motherhood*. Sydney: Allen & Unwin.

Whorf, B. L. (1956) *Language, Thought and Reality* (edited and introduced by J. B. Carroll). Cambridge, Mass.: MIT Press.

7 Speech genre, semiotic mediation and the development of higher mental functions

Abstract

In contrast to Piaget's genetic individualism, Vygotsky maintained that the *development of higher mental functions* is sociogenetic, arguing that any function in the child's cognitive development appears twice, first on the social plane and then on the psychological plane. The move from the social plane to the psychological is *semiotically mediated*; in fact, this semiotic mediation is the deep meaning of human social interaction. And since due to its inherent characteristics, language is the most pervasive modality for social interaction, it follows that language is also the most powerful tool for *semiotic mediation*. This theory of human cognitive development offers powerful insights into the relations between mind, language and society; however, its formulation does give rise to certain problems. The first part of this paper examines the two key concepts of *higher mental function* and *semiotic mediation*, drawing attention to some of the problems in Vygotsky's conceptualization of the relation between the two. It is argued that being intimately related to social interaction, semiotic mediation is susceptible to variation, but the Vygotskian framework fails to assign a coherent place to such variation. Further, to accord a central place to verbal interaction in this sociogenetic process calls for some element in the theory which would account for the over-all nature and forms of social interaction, but no such theoretical apparatus is to be found in the Vygotskian framework. It has been suggested recently that these crucial problems in Vygotsky's framework might be resolved by appealing to Bakhtin's concept of *speech genre* – the more so since in Bakhtin's view of speech genre, heteroglossia forms an integral element. Although at first glance this suggestion appears reasonable, a closer examination of Bakhtin's writing reveals that our optimism might be premature, that in fact there are features of Bakhtin's writing which make it almost impossible to use his notions in the analysis of speech genre – a concept very close to that of *register* in the systemic functional model. In drawing attention to these problems, the second part of the paper briefly compares Bernstein's views on the role of verbal interaction in the creation of variant forms of human consciousness. The paper concludes by a discussion of certain foundational issues in relating language, society and mental development.

Introduction

Much can be said in favour of technical terminology, but a title such as mine cries out for translation into 'ordinary, simple' language. So translated, it declares a concern with the role of everyday talk in creating human minds. As a topic, it is perhaps not very highly favoured. As a matter of fact, for most self-respecting linguists, if talk appears at all important it is usually because it can reveal something about language; further, in most scientific linguistic models, it is far more acceptable to argue that mind makes language than that language makes mind. I hope the development of this paper will reveal that an exploration of the relations between the three concepts invoked in the title – 'Speech genre, semiotic mediation, and the development of higher mental functions' – is relevant to some of the foundational issues in linguistic theory. As a first step in the development of this theme, it will be necessary to present an interpretation of the three terms, which are reminders of the intense intellectual activity that characterized the early days of Russian revolution. The term *speech genre* is used here to invoke the views of Bakhtin (Volosinov 1983; Todorov 1984; Bakhtin 1984; 1986), while *semiotic mediation* and *higher mental functions* form important elements in the psychological theory of Vygotsky, whose ambition was to 'create a Capital for psychology using Marx's method' (Lee 1987, 96).

In order to examine the relevance of these notions to each other and the relevance of the entire debate to the foundations of linguistic theory, the paper is designed to have three movements. The first movement will consist of the second and third sections. In the second section I will be concerned with interpreting the two Vygotskian terms. In the third, I will point out some residual problems in his conceptualization of the relation between the two. It has been suggested (Wertsch 1985c) that Bakhtin's views on speech genre and allied concepts can resolve some of these problems. The second movement of the paper will consist of the fourth section, where I will discuss Bakhtin's views in order to ask if they can resolve the residual problems in Vygotsky's approach. In the discussion of Bakhtin's views, it will be seen by those who are familiar with the systemic functional (henceforth SF) model, that there exist many points of similarities between the two approaches. Of course, there are also significant differences. Although from time to time, I shall refer to some aspect of SF linguistics, it is not the aim of my presentation to compare the two approaches, which is a much bigger enterprise, and must await another occasion. I shall however, draw attention to theoretical problems in the Bakhtinian approach which, in my view, prevent it in its present state, from contributing to Vygotsky's theory. The third and final movement of the paper will identify those features that will be needed in a linguistic theory capable of contributing positively to a clarification of the issues raised in the third section with reference to semiotic mediation and the genesis of higher mental functions. This discussion will raise some foundational issues of linguistic theory. Halliday has always maintained (1973; 1974) that the sharp distinction between the intra-organic and interorganic basis of language is intellectually incoherent. The Vygotsky–Luria approach to the genesis of mind in society provides the kind of detailed argument needed to support Halliday's rejection of the above distinction. The other widely accepted antinomy in linguistic theory, Saussure's uncompromising separation of *langue* and *parole*, is seriously questioned by the SF model's view of functionality (Halliday 1975; Halliday and Hasan 1989; Martin 1991; Hasan 1995). In general, the Bakhtin–Volosinov perspective on the nature of language supports the SF stance. A functional linguistic theory of the type that SF aspires to be is truly a transdisciplinary theory, which is located at the intersection of semiology, sociology and psychology. The concluding section argues that in the nexus of Vygotsky–Luria, Bakhtin –Volosinov and Halliday, the element lacking is a theory of society such as perhaps that of Bernstein who is able to provide principles for linking semiotic variation with the material social conditions of human existence.

Semiotic mediation and higher mental functions

In presenting an interpretation of the two Vygotskian concepts, much of what I say is naturally derivative: for an understanding of these concepts, I have relied on the translated works of Vygotsky (1962; 1978) and Luria (1976), and on the recent growing literature in social psychology (e.g. Mertz and Parmentier 1985; Hickman 1987); I am particularly indebted to Wertsch (1981; 1985a; 1985b; 1985c; 1990; and Wertsch and Hickman 1987), whose work has made a significant contribution to the revived interest in Vygotsky's ideas. It is important to add though that I alone am responsible for the views expressed here.

To appreciate the importance of the concept of semiotic mediation, we need to understand its role in Vygotsky's theory of psychological development. Some of the important aspects of this theory are highlighted by Wertsch (1990, 64):

> Vygotsky's theoretical vision can be outlined in terms of three general themes that run through his writings:
> 1. a reliance on a genetic or developmental method;
> 2. the claim that higher (i.e. uniquely human) mental functioning in the individual has its origins in social activity;
> 3. the claim that a defining property of human mental action is its mediation by tools ('technical tools') and signs ('psychological tools').

By *genetic* Vygotsky did not mean something inherited in some specific form once for all as in the phrase *genetic defect*; rather he relates the term to *genesis* in the sense of *origin* or *growth*. Reliance on a genetic, i.e. developmental, method in explaining the nature of some phenomenon implies an enquiry into how and why this phenomenon develops the way it does: in the celebrated words of Blonsky 'behaviour can be understood only as the history of behaviour' (quoted in Vygotsky 1978, 65). According to Vygotsky, mental functioning was not an exception to this principle: if we wish to understand the nature of such higher mental functions as generalization, abstraction, or the formation of scientific concepts, then we need to understand the trajectory of their development. Within the confines of this paper it is not possible to do justice to all elements of Vygotsky's genetic theory of human mental functioning which covers a wide area (Lee 1987; Wertsch 1985b; 1990); I shall restrict myself here simply to the ontogenetic perspective, asking what the role of semiotic mediation is in the development of higher mental functions in an individual.

From this point of view, Vygotsky identified two 'lines' of development – the first, a natural line of development, and the second, a social line. Corresponding to these lines of development are two categories of mental functioning: the elementary and the higher. Elementary mental functioning develops along the natural line, while for the development of higher mental functioning, the social line is considered necessary. The two lines are not unrelated; in fact, in human beings mental development results from 'the interweaving of these two lines' (Vygotsky 1978, 46). By granting the natural line of development a definite status in human psychological development, Vygotsky side-stepped the sterile polarization whereby either mental functions are biologically given or they are not. Elementary mental functioning, made possible due to the natural line, and forming the biogenetic foundation for mental development, is necessary but not sufficient to account for those qualities of mental functioning which are distinctively human. Vygotsky maintained that the uniquely human, higher mental functioning develops along the social line; its roots are to be found in the social nature of human existence. The association between the social line and the higher functioning in Vygotsky's framework is indissoluble. In fact, Wertsch (1985b, 24) points out that 'Vygotsky... sometimes used the term "cultural" (versus "natural") in place of "higher" (versus "elementary") when describing mental function'. Human and social are, thus, closely related terms in Vygotsky's writing, as they are in Marx's work. But what did Vygotsky mean by higher mental functioning?

In general terms, the distinction between elementary and higher mental functioning is qualitative. Four closely related distinguishing criteria for this kind of mental functions are enumerated by Wertsch (1985b, 25):

> (1) the shift of control from environment to the individual, that is, the emergence of voluntary regulation; (2) the emergence of conscious realization of mental processes; (3) the social origins and the social nature of higher mental functions; and (4) the use of sign to mediate higher mental functions.

That the four attributes are logically related can be seen from Vygotsky's discussion of the development of memory as an example of a mental function. As an elementary mental function, where it is activated by the natural line of development, memory is:

> characterised by the non-mediated impression of materials, by the retention of actual experiences as the basis of mnemonic (memory) traces... it arises out of

the direct influence of external stimuli ... the entire process is characterised by a quality of immediacy. (Vygotsky 1978, 38)

By contrast, even in communities lacking advanced technology, human memory may not depend simply on the 'retention of actual experience'. It may be activated by some mediating device such as the use of 'notched sticks and knots'. This particular instance of a mediating device is fairly simple, but the fact of mediation itself has deep implications. According to Vygotsky (1978, 51):

> When a human being ties a knot in her handkerchief as a reminder, she is in essence, constructing the process of memorizing by forcing an external object to remind her of something; she transforms remembering into an external activity ... In the elementary form something is remembered; in the higher form humans remember something.

And although in its potential for mediation, this particular mediating 'tool' is itself quite limited by comparison with, say, writing, its use still shows that human beings in even the most primitive conditions will:

> go beyond the limits of the psychological functions given to them by nature and proceed to a *new culturally-elaborated organization* of their behaviour ... The central characteristic of elementary functions is that they are totally and directly determined by stimulation from the environment. For higher functions, the central feature is *self-generated stimulation,* that is, the creation and *use of artificial stimuli which become the immediate cause* of behaviour. (Vygotsky 1978, 39; emphasis added)

The externalization or voluntary regulation of a mental function is closely related to the possibility of its conscious mental realization: a process that can be voluntarily regulated can become the object of reflection, of 'intellectualization'. To take once again the case of memory as a higher mental function, 'to recall means to think' (Vygotsky 1978, 51). Translating directly from his *Thinking and Speech: Psychological Investigations* Wertsch (1985b, 26) quotes Vygotsky's view on higher psychological functions:

> ... [their] basic and distinguishing features are intellectualization and mastery, that is, conscious realization and voluntariness.
> At the centre of development during the school age is the transition from the lower functions of attention and memory to higher functions of voluntary attention and logical memory ... the intellectualization of functions and their mastery represent two moments of one and the same process – the transition to higher psychological functions. We master a function to the degree that it is intellectualized. The voluntariness in the activity of a function is always the other side of its conscious realization. To say that memory is intellectualized in school is exactly the same as to say that voluntary recall emerges; to say that attention becomes voluntary in school age is exactly the same as saying ... that it depends more and more on thought, that is, on intellect.

Free regulation and conscious realization require the 'use of artificial stimuli': only 'artificial stimuli' are by definition under the control of the user, and can be subjected to intellectualization and auto-stimulation. But the artificial nature of the stimuli highlights the socio-cultural mediation of higher mental functioning. To go back to the knot in the handkerchief, here memory is freely regulated, and cannot be attributed to the 'retention' of actual subjective experience, and both the mediating means and the kind of higher mental function mediated by it implicate contexts of human communal living. In explaining the development of such mediated mental acts, it becomes necessary to refer to the socio-cultural dimension. If mediated mental functions are by definition higher mental functions, then also by definition, higher mental functions are 'socio-genetic'. Just as free regulation and conscious realization of mental functions presuppose mediation by artificial stimuli, so also the fact of mediation presupposes socio-genesis: socio-genesis is a necessary attribute of mediated mental functions.

It is difficult to dissociate Vygotsky's notion of *mediation* from that of *tools*. In Vygotsky's theory, the tool was transformed from being a simple adjunct of activity to an active principle, contributing to its mental management. He recognized two basic types of mediation on the basis of the kind of tools that served as the means for mediation: mediation by means of *technological, concrete tools*, and mediation by means of *psychological, abstract tools*. Both sorts of tools lead to a higher level of activity than could be achieved by pursuing simply the natural line of development: the technological tool primarily influences via its effect on the sphere of physical activities; the abstract, via that of mental activities:

> the psychological tool alters the entire flow and structure of mental functions. It does this by determining the structure of a new instrumental act just as a technical tool alters the process of a natural adaptation by determining the form of labour operation. (Vygotsky 1981, 137)

From this point of view, *semiotic mediation* could be paraphrased as 'mediation by means of semiosis'; semiosis, the use of sign systems, thus becomes an abstract tool, acting on the mental make-up of the user (Vygotsky 1978, 40):

> The use of signs leads humans to a specific structure of behaviour that breaks away from biological development and creates new forms of a culturally-based psychological process.

Although Vygotsky was keenly aware of the contribution of other semiotic modalities to higher mental development, semiotic mediation became almost synonymous in his writing with 'mediation by means of semiosis-by-language'. This 'privileging of language', as the situation would be described in the pseudo-revolutionary intellectual discourses of the last few decades, arose from Vygotsky's conviction that amongst the various semiotic modalities, language alone *maximized* the attributes essential for the development of higher mental functions. For example, to go back to memory again, language as an abstract tool permits the free regulation of memory to the greatest degree: this cannot be seriously doubted if we consider the role of writing in this context. But writing is not language's only contribution to the regulation of memory: the conscious realization of memory is maximally assisted by the internalizing nature of language. The use of the sign system 'is a means of internal activity aimed at mastering oneself; the sign is internally oriented' (Vygotsky 1978, 55). As a mediating means language is far more supple, far more pervasive than any other variety of 'abstract tool'. Amongst all the semiotic systems operative in any community, language alone has the potential of representing the reality that is lived by the members of the community in their everyday existence. That language is active in the creation, maintenance and alteration of all human social institutions is simply one aspect of this potential. The meta-semiotic nature of language is another very important factor in its efficacy. The meta-semiotic nature of language explains why as an apprentice to culture, the child's access to other abstract tools current in the community depends to such a very large extent on verbal semiosis. This importance of verbal semiosis is not negated even though there certainly exist cultures (John 1972; Dumont 1972; Phillips 1972) where verbal semiosis is sparingly used in actual direct instruction. It is not surprising, then, that verbal interaction, which is itself an expression of social relations, assumes a crucial role in Vygotsky's theory of the development of higher mental functions: by its very nature, everyday talk becomes an active force in the process of acculturation. To quote Vygotsky (1981, 163) once again:

> Any function in the child's cultural [i.e. higher] development appears twice, or on two planes. First, it appears on the social plane, and then on the psychological plane. First, it appears between people as an inter-psychological category, and then within the child as an intra-psychological category. This is equally true with regard to voluntary attention, logical memory, the formation of concepts, and the development of volition. We may consider this position as a law in the full sense of the word, but it goes without saying that internalization transforms the process itself and changes its structure and functions. Social relations or relations among people genetically underlie all higher functions and their relationships.

This brief discussion leaves out many important elements of Vygotsky's theory, presenting merely the gist of the relation between semiotic mediation and the development of higher mental functions. Before turning to a discussion of the problems in this view, it may be useful to draw attention to some implications that follow from an acceptance of the relationship between these two pivotal concepts.

First, if in the development of higher mental functions, the inter-psychological categories precede the intra-psychological ones, and if consciousness is another name for higher mental functions, then from a genetic point of view 'the social dimension of consciousness is primary in time and

SPEECH GENRE AND SEMIOTIC MEDITATION 159

fact. The individual dimension is derivative and secondary' (Vygotsky quoted in Wertsch 1990, 66). These sentiments are in close harmony with the famous claim made by Marx: 'it is not the consciousness of men that determines their being, but on the contrary their social being that determines their consciousness' (quoted in McLellan 1975, 40). It is certainly true that individuals have (degrees of) freedom and capacity to control their environment, that they are autonomous in a manner of speaking, so far as their internal psychological processes are concerned. But in the last analysis what actually enables this psychological autonomy, this freedom from dependence on purely external stimuli, is their consciousness in the sense of higher mental functioning, and we have seen that the genesis of this consciousness is not to be discovered by looking simply inside the brains of an *isolated* human organism; these origins lie in the external processes of social life characterized by interpersonal interaction. This leads Luria to suggest that 'the Cartesian notion of the primacy of self-consciousness', which assigns a secondary rank to 'the other' must be rejected. The growth of specifically human mental acts presupposes an *other*. To quote Luria (1976, 19):

> The perception of oneself results from the clear perception of others and the processes of self-perception are shaped through social activity, which presupposes collaboration with others and an analysis of their behavioural patterns.

It follows that an individual who has already attained such consciousness should not be confused with the biological human organism. The same point is made very effectively by Volosinov (1983, 34) in the following extract:

> A rigorous distinction should always be made between the concept of the individual as natural specimen without reference to the social world (i.e., the individual as object of the biologist's knowledge and study) and the concept of individuality which has the status of an ideological semiotic superstructure over the natural individual and which, therefore, is a social concept. These two meanings of the word 'individual' (the natural specimen and the person) are commonly confused, with the result that the arguments of most philosophers and psychologists constantly exhibit *quaternio terminorum*: now one concept is in force, now the other takes its place.

The *second* implication of accepting Vygotsky's views follows partly from these comments. Vygotsky emphasized socio-genesis, but, in doing so, he did not abandon the contribution of the biogenetic foundation in human development. Thus his approach neatly side-stepped the pointless opposition between nature and nurture, individual and collectivity, between the biological and the social. What he postulated in place of these oppositions was a dynamic theory in which the biological and the social are united by a co-genetic logic (Markova 1990, 14). It is a theory that explains change both in society and the individual by virtue of the part one plays in the evolution of the other (Vygotsky 1978, 60):

> The dialectical approach [to the psychological development of humans] while admitting the influence of nature on man, asserts that man, in turn, affects nature and creates through his changes in nature new natural conditions for his existence.

Finally, Vygotsky emphasized the 'empowering' nature of higher mental functions, how they contribute to the evolution of humanity. In this argument, the theme of control over the natural conditions of existence is important as revealed in the following comments (Vygotsky 1978, 51):

> It may be said that the basic characteristic of human behaviour in general is that humans personally influence their relations with the environment and through that environment personally change their behaviour, subjugating it to their control.

Vygotsky suggests that this empowering human characteristic which represents 'the qualitative leap from animal to human psychology' (Vygotsky 1978, 57), is at the basis of human evolution (Vygotsky 1978, 60):

> It is my belief, based upon a dialectical materialist approach to the analysis of human history, that human behaviour differs qualitatively from animal behaviour to the same extent that the adaptability and historical development of humans differs from the adaptability and development of animals. The psychological development of humans is part of the general historical development of our species and must be so understood.

If it is true that what is essentially human in human beings is created by their socio-cultural history, it is also equally true that human beings are not simply made by their history; they themselves make their own socio-cultural history. We have already seen that this human characteristic of psychological autonomy, which enables control over the environment, itself derives from the internalization and intellectualization of those mental activities which are sociogenetic, nurtured largely by semiotic mediation. And when the logical connections that link the arguments in Vygotsky's model are taken into account, he can be heard as suggesting that human evolution and semiotic mediation are related phenomena. These Vygotskian statements foreshadow the idea of *exo-somatic evolution* which was to be put forward years later by such famous scholars as Popper, Medawar, and Eccles, though in a qualitatively different framework where the role assigned to language makes the framework problematic. It is not necessary to elaborate on this point here; it is sufficient simply to note that an acceptance of Vygotsky's views on semiotic mediation and the genesis of higher mental functions implies an acceptance of the role of languaging in human evolution.

The problems of semiotic mediation

The above account shows that in its broad outlines Vygotsky's theory of the genesis of mind in society is a powerful means for explaining some of the most serious issues in human and social development. But while in general terms, the role of semiotic mediation in the development of specifically human mental functions as outlined by Vygotsky appears convincing, some serious problems surface as soon as we begin to consider particular cases of higher mental functioning. For example, take the role of semiotic mediation in the development of such higher mental functions as those of categorization, generalization, abstract thinking, syllogistic reasoning, and so on. These mental functions are so often cited as instances of higher mental functioning that it seems reasonable to think of them as paradigm cases. But if so, then it would seem that we need to be more precise in talking about semiotic mediation: verbal semiosis may be a necessary condition for the development of such functions, but it is not just any kind of verbal semiosis that will necessarily lead to their emergence. Here the discussion of Luria's research in Uzbekistan (Luria 1976) is particularly relevant. Luria found that different groups of the Uzbek community functioned significantly differently with respect to these specific mental functions, the variation correlating with the absence or presence of 'formal' schooling which subsumes contact with literacy. According to Luria (1976, 48–49):

> Categorical classification involves complex verbal and logical thinking that exploits language's capacity for formulating abstractions and generalizations for picking out attributes, and subsuming objects within a general category ... 'categorical' thinking is usually quite flexible; subjects readily shift from one attribute to another and construct suitable categories. They classify objects by substance (animals, flowers, tools), materials (wood, metal, glass), size (large, small), and colour (light, dark), or other property. The ability to move freely, to shift from one category to another, is one of the chief characteristics of 'abstract thinking' or the 'categorical behaviour' essential to it.

There was no evidence of 'categorical, abstract thinking' amongst those of Luria's Uzbeki subjects who did not have the benefit of formal education, and who were functionally illiterate. Luria (1976, 77) comments:

> Every attempt to suggest the possibility of categorical grouping met with protest ... They either disregarded generic terms or *considered them irrelevant*, in no way essential to the business of classification. *Clearly, different psychological processes determined their manner of grouping which hinged on concrete, situational thinking rather than abstract operations which entail the generalizing function of language.* (emphasis added)

The subjects showed a marked tendency for 'concrete, situational thinking'. This raises several disturbing questions. First: is 'concrete, situational thinking' as much an instance of higher mental functioning as is 'categorical, abstract thinking'? If it is not, then, for very obvious reasons, *higher* in the expressions 'higher mental functions' or 'higher consciousness' cannot be equated with *specifically human*, unless the quality of humanity is defined by the ability to think in a particular way. This 'elitist' position is obviously far from the intentions of a psychological theory which would emulate Marx's

Capital! If, on the other hand, *both* types of thinking are seen as cases of higher mental functioning, then the two different sorts of psychological processes (if indeed they are two qualitatively different processes) – the one underlying 'concrete, situational thinking' and the other underlying 'categorical, abstract thinking' – are being hierarchized; the latter kind of thinking is obviously treated as more desirable than the former. I shall not question at this point the rationale for this valuation; but note what is implied with regard to semiotic mediation in accepting the need for the hierarchization of the forms of higher consciousness.

First, both the more 'valued' and the less 'valued' forms of thinking would have to be accepted as being sociogenetic. Note Luria's unequivocal claim (1976, 79):

> concrete thinking is neither innate nor genetically [i.e. *by heredity*] determined. It results from illiteracy and the rudimentary types of activity that have prevailed in these [i.e. the unschooled Uzbeki] subjects' daily experience.

Clearly 'concrete, situational thinking' is not just an instance of the natural line of development, and if its emergence is sociogenetic, then it must be – at least in part – semiotically mediated. This leads to the *second* implication: the more highly valued 'categorical, abstract thinking' cannot be attributed to *semiotic mediation per se*: rather, its emergence must be attributed to *particular forms of semiotic mediation* – to particular *fashions of speaking*, to use the Whorfian phrase, or to distinct *coding orientations* as Bernstein would say. These fashions of speaking or coding orientations would be the ones where speakers 'exploit language's capacity' for mediating precisely these sorts of functions; and this may be because speakers consider such functions relevant. *Third*, it follows that there is variation in semiotic mediation. This, in turn, raises two further questions: one, how should that particular variety of semiotic mediation be characterized which underlies the genesis of abstract categorical thinking – what are the internal linguistic attributes of such semiotic mediation?, and two, what, if any, is the relation between the material conditions of social existence and variant forms of semiotic mediation, in other words, what underlies the appearance of the internal linguistic attributes that characterize the variant forms of semiotic mediation?

Rational thinking which is said to be based on inference and deduction is also taken to be a higher mental function. Similar problems are encountered when we examine the development of deduction and inference, the classic case of which is said to be syllogistic reasoning. Here is how Luria (1976, 101) describes the nature and function of syllogistic reasoning:

> One of the objective devices that arises in the process of the development of cognitive activity is the syllogism – a set of individual judgments of varying degrees of generality in certain objectively necessary relationship to one another. Two sentences, of which the first ('precious metals do not rust') is in the nature of a general judgment ... while the second ('gold is a precious metal') is a particular proposition, are not perceived by the developed consciousness as two isolated

SPEECH GENRE AND SEMIOTIC MEDITATION 163

phrases in juxtaposition. A human being whose theoretical thought processes are well developed will perceive these as a completed logical relation implying the conclusion, 'hence gold does not rust.' This conclusion does not require any personal experience; it is arrived at through a syllogism created objectively by historical experience. A considerable proportion of our intellectual operations involve such verbal and logical systems; they comprise the basic network of codes along which the connections in discursive human thought are channelled.

Luria's subjects were 'exposed' to two categories of syllogisms: syllogisms the content of whose propositions was taken from the subjects' immediate practical experience, and those where the content of the propositions was divorced from such experience. The results of this experiment correlated with very finely graded social attributes in the subjects (see discussion Luria 1976, 113ff.). Reporting on one set of results, this is what Luria (1976, 114) says:

> For the non-literate subjects, the process of reasoning and deduction associated with immediate experience follows well-known rules. These subjects can make excellent judgments about facts of direct concern to them and draw all the implied conclusions, displaying no deviation from the 'rules' and revealing much worldly intelligence. The picture changes, however, just as soon as they have to change to a system of theoretical thinking – in this instance making syllogistic inferences.

Luria cites three factors in explanation of this finding which shows that the non-literate subjects have limited 'capability for theoretical verbal-logical thinking':

> ... [1] mistrust of an initial premise that does not reproduce personal experience ... [2] the unacceptability of the premise as universal ... [3] a consequence of the second ... [the] ready disintegration of the syllogism into three independent and isolated particular propositions with no unified logic and thus no access for thought to be channelled within this system.

It is obvious from the discussion that deduction and inference from the second category of syllogisms – whose propositions are not embedded in the practical experience of the subjects – are thought of as indicative of even *higher* mental functioning. But how do we interpret the inability to relate to any premise that does not 'reproduce personal experience'? What underlies the failure to recognize 'universal facts'? What sort of consciousness do these processes indicate? Could these questions be answered satisfactorily if the defining attributes of that variety of semiotic mediation are identified which underlies the emergence of the valued forms of higher consciousness?

Any attempt to answer the last question turns us inevitably to Vygotsky's views about language. And although it is important to discuss both his views on the system of language as the potential and on that variety of language which selectively actualizes precisely that part of the potential which underlies the emergence of the valued forms of higher consciousness, I shall argue that for Vygotsky's framework it is language use that is absolutely crucial; this is because in Vygotsky's approach, interpersonal languaging, social speech, forms the fulcrum of semiotic mediation. To begin again by quoting Wertsch (1985c, 53ff.), who identifies two apparently 'opposing tendencies' recognized by Vygotsky as basic to 'the organization and use of human language':

> On the one hand, language has *the potential to be used* in abstract, decontextualized reflection. This led to the study of concept development, categorization, and syllogistic and scientific reasoning, and to a focus on the decontextualization of the 'meaning' of words. On the other hand, there is a side of linguistic organization rooted in contextualization ... Vygotsky considered the ways in which the structure and interpretation of utterances depend on their relationships with their extralinguistic and intralinguistic contexts ... this provides the foundation for an account of inner speech and the notion of 'sense'. (emphasis added)

In discussing Luria's research, we have already seen that what is at issue is not 'the *potential* of language to be used in abstract decontextualized reflection'; rather, the valued higher mental functions develop only if this potential is *actualized* in verbal interaction. It is, of course, necessary to demonstrate that such a potential inheres in language as a system, but this demonstration cannot explain the genesis of the actualization of any part of the postulated potential. The crucial question is when and why does it appear relevant to speakers to 'exploit language's capacity for formulating abstractions', for categorization, syllogistic reasoning, and so on. One must mention here Vygotsky's repeated references to pedagogic discourse as one type which could perhaps be viewed as maximizing the possibility of developing the higher mental functions in the pupils. But against this claim, we must also remember that the actual mental development of pupils, in this sense of mental development, is subjected to evaluation; that the rate of educational success for pupils, according to repeated findings, is not the same; and that variation in levels of educational success correlates typically with the pupils' social positioning. Why should this be so? and what aspect of semiotic mediation in pedagogical contexts could be cited as a possible explanation for this differential outcome in mediating the development of mental functions?

In the literature, a distinction is made between the concrete context-bound use of a word to refer to something that is physically present to the senses, as a child might say 'horse' when a horse is present. This is using the linguistic sign as a *signal*; this contrasts with the use of the linguistic sign, the word, as a *symbol*. The word is said to be used as a symbol, when the meaning structure underlying the linguistic sign is so well internalized by the speaker that s/he can use it to recount, to pretend, to hypothesize – in short, s/he can use it *in displacement*. It seems to me that four closely related points need to be made here. *First*, the move from signal to symbol is a significant step in learning how to mean (Halliday 1975; Painter 1984), as it turns the sign into a creative 'tool' rather than one which is constrained to 'correspond' to or 'reproduce' a concrete reality existing in the here and now of the speech situation. Thus the identification of this feature as important in the development of mental functions appears fully justified. *Secondly*, the emergence of this stage in the child is a classic example of the 'interweaving of the two lines' of development (Vygotsky 1978, 46); the internalization of the specific meaning structure of the word in the child relies no less on sociogenetic foundations (Malinowski 1923; 1935; Painter 1984) than on the biogenetic ones. The specific character of the meaning structure internalized by the child is a major step in the creation of that intersubjectivity which makes communication possible between the child and her *speech fellowship* (Firth 1957a, 186ff.). *Thirdly*, by the same token, to speak as a normal adult is to have arrived at this stage of using the linguistic sign as a symbol. No matter how far a particular group of Uzbeki fell from the standards of 'abstract thinking' as defined in Vygotsky and Luria, their use of the linguistic sign could not have been a signalling use; it *had* to be a symbolic use in the definition of the term offered here, for such use is a *condition* of all adult communication. Any examination of language use even in the most primitive communities, irrespective of how primitiveness is defined, would reveal that the sign system of language is used symbolically by normal adults everywhere. It is on this basis that 'displacement' has been recognized as an inherent quality of the linguistic sign system. *Finally*, it follows from this that if all language use presupposes 'decontextualization' of word meaning – as this situation is sometimes described – then 'the decontextualization of the "meaning" of words' *by itself* cannot be responsible for the emergence of the *valued* higher mental functions, repeatedly mentioned by Vygotsky–Luria. Since the quality of 'decontextualization' of word meaning is ubiquitous, this quality must underly both the less and the more valued higher mental functions. The Uzbekis used language signs as symbols, no less than did the famous scholars of their time who used the Uzbekis as subjects in their experiments. As Wertsch (1985c, 55) points out:

> the Vygotsky–Luria argument ... concerns the *process of reflecting on decontextualized word meanings*. The 'latent or potential content of speech' (Sapir 1921, 15) is a necessary but not a sufficient condition for this form of abstract reasoning to appear. (emphasis added)

The 'process of reflecting on decontextualized meanings' has to be seen as a *specific kind of social process*, a particular kind of language use, as for example in certain cases of classroom discourse (Butt 1989a; 1989b), or in explaining the steps in problem solving. The results of my research in Australia (Hasan 1989; 1991; 1992a; 1992b; Hasan and Cloran 1990) indicate that engagement in this kind of language use is the prerogative of a speaker's privileged socio-economic position in the wider community. In the context of such complex communities as the capitalist democracies of today, it becomes problematic then to even relate this social process directly to the 'socio-cultural history' of a speech community as a whole. What would it mean to say that the socio-cultural history of the working-class mother in Australia is less evolved than that of the middle-class mother? That this explains why the working-class mother's higher mental functions, her consciousness, are less evolved by comparison with the middle-class mother? It seems to me that the Vygotsky–Luria framework for the sociogenesis of mind calls not only for a more sophisticated theory of language as suggested by Wertsch; it also needs a sophisticated theory of social organization.

Suppose it is granted that what underlies the genesis of higher mental functions is reflection on decontextualized meanings of the verbal sign, and the readiness to use language to construe experience which is not simply remote from one's actual personal experience but might even run counter to it. Even so, it is clear that what we are talking about here are *qualities of language use*; these qualities are, as it were, permitted (not demanded) by the inherent nature of the language system. So, in identifying the 'desirable' variety of semiotic mediation by languaging, it is not a question of what there is in the system of language, but rather of how that system is deployed. And we may formulate a general rule: how a linguistic system is deployed is never a simple question of manner; it is, rather, a question of the social situatedness of speakers and their speech process – who is talking to whom and why. In order to be able to intellectualize the social situatedness of the varieties of verbal interaction, what we need is a theory of social context. In Vygotsky's work this necessary element of the theory of language is virtually absent. Certainly Vygotsky does mention some specific contexts of talk, e.g. the pedagogic contexts of the classroom, peer interaction, adult–child interaction, but the attributes of the talk situation identified by him will be found to be incidental to his concern with whatever specific kind of mental activity is under discussion. Moreover as Wertsch points out, Vygotsky's analysis of language focused most often on the unit word and its characteristics. The natural unit for semiotic mediation is not the word, but text/ discourse – language operational in a social context (Halliday and Hasan 1989). Obviously the analysis of forms of semiotic mediation would stand to gain if the concepts of text and context in relation to each other can be utilized. It is to achieve this goal that Wertsch turns to Bakhtin's notion of *speech genre*.

Speech genre and semiotic mediation

Over the past two decades, Bakhtin's views on the nature of language have attracted a good deal of attention. Particularly his concepts of *speech genre, intertextuality, social language,* and *ideologically based communication* are cited as making a much needed contribution to linguistic theory. Though I shall touch briefly on all of these concepts, my main concern in this section, will be with the Bakhtinian views on speech genre, in the discussion of which I shall rely largely on his 'The Problem of Speech Genres' (1986). I shall refer also to Volosinov (1983), especially with respect to the ideological basis of human consciousness and communication, though recognizing Todorov's cautionary comments (1984, xii) against assuming authorial identity between the two. It may be true that *Marxism and the Philosophy of Language* was not penned by Bakhtin, but surely the principles of intertextuality and dialogism would make it closely related to his views. This exclusive reliance on Bakhtin–Volosinov's writing is not to deny the contributions of other scholars to the interpretation of these authors' views; it is simply that this would introduce a dimension of complexity to which the scope of this paper cannot do justice. The bond of intertextuality also links Vygotsky and Bakhtin, though perhaps not so closely as Bakhtin–Volosinov. I do not know that the former two scholars were specifically aware of each other's work, but without doubt the themes of one are to be found also in the works of the other: as Bakhtin might say each epoch has its own concerns, its own web of intertextuality, and the contemporaneousness of these scholars makes it likely that their writings would be mutually complementary. In what follows, I shall first present an account of Bakhtin's concepts; each such presentation will be followed by a critique in an attempt to evaluate the explanatory and descriptive power of the Bahktinian framework. This will furnish the basis for answering the main question: would Bakhtin's concept of speech genre, utterance, intertextuality, social language, etc. successfully resolve those problems in Vygotsky's framework that were outlined in closing the last section?

From this point of view, the perspective on language adopted by Bakhtin promises well. He is deeply committed to the importance of *parole* – language as it is actualized in verbal interaction, making a sharp distinction (1986, 67) between 'utterance as a unit of speech communion' and 'the units of language (words and sentences)'. For Vygotsky's theory of mental development language use is more relevant than language system. Further, as pointed out by Wertsch (1985c; 1990), one of the problems in Vygotsky's discourse on semiotic mediation is that he often describes the nature of semiotic mediation in terms of words; Bakhtin's commitment to utterance as the natural unit of verbal interaction could be valuable in providing a means of examining the crucial characteristics of that variety of semiotic mediation which leads to the emergence of the valued kinds of higher mental functions. Not only is Bakhtin concerned with utterance as a whole, but he is able to suggest a means for classifying utterances by linking them to his notion of speech genre. This is how Bakhtin (1986, 60) introduces the concept of genre:

> All the diverse areas of human activity involve the use of language ... the nature and forms of this use are just as diverse as are the areas of human activity ... Language is realized in the form of individual concrete utterances (oral and written) by participants in the various areas of human activity. These utterances reflect the specific conditions and goals of each such area not only through their content (thematic) and linguistic style, that is, the selection of lexical, phraseo-

logical, and grammatical resources of the language, but above all through their compositional structure. All three of these aspects – thematic content, style, and compositional structure – are inseparably linked to the *whole* of the utterance and are equally determined by the specific nature of the particular sphere of communication. Each separate utterance is individual, of course, but each sphere in which language is used develops its own *relatively stable types* of these utterances. These we may call *speech genres*. (emphasis as in original)

It is obvious from this extract that the two terms *utterance* and *human activity* are closely related, and both appear criterial to the discussion of speech genre. 'We speak only in definite speech genres, that is, all our utterances have definite and relatively stable typical forms of construction of the whole' (Bakhtin 1986, 78). As a term, *speech genre* might be paraphrased as *utterance type* ... 'utterances and their types, that is, speech genres' (Bakhtin 1986, 65). It follows that every 'concrete utterance' is an actual instance of some speech genre. Such concrete utterances belong to 'various spheres of human activity and communication' (Bakhtin 1986, 62); this line of reasoning argues that there exists a definite relation between utterances, utterance types, and spheres of human activity. So what does the term *human activity* refer to?

One point that is obvious from the longer extract given above (Bakhtin 1986, 60) is that human activity is relevant to utterance since it is 'reflected' or it 'determines' both the wording and the compositional structure of the utterance. If so, then another term for *human activity* might be *social situation* since this is precisely how social situation too is said to act on utterances: 'The immediate social situation and the broader social milieu wholly determine – and determine from within, so to speak – the structure of an utterance' (Volosinov 1983, 86). The deep relationship of human activity or social situation to utterance is again and again pointed out by Bakhtin–Volosinov. Consider for example the following claims (Volosinov 1983, 93; emphasis added):

> The organizing centre of any utterance ... is not within but outside – in the social milieu surrounding the individual being. Only the inarticulate cry of an animal is really organized from inside the physiological apparatus of an individual creature ... even the most primitive human utterance produced by the individual organism is, from the point of view of its content, import, and meaning, organized outside the organism, in the extra-organismic conditions of the social milieu. Utterance as such is wholly a product of social interaction, both of the immediate sort *as determined by the circumstances of the discourse, and of the more general kind, as determined by the whole aggregate of conditions under which any given community of speakers operates.*

The social 'situation shapes the utterance, dictating that it sound one way and not another' (Volosinov 1983, 86). This relationship between the utterance and the social situation is also viewed dialogically: 'language enters life through concrete utterances (which manifest language) [*sic!*] and life enters language through concrete utterances as well' (Bakhtin

1986, 63). As instances of speech genres, utterances that are shaped by situation, act as a bridge between the history of society and the history of language: 'Utterances and their types, that is, speech genres, are the drive belts from the history of society to the history of language' (Bakhtin 1986, 65).

Such comments make it very clear that human activity *alias* social situation should have a crucial role in a theory of utterance and utterance types, i.e. in the theory of speech genre. It is interesting to note then that the concept of social situation is breathtakingly wide and inclusive – this is certainly the case if we take Volosinov (1983) as indicative; but, at the same time, and quite paradoxically, the notion of social situation remains underdeveloped both in Volosinov and in Bakhtin. What I mean by this is the marked absence of a schema of any sort which might give the terms *social situation* and *social milieu* a tangible quality, making it obvious what would count as elements of social situation and why. Using the terms in Vygotsky's theory, one might say that the concepts are not sufficiently 'intellectualized'. However, their complexity is quite obvious. Volosinov (1983, 47) himself accepts the need for their clarification:

> the fact of the matter is that the organized social milieu into which we have included our complex [spheres of reality – physical, physiological, and psychological. see p. 46; loc. cit] and the immediate social communicative situation are *in themselves extremely complicated* and involve hosts of multifaceted and multifarious connections, *not all of which are equally important for the understanding of linguistic facts* ... (emphasis added)

A developed theory of social context would at least have two attributes: one, it would explain the principle whereby the immediate social situation is related to social milieu; and two it would specify the composition of social situation itself, making salient those of its significant elements which are relevant to the understanding of the linguistic facts as they impinge on utterances and utterance types. Ideally, the theory would attempt to specify the *principles* by virtue of which the elements of the social situation happen to be related to the wording and the compositional structure of the utterance (types). If these steps are not taken, and the notion of context is allowed to remain 'elastic' (i.e. theoretically underdeveloped) if individual elements of situation are deployed adventitiously to 'explain' the nature or the wording and/or the structure of concrete utterances wherever, whenever they suit the analyst's purpose, then clearly this would create descriptive problems (Firth 1957b; Cook 1990). This kind of theoretical elaboration is lacking in Bakhtin–Volosinov; and since they provide no clear criteria for making judgments, the reader is left to infer from a scattering of their comments what they might consider the relevant elements of the social situation; inevitably, such inferences contain lacunae. For example, a category of speech genres is said to be 'extremely varied depending on the *subject matter, situation, and participant*' (Bakhtin 1986, 60; emphasis added). But in such comments it is not clear whether *subject matter* is a part of *human activity*, whether it is at the same level of abstraction as the next two terms *situation* and *participant*, whether *situation* is inclusive of *participant* or simply on par with it, and in what way these two relate to *human activity*.

The element of social situation that is emphasized most often in both authors is the interpersonal one. Thus (Bakhtin 1986, 70):

> These genres [i.e. *speech genres*] are so diverse because they differ depending on the situation, social position, and personal inter-relations of the participants in the communication.

Here 'social position' and 'personal inter-relations of the participants', in effect, refer to the interpersonal aspect of the social situation. Consider again (Bakhtin 1986, 95):

> Both the composition and, particularly, the style of the utterance depend on those to whom the utterance is addressed, how the speaker (or writer) senses and imagines his addressees, and the force of their effect on the utterance. Each speech genre in each area of speech communication has its own typical conception of the addressee, and this defines it as a genre.

Two further extracts on this topic, this time from Volosinov (emphasis added)

> the forms of signs are *conditioned above all by the social organization of the participants* involved and also by the immediate conditions of their interaction. (Volosinov 1983, 21)

> to observe the phenomenon of language, both the producer and the receiver of sound and the sound itself must be placed into the social atmosphere ... After all, the speaker and the listener must belong to the same language community – to a society organized along certain particular lines. Furthermore, our two individuals must be encompassed by unity of *the immediate social* situation, i.e., they must make contact, as one person to another, on *a specific basis*. Only on a specific basis is a verbal exchange possible. (Volosinov 1983; 46)

Here in the first extract the context of the discussion makes it quite clear that the 'forms of sign' should be read as 'forms of utterance'. Turning to the second extract, it seems that the *social atmosphere* is the *social milieu*, since it appears to be equated with language community and societal organization. The speaker and the listener need also to 'be encompassed by the unity of the immediate social situation': are the 'two individuals', then, elements of the immediate social situation, or do they come together in a pre-existing social situation as actors come together upon a prearranged scene on the stage? And what is 'a specific basis'? Is it another word for social situation, or is it an element therein? To ask that concepts such as human activity, immediate social situation, and the relation of these to social milieu should be clarified is not just a pedantic demand. These concepts are needed so

SPEECH GENRE AND SEMIOTIC MEDITATION

that we may establish whether the claims being made about the determination of the utterance by social situation are indeed tenable, and if so, what is the nature of those concepts and arguments that are offered in support of the claim. If the concepts of human activity and utterance are to be used in explicating how different forms of semiotic mediation differ from each other, we shall certainly need this degree of explicit clarification; but, without denying the richness of Bakhtin's writing, it has to be conceded that this kind of explicitness will be hard to find in his writing.

Let me turn now to the concept of utterance in Bakhtin's discussion of speech genres. The term *utterance* is used in Bakhtin (1986) in at least two senses: it is the 'natural unit' of verbal interaction, corresponding to 'discourse' and/or 'text'; secondly, it is also used to refer to a unit that is much closer in its sense to a *turn* as in turn-taking in dialogue. It is only in the first sense that utterance type and (speech) genre are exchangeable terms as is evident from the following locutions: 'the novel is a secondary (complex) utterance' (Bakhtin 1986, 62); 'concrete utterances (written and oral) belong to various spheres of human activity and communication: chronicles, contracts, texts of laws, clerical and other documents ... ' (Bakhtin 1986, 62); and so on. From this view of the utterance, we are moved to another conception of the term. Deploring the linguists' 'imprecise' use of the word *speech*, which might stand for 'the speech process', i.e. speaking, or for the 'individual utterance', or for 'an entire long indefinite series of such utterances, or a particular genre' as in 'he gave a speech' (Bakhtin 1986, 70), Bakhtin comments that these confusions 'result from ignoring the *real unit* of speech communication: the utterance' (Bakhtin 1986, 71):

> Speech is always cast in the form of an utterance belonging to a particular speaking subject, and outside this form it cannot exist. Regardless of how varied utterances may be in terms of their length, their content, and their compositional structure, they have common structural features as units of speech communication, and, above all, quite clear-cut boundaries ... The boundaries of each concrete utterance as a unit of speech communication are determined by a *change of speaking subjects*, that is, a change of speakers. Any utterance – from a short (single-word) rejoinder in everyday dialogue to the large novel or scientific treatise – has, so to speak, an absolute beginning and an absolute end: its beginning is preceded by the utterances of others, and its end is followed by the responsive utterances of others (or, although it may be silent, others' active responsive understanding, or, finally, a responsive action based on this understanding). The speaker ends his utterance in order to relinquish the floor to the other or to make room for the other's active responsive understanding.

I have quoted extensively to reveal the basis of my claim that Bakhtin's use of the term *utterance* is ambivalent. It is of course ingenuous to claim, as Bakhtin does by implication, that there is no ambivalence, that in actual fact utterance in the sense of a turn in a dialogue and in the sense of a text/ discourse is the same thing at the deepest level of analysis. It seems that

Bakhtin is aware of the problematic nature of his claim; he argues at some length in its support (Bakhtin 1986, 75–76):

> Let us turn to the real-life dialogue ... this is the simplest and the most classic form of speech communication. The change of speaking subjects (speakers) that determines the boundaries is especially clear here. But in other speech communication as well ... the nature of the boundaries of the utterance remains the same.
>
> Complexly structured and specialized works of various scientific and artistic genres, in spite of all the ways in which they differ from rejoinders in dialogue, are by nature the same kind of units of speech communication. They too are demarcated by a change of speaking subjects, and these boundaries, while retaining their *external* clarity, acquire here a special internal aspect because the speaking subject – in this case, the *author* of the work – manifests his own individuality in his style, his world view, and in all aspects of the design of his work ...
>
> The work, like the rejoinder in a dialogue, is oriented toward the response of the other (others), towards his active responsive understanding ... Like the rejoinder in the dialogue, it is related to other work-utterances: both to which it responds and which respond to it. At the same time, like the rejoinder in the dialogue, it is separated from them by the absolute boundaries created by a change of speaking subjects.
>
> Thus the change of speaking subjects ... is the first constitutive feature of the utterance as a unit of speech communication ... [a] second feature, which is inseparably linked to the first ... is the specific *finalization* of the utterance.

There are, however, serious difficulties in maintaining this ingenuous claim of deep identity between a complete text/discourse and a dialogic turn, which could simply be part of a text/discourse. Let us ignore, for the moment, the problems of self-contradiction in maintaining on the one hand that different genres allow different degrees of discretion for 'reflecting individuality' (Bakhtin 1986, 63), and on the other, claiming that authorial individuality is an ever-present feature of all utterances. Reliance on the 'imprint of individuality' – even if this were equally available to all utterance types – is hardly likely to distinguish one utterance/text from another *where the same author is concerned*. And while there certainly are many advantages in viewing the entire *oeuvres* of an author as one unified utterance/text, this will equally certainly pose problems for genre typification: the notion of genre demands a clear articulation of the principles which will define and distinguish the boundaries of individual utterances (in the sense of text/discourse) one from another. As I have claimed before, Bakhtin is well aware of these problems and he offers 'three indicators of the *wholeness* of the utterance' which will apply to both senses of the term 'utterance'. He reiterates that what gives an utterance its identity as an utterance is 'subject neither to grammatical nor to abstract semantic definition' [but note first indicator below!] (Bakhtin 1986, 76):

> This finalized wholeness of the utterance, guaranteeing the possibility of a response ... is determined by three ... factors that are inseparably linked in the

organic whole of the utterance: 1. semantic exhaustiveness of the theme; 2. the speaker's plan or speech will; 3. typical compositional and generic forms of finalization.

The 'possibility of response' on which Bakhtin relies almost implicitly, is itself a double-edged sword in his framework. To Bakhtin's credit, unlike most scholars, his view of response and understanding are truly dynamic – as such, they are, certainly, an ongoing feature of the dialogue. In a dialogue then the possibility of response must characterize both *utterance* in the sense of individual turns (or even parts thereof), and *utterance* in the sense of (a substantial fragment of) the overall verbal interaction. How else could one account for a 'retrospective' response? Since admirably, in Bakhtin, response is not a uniquely situated phenomenon, since it is an ongoing quality of engagement in the speech process, the 'possibility of response' is indeed incapable of acting as a criterion for boundary demarcation, since such dynamic response is ever-present. Turning to the three factors enumerated above, each one of these remains equally vague (see Bakhtin's discussion 1986, 77ff.) to an extent that makes it quite doubtful that they could be actually used effectively for the recognition of utterance boundaries. As I see it, the reasons for this vagueness have to do with the lack of theoretical development. This point can be elaborated, by stating exactly what sort of relations are missing from Bakhtin's genre theory.

First, take the theorization of the relation between context and text. I have already commented on the pre-theoretical status of the notion of social situation. Since social situation and the wordings and compositional structure, that is to say, generic structure, of utterance/text are so closely related, it is reasonable to suppose that the three indicators of 'the finalized wholeness of the utterance' mentioned above can be clarified by reference to social situation: indeed, in the SF model, this issue has been debated and developed for some time (Hasan 1978; 1984; 1995; Ventola 1984; 1987; Martin 1985; 1992; Gregory 1988). But to do this successfully, it is necessary to know the specific details of what may be the significant elements of the social situation, and which element is related to which aspect of the utterance. What are those aspects of the social situation to which is related the semantic exhaustiveness of the theme in an utterance/text? Could it be the nature of the social activity, i.e. the *field of discourse*, to use SF terminology (Halliday and Hasan 1989)? What is that quality of the speech process that allows us to 'embrace, understand, and sense the speaker's speech plan or speech will, which determines the entire utterance, its length and boundaries'? And a similar question can be asked also about the basis on which we 'guess' the genre 'from the very first word' uttered by the speaker. Bakhtin (1986, 78) reiterates the nexus between utterance and the social situation:

> the choice of a particular speech genre ... is determined by the specific nature of the given sphere of communication, semantic (thematic) considerations, the

concrete situation of the speech communication, the personal composition of its participants, and so on.

But as I have said before such assertions are pre-theoretical; they cannot provide the foundation for a viable description. What Bakhtin passes over as 'the speech process' is a functionally organized configuration of linguistic meanings. This configuration addresses the extra-linguistic situation on the one hand, and the linguistic form – grammar, lexicon, intonation – on the other. A viable description has to find some means of bringing together these distinct orders of abstractions.

This brings me to the *second* point: the Bakhtinian framework has no apparatus for distinguishing different orders of abstraction, much less for relating them to each other on a principled basis. Although such words as *manifestation, actualization, realization, expression*, etc, are used by Bakhtin–Volosinov, this use remains informal. To explain the relations between social situation, utterance/text, and the 'units of language' such as words, phrases, sentences, we need to recognize *stratification* and *realization* as formal concepts in the descriptive model (Halliday 1992; Hasan 1995). This would allocate different orders of abstraction to different strata and yet permit them to be linked by realization to each other. Bakhtin's claim that utterance/text cannot be described in terms of words, phrases, and sentences is echoed in SF (Halliday 1977; Halliday and Hasan 1989). Utterance/text is not *made up* of sentences, phrases, etc.; rather, it is *realized* as sentence(s), phrase(s) etc. This realizational relationship (see for discussion, Halliday 1992) links context, text, and lexicogrammar (Halliday and Hasan 1989; Martin 1991; Matthiessen 1992; 1996). Just as a text realizes its context, similarly it is itself realized by the lexicogrammatical units of language. It seems to me that some consistent means of linking the social situation and the language of the utterance (i.e., what the utterance manifests, and what manifests the utterance) is a necessity in the theory of genre. Assertions about the nature and attributes of utterance/text will tend to create a 'mystification', unless they are grounded in the social and the verbal systems. If 'stylistic effect', almost as a rule, is not produced by the functioning of the categories of the system of language in context, then by implication its source is mysterious, and in explaining its appearance, we may need to appeal to something akin to the individualistic subjectivism, which Bakhtin so categorically rejected as having no basis in reality. Like most linguists Bakhtin appears to think that appeal to the system of language can be made to explain the actualization of *only* those categories which conform to the system, replicating the norms exactly. However, as Firth (1957a) pointed out, divergence, originality, individuality in language use cannot be described coherently except by relation to the language system operative in some social context.

Bakhtin–Volosinov are incisive critics of the approaches in linguistics that they described as *abstract objectivism* and *individual subjectivism*. They advocate a linguistics committed to the analysis of whole utterances in the speech process. However, in supporting the linguistics of *parole*, they are inclined to underplay the importance of *langue*. Superficially this may appear to be a corrective step, but in fact it simply replicates the Saussurian situation in reverse: with Saussure system was everything; with Bakhtin, process is everything. Neither stance can support a dialectical approach; both are monological. A *third* sense in which I find Bakhtin's framework theoretically underdeveloped is precisely its inability to relate language process to language system. Naturally I am not implying that Bakhtin–Volosinov are unaware of the fact that speech process creates, maintains, and alters the system so that the system is always 'becoming', always being 'renewed'. In fact we owe some of the most illuminating comments to Bakhtin–Volosinov on the relation of *langue* and *parole*. Consider the following comments by Volosinov:

> From the standpoint of observing language objectively, from above, there is no real moment in time when a synchronic system of language could be constructed. (Volosinov 1983, 66)

> the constituent factor for the linguistic form, as for the sign, is not at all its self-identity as signal but its specific variability; and the constituent factor for understanding the linguistic form is not recognition of the 'same thing', but understanding in the proper sense of the word, i.e., orientation in the particular, given context and in the particular, given situation – orientation in the dynamic sense of becoming and not 'orientation' in some inert state. (Volosinov 1983, 69)

There is abundant proof in their writing that Bakhtin–Volosinov are fully aware of the importance of parole as 'an essential factor in the history of language' (Volosinov 1983, 61); 'speech genres are the drive-belts from the history of society to the history of language' (Bakhtin 1986, 65). So I am not suggesting that Bakhtin is unaware of the fact that 'process becomes system'; rather, I am claiming that in Bakhtin's framework, *there exists no apparatus for modelling this symbiosis of process and system*, for explaining how it is that process *could* become system. Volosinov (1983, 67) asks a rhetorical question in order to reject a particular conception of language system:

> Does language really exist for the speaker's subjective consciousness as an objective system of incontestably, normatively identical forms? ... Is the mode of being of language in the subjective speech consciousness really what abstract objectivism says it is?
>
> We must answer this question in the negative. The Speaker's subjective consciousness does not in the least operate with language as a system of normatively identical forms. That system is merely an abstraction arrived [at] with a good deal of trouble and with a definite and practical focus of attention. The system of language is the product of deliberation on language, and deliberation of a kind by no means carried out for the immediate purpose of speaking.

It would seem that the 'verbal consciousness of speakers has ... nothing whatever to do with linguistic form as such or with language as such' (Volosinov 1983, 70). He goes on to suggest (1983, 71) that:

for the consciousness of a speaker of a language, the real mode of existence for that language is not a system of normatively identical forms. From the viewpoint of the speaker's consciousness and his real-life practice in social intercourse, there is no direct access to the system of language envisioned by abstract objectivism.

Here I would make three points. *First*, according to Bakhtin–Volosinov, both speaking and understanding are constituted ideologically. But does this imply that for communication to occur, the community of speakers capable of engaging in verbal interaction must subscribe to (largely) the same ideology? This is problematic, if for the simple reason that social domination requires verbal intercourse with the dominated (Hasan 1986). Besides, if speaking and understanding are constituted by a single ideology, how do we explain the creation of such sophisticated utterances as Dostoevsky's novels? Thus there has to be some qualification, some elaboration of the notion of ideologically governed speaking and understanding. I believe I am right in saying that this qualification and elaboration would throw into question some of the views expressed by Bakhtin–Volosinov on the verbal consciousness of speakers.

The *second* point is closely related to this. If the need for recognizing not one but several coexisting ideologies is granted, then we have to grant also that in the speakers' consciousness there must be a representation of some kind of language system which permits a wider play for intersubjective objectivity: there has to be some response to the other coexisting ideologies in the same social milieu, even if it is to contest, to resist, to engage in a struggle. What would this language system be like, the representation of which in the verbal consciousness of the members of the wider community is essential for the necessary presupposition of intersubjective objectivity? What would be the attributes of a system of this kind? How is this system activated in the speech process?

This brings me to the *third* point: in their disdain against language system, Bakhtin–Volosinov always seem to operate with the same conception of language and linguistics which they have already given us grounds for rejecting. It is as if linguistics and language system were immutable realities, which no amount of reasoned debate could hope to alter. When Volosinov (1983, 78) claims:

> Formal, systematic thought about language is incompatible with living, historical understanding of language ... The structure of a complex sentence ... is the furthest limit of linguistic reach.

or when Bakhtin (1986, 72) declares that:

> The relations among whole utterances cannot be treated grammatically since, we repeat, such relations are impossible among units of language, and not only within the system of language, but within the utterance as well.

SPEECH GENRE AND SEMIOTIC MEDITATION 177

both authors are implicitly operating with the same conception of language system and of language study, that same authoritarian sense of grammar, which can be traced back to antiquity: Saussure's was simply the most persuasive voice commending these views early this century. But what if the Saussurian conception of language system itself is erroneous, as Bakhtin–Volosinov have already argued? What if, ideational meaning (Bakhtin's 'thematic content') is not the only meaning to be considered integral to the system of language? What if, the system of language is functionally organized as suggested by Halliday? And grammar is concerned with describing not only single (complex) sentences but with the description of utterance/text? What if the system of language is inherently variable? Through their brilliant analysis of why linguistics should not be construed the way it is, why the system of language with which we function could not be the way it is said to be in Saussurian linguistics, Bakhtin–Volosinov tantalizingly take us so far, but they abandon us at the end of their negative polemics. They do not provide any set of relations which would explain how speech process can intervene in the internalization of the living, variable, valuated system of language that they wish to attribute to the speakers' verbal consciousness. In fact Bakhtin (1986) is vehement that evaluation of linguistic phenomena cannot be ever explained by reference to language system. But he could be quite wrong; it can be argued that the textual and interpersonal metafunctions are part of the potential of language (Halliday 1973; 1977; Lemke 1992; Matthiessen 1992). Bakhtin–Volosinov do not tell us what a linguistics model needs to be like in order to account for the conception of language as implied by their views; instead they simply denounce that same system whose fictitious nature calls for its rejection. Language use and language system as needed to support their conception of language use are thus not *anchored* together in their theory. How, then, should we interpret the claim that 'behind each text stands a language system' (Bakhtin 1986, 105), except as a trivialization of the notion of system as potential.

One of the most valuable contributions made by Bakhtin (1984; 1986) to our understanding of the speech process is via the constellation of notions that revolve around his conception of *understanding* as an integral element of the speech process. Bakhtin rejected 'fictions' such as that of a speaker who actively produces speech and the listener who passively understands it. To him understanding and responding are two aspects of the same activity: 'understanding is inherently responsive' (1986, 68); the responsiveness may be manifested in different ways, one of these being responsive speaking. But if one possible form of responding is speaking then this is tantamount to claiming that responsive speaking should be treated as the active form of understanding. This is a critical conclusion for it implies that the boundary between understanding and speaking is tenuous – the two could be seen as symbiotic:

> all real integral understanding is actively responsive, and constitutes nothing other than the initial preparatory stage of a response (in whatever form it may be

actualized). And the speaker himself is oriented toward such an actively responsive understanding ... any speaker is a respondent to a greater or lesser degree. He is not after all the first speaker, the one who disturbs the eternal silence of the universe. (Bakhtin 1986, 69)

To speak is to be located socio-historically by virtue of your participation in all those speech processes in which you have ever engaged. We can already begin to see the genesis of the notion of *intertextuality* in these claims. If an utterance is a response to some utterance(s) and if all saying has some generic identity or other, then it follows that each saying is intertextually related to (some) sayings (at least) in that genre within that area of social existence. 'The speaker is not the biblical Adam' (Bakhtin 1986, 93). This is true not only with respect to generically differentiated vocabulary, but with respect to the entire speech process (Bakhtin 1986, 91).

> Any concrete utterance is a link in the chain of speech communion of a particular sphere ... Utterances are not indifferent to one another, and are not self-sufficient; they are aware of and mutually reflect one another ... Each utterance is filled with echoes and reverberations of other utterances to which it is related by the communality of the sphere of speech communion ... Our thought itself – philosophical, scientific, and artistic – is born and shaped in the process of interaction and struggle with others' thought, and this cannot but be reflected in the forms that verbally express our thought as well.

Virtually the same sentiments are voiced by Volosinov (1983, 72):

> 'Any utterance – the finished, written utterance not excepted – makes a response to something and is calculated to be responded to in turn. It is but one link in a continuous chain of speech performances. Each monument carries on the work of its predecessors, polemicising with them, expecting active, responsive understanding in return. Each monument in actuality is an integral part of science, literature or political life. The monument, as any other monological utterance is set toward being perceived in the context of current scientific life or current literary affairs, i.e., it is perceived in the generative process of that particular ideological domain of which it is an integral part.'

These ideas are potentially relevant to the problems I have identified in Vygotsky's framework. Can they be employed for explaining the existence of variant forms of semiotic mediation which may be said to underly the genesis of variant forms of mental functions, variant forms of consciousness? It is at this point that we need to turn to Bakhtin's ideas about social language and the ideological basis of communication. To quote two extracts from Volosinov:

> Signs can arise only on *interindividual territory*. It is territory that cannot be called 'natural' ... signs do not arise between any two members of the species *Homo sapiens*. It is essential that the two individuals be organized socially, that they compose a group (a social unit); only then can the medium of sign take shape between them. (1983, 12)

The only possible objective definition of consciousness is a sociological one. Consciousness cannot be derived directly from nature ... ideology cannot be derived from consciousness. Consciousness takes shape and being in the material of signs created by an organized group in the process of its social intercourse. The individual consciousness is nurtured on signs; it derives its growth from them; it reflects their logic and laws. The logic of consciousness is the logic of ideological communication, of the semiotic interaction of a social group. (1983, 13)

It is here that Bakhtin–Volosinov and Vygotsky–Luria most closely share a common ground; and it is in the idea that members of different social groups might experience different forms of verbal interaction that the heterogeneity of semiotically mediated consciousness could find a 'rational' explanation. Language seen socially is discourse specific to a particular stratum in society, defined by some social attribute such as class, profession, race, gender, age. At any one point in the history of a community, there might exist many such 'social languages'. This amounts to saying that the natural experience of language is in the form of specific dialects, specific registers/genres, and specific codes displaying distinct semantic orientation. Moreover members belonging to distinct social groups experience a different subset of these varieties, and this experience actively shapes their own verbal consciousness, their own ways of saying and meaning. It is these habitual fashions of speaking – and coding orientations to meanings – that mediate specific forms of human consciousness. The three elements of such an argument are summed up by Volosinov (1983, 21):

1: ideology may not be divorced from the material reality of sign ... ;
2: the sign may not be divorced from the concrete forms of social intercourse ... ;
3: communication and the forms of communication may not be divorced from the material basis.

What we need now to give substance to these claims about linguistic varieties, about differing experience of intertextuality, about ideologically constituted limits on speaking and understanding, is a theory that will specify why human communities stratify, why subgroups are created, how members are 'recruited' in a subgroup, why they tend to stay there despite the fact that 'objectively' speaking membership in a subgroup might not be advantageous, and why or how these social relations might ever change. As before behind the fascinating and perspicacious analyses of language phenomena offered by Bakhtin–Volosinov, we will not find the kind of theoretical precision which would assist in an empirical enquiry of the kind that is needed.

The socio-semiotically constituted human consciousness, the socio-historical nature of verbal semiosis, the heterogeneity of voices, the centrality of utterance as the unit of social interaction, the recognition of the centrality of social situation and milieu – these elements are indeed potentially important in the clarification of some of the problematic themes found in Vygotsky–Luria. If my reading is correct then it does seem rather improbable that this potential of the Bakhtin–Volosinov framework could be fully actualized. This is because its concepts and relations lack the kind of precision that is needed for a definitive study of the problems: the principles along which the Bakhtinian explanations might proceed are clear; what is not clear is the nature of the very constructs which are to be used in the explanation.

I should add, before leaving this debate, that my reading is partial and derivative; it is limited by my own inability to experience directly the literature relevant to the Bakhtin–Volosinov positions. But even so, perhaps one could justifiably place some of the responsibility with Bakhtin, who himself commented that:

> in my work there is also considerable incompletion, incompletion not of thought but of its expression ... My penchant for variation and a plurality of terms to name the same phenomenon. The multiplicity of perspectives. The convergence with the distant without any indication of the intermediate links. (quoted in Todorov 1984, xii)

Mind, society and language: foundational issues

My critique of Vygotsky and Bakthin is actuated by an interest in a positive outcome. I am not so much concerned with what was lacking in Vygotsky and/or Bakhtin's frameworks simply to record the negative fact of some lack in their theory. My approach has been to accept most of the theoretical and pre-theoretical statements made by these two great scholars, while at the same time trying to understand how the questions raised by these 'incompletions' in their accounts can be answered, and what would these answers imply with regard to the foundations of a linguistic model. I can hardly do better than repeat Bernstein (1990, 168), with apologies for introducing minor changes to his comments made in a similar but different context:

> my criticisms should not be read as acts of dismissal. The criticisms should not be considered as part of a methodology of disposal; a field procedure for the displacement of theories of others. The concern here was to show what such theories and approaches presuppose, and, perhaps, inadvertently, what cannot be addressed as a consequence of the form the theories take.

In this final section of the paper, I turn to the questions posed by the Vygotskian approach. I will try to outline what is implied for a linguistic theory in any attempt to provide viable answers. Let me begin, then, by stating clearly three assumptions, which are based on the acceptance of Vygotsky's arguments and of Luria's findings in Uzbekistan:

Assumption 1:
    The socio-genesis of higher mental functions entails semiotic mediation using language as the mediational means;

Assumption 2:
> within the same speech community, variant forms of higher mental functioning exist all of which are socio-genetically produced;

Assumption 3:
> it follows from 1 and 2 that in every speech community, there must exist variant forms of semiotic mediation using language as the mediational means.

These assumptions carry certain implications attention to which has already been drawn in the course of the discussions in the third and fourth sections; but it may be useful briefly to summarize them here once again.

(1) Since all sociogenetically produced higher mental functions are semiotically mediated by language, whatever language attributes are cited as important to semiotic mediation of any kind whatever, must refer to properties such that the system of language is capable of 'supporting them'. This includes the potential of language to refer to phenomena not present to the senses in the here and now of speech; it includes the inherent efficacy of language in the classification of phenomena, in the definition of experience, in concept formation, in enabling metalinguistic reflection, and so on. The potential for being used in these ways inheres in all human languages, irrespective of whether and/or how habitually which of these potentials might be deployed. Human languages are not 'primitive' in the sense of not being capable of being used for some purpose or other. It follows that in a viable linguistic theory language must be viewed as an inexhaustible resource, such that the system of language itself is infinite, while the texts already instantiated by it are finite (Halliday 1992).

(2) The notion 'semiotic mediation' properly understood is 'participation in language use'. Since language use is a socio-historically situated (convergent or divergent) instantiation of (some features of) the system of language, any account of semiotic mediation must involve an analysis of language as code and language as behaviour in social contexts (Halliday 1984). To be able to describe the details of semiotic mediation, the linguistic theory must postulate three orders of abstraction: language system, language use, and the social context; this in turn means that such a theory must provide a coherent set of relations between these orders of abstraction. Notions such as those of genre, intertextuality, ideological basis of communication pertain to the general theory of semiotic mediation as such, in that no accounting of any form of semiotic mediation is at all possible without these postulates.

(3) Semiotic mediation as conceptualized above makes meaning the most central concept of linguistics. By definition these meanings are *linguistic* meanings, and they are not limited to word meaning; the meaning or language in use is not a sum of the meanings of individual words, phrases, and sentences. A viable theory of linguistics will need to explain how participants construe the meanings of their own interaction when using language; whether these meanings are related in any way to the social context which includes the participants' experience of interaction; whether

the forms – the lexicogrammar – of a language is related to the meanings being construed. It will be seen that a theory which attempts to explain the activation, construal, and ongoing interpretation of meaning in language use will need to recognize the Whorfian notion of cryptogrammar as central to the description of linguistic form.

Let me reiterate also the three basic questions posed by the existence of variant forms of semiotic mediation below:

Question 1:
How can the fact be explained that within 'the same' wider community there exist variant forms of human consciousness and of semiotic mediation?

Question 2:
What does a linguistic theory need in order to describe those linguistic features which distinguish the variant forms of semiotic mediation, one from another?

Question 3:
What is the basis for assigning some value to some particular form of semiotic mediation and its corresponding human consciousness?

To take the first question first, the explanation for the existence of variant forms of semiotic mediation cannot really be given in terms of Bakhtin's notion of linguistic heterogeneity: the recognition of heterogeneity is simply another way of saying that the possibility of the existence of variant forms of semiotic mediation exists. What is needed is an explanation for the genesis of heterogeneity, the presence of distinct 'voices', different fashions of speaking. Following Marx's lead Bernstein (1971; 1982; 1987; 1990) explains the existence of distinct forms of semiotic mediation by relating them to the material conditions of social existence, which act on human action and relation, thus affecting and being affected by the forms of consciousness. Bernstein's explanatory base is more specific than the 'large' expression 'socio-cultural history', but appears to add substance both to Volosinov's maxim (1983, 21) that 'communication and forms of communication may not be divorced from the material basis' as well as to Marx's claim that:

> In the social production of their life men enter into definite relations that are independent of their will .... The sum total of these relations of production constitutes the economic structure of the society... to which correspond different forms of consciousness. The mode of production of material life conditions the social, political, and intellectual life processes in general. It is not the consciousness of men that determines their being, but on the contrary, their

social being that determines their consciousness. (quoted in McLellan 1975, 40)

These relations of production which constitute the economic structure of the society, translate themselves into the relations of power and control via practices of division of labour in society, thus entering into everyday human life as differential privilege of access to social processes and different structures of human relation. Bernstein suggests a relation between material basis and orientation to meaning – i.e., coding orientation (Bernstein 1982, 310): the more specific and local the relation between an agent and the material base, the more direct the relation between meanings and [this] specific material base; what appears relevant is itself local relations. Conversely, the less specific and local the relation between the agent and the material base, the less direct the relation between the meanings and the specific material base. The experience of languaging in the former segment of the community is critically different from that in the latter. On the basis of their social positioning, infants are 'recruited' as apprentices to 'different spheres of human social existence' each of which stands in some specific relation to the distribution of power and control: to the extent that their material base is different in the ways specified above, to that extent their experiences of discourse are diverse, and variant forms of consciousness are created (Bernstein 1971, 144):

> the particular forms of social relation act selectively upon what is said, when it is said, and how it is said ... [they] can generate very different speech systems or codes ... [which] create for their speakers different orders of relevance and relation. The experience of the speaker may then be transformed by what is made significant or relevant by different speech systems. As the child ... learns specific speech codes which regulate his verbal acts, he learns the requirements of his social structure. The experience of the child is transformed by the learning generated by his own, apparently, voluntary acts of speech.... From this point of view, every time the child speaks or listens, the social structure is reinforced in him and his social identity shaped. The social structure becomes the child's psychological reality through the shapings of his acts of speech.

It seems obvious that Bernstein's explanations would apply to the results of Luria's research in Uzbekistan. There is a crucial difference between Bernstein's account of semiotic mediation and that which one finds in Vygotsky or Bakhtin. In Vygotsky's account it seems as if all that is needed for the genesis of a particular form of higher mental functioning is 'contact' with a particular fashion of speaking, a specific kind of language use. With Bakhtin the ever-enlarging circle of intertextuality implies almost unlimited access to any voice; it is not clear at what point, why, and how the material basis and the forms of communication constrain this pervasive intertextuality. By relating the distribution of power and control to the regulation of social interaction and personal experience, Bernstein's approach is able to provide answers to these questions. The specific relations he has postulated can begin to explain why different sections of the wider community might have different patterns of engagement in social processes, why there would be different orders of relevance, different interpersonal relations. Moreover through his theory of socialization – which is in fact a theory of how different forms of consciousness are produced – Bernstein is able to explain why pedagogic discourse is one thing for one set of learners and another for another set. The concepts of 'official' and 'local pedagogy' (Bernstein 1990, 179ff.) become a means for showing how 'social milieu' enters into 'immediate social situations', and vice versa. Both Vygotsky and Bakhtin need a theory of societal organization – a framework that explains why human activities take this form here, and another form there, why access to human activities is not universal in any community, and how in the creation of consciousness both the socialized and the socializing parties make an active contribution.

How are these facts relevant to a linguistic theory? Consider the earlier claim that a viable theory will need to bring social context, language use and language system in relation. A sophisticated sociological theory will provide a 'good' account of those aspects of societal organization by reference to which it can be surmised who will engage in what sort of social activities, what would be the quality of their interpersonal relations, their access to means of semiotic management. It would identify viable principle(s) to account for significant variation in social action, by relating this variation to variables with fundamental function in the management of the community's life. Such a theory will clearly tell us about those elements which are indispensable in conceptualizing the relation between the wider context of culture and the more immediate context of situation. Judgements about relevance are judgements about meaning. If social contexts act on speakers' ideas about what is relevant, then they also act on what is meaningful. The need to explicate the relation of context to meaning, and of meaning to wording is further reinforced as a desirable goal of any linguistic theory that would aspire to describe semiotic mediation. Moreover, if as Bakhtin–Volosinov imply the system of language is always 'becoming', always being 'renewed', there can be only one source of this renewal – and that is in language use. From this point of view, whatever impinges upon language use, whatever functions as an active principle in explaining the character of language use needs to be incorporated in the larger design of the linguistic theory, for it is only then that it can be coherently brought in relation with the system of language. If the notion of context is important to linguistics, linguistics needs to understand the sociological basis of both who recognizes what as a context and who engages in which contexts.

Turn now to the second question. If semiotic mediation is centrally concerned with meaning, it seems very probable that the characterization of variant forms of semiotic mediation will be semantic in character. But this use of the term 'semantic' is very far from what passes as semantics in linguistics in general. Traditionally, in linguistics the conception of meaning is limited; all meaning is just 'cognitive', 'referential', or 'experiential'. Semiotic mediation takes the form of text in context; therefore the notion of semantics has to be rich enough in linguistics to be able to account for 'text-ness', for how meanings and wordings realize the generic identity of some communication. By the same token, a linguistic theory must be able to account for the interpersonal meanings construed in a verbal interaction. The limited notions of meaning which linguistic models have seen it fit to operate with, break down each time they confront the reality of human communication as it occurs in social contexts. This is not because by some inevitable *fiat* linguistics is concerned with language system and language system cannot be used for explaining any of these phenomena as Bakhtin–Volosinov imply. It is only because the ideas about language and about linguistics propagated by formalist models are inadequate. They need revision. And this revision would require a recognition of language as a resource for meaning – for construing our experience, for enabling the construal of complex relations, for expressing interpersonal meanings and for enabling meanings that will construe coherence, both within the communication and between that communication and its social context (Halliday 1985; Halliday and Hasan 1989; Martin 1991; Hasan 1995). Where language is seen as a resource, the theory can represent the form of a verbal interaction as choice of meaning in social context, thus being able to account for variation as well as similarities between texts and contexts.

Finally, to turn to the last question, which has the least direct relevance to the theory of linguistics: what is the basis for assigning value to forms of semiotic mediation: why are some forms of human consciousness considered more desirable, others not? This issue relates very closely to the genesis of variation in semiotic mediation. One possibility is to limit the scope of the reference of the expression 'semiotic mediation', so that it refers only to that kind of language use which is instrumental in the creation, transmission, internalization of scientific concepts, of mathematical operations, of decontextualized reflection – in short only to what Vygotsky–Luria typically presented as instances of higher mental functioning. This will pose certain problems. For example, the boundary between scientific and everyday concepts is not crystal clear; and Vygotsky certainly accepts this. Moreover, if this is how semiotic mediation is to be understood, then a simpler equivalent for that kind of use of language is 'official pedagogic discourse' (Bernstein 1990) or 'instructional registers'. There are however communities, where at least some members have never experienced such discourse. It would therefore be necessary to dissociate the notion of semiotic mediation from the genesis of human consciousness, for obvious reasons. This makes the theory far less powerful, leaving the role of language in the construction of everyday experience completely undescribed. It also creates another serious problem: is semiotic mediation to be referred to as semiotic mediation only if it is successful in producing this specific sort of consciousness? or is it simply a label applied to language with certain semantic properties? If the former, then semiotic mediation in the sense of official pedagogic discourse would be semiotic mediation for some but not for others (Bernstein 1971; 1990). If it is the latter, then it has acquired a rather static character, and it would not necessarily enter into the discourse of the sociogenesis of higher mental functions. These are serious problems. And it has seemed to me nearer Vygotsky's usage to think of semiotic mediation as 'learning through the mediational means of language in use', without making the nature of that which is learned criterial to the definition of the term.

But this solution brings us back to the problem of valuation, for valuation of variant forms of consciousness, and hence of semiotic mediation, does exist. I suggest that essentially the valuation of the variant forms of human consciousness is irrational. I agree with Marx when he says that 'ideas of the ruling class are, in every age, the ruling ideas' (quoted in Bottomore and Rubel 1976, 93); and the ways of meaning and saying (the form of human consciousness) we consider desirable are those that belong to the power group, whoever they may be and whatever their source of power. However, the valuation is *rationalized* by appeal to our ideas about what counts as human evolution, what is construed as human progress. Those ways of meaning and saying which appear to contribute to 'control over environment', to the subjugation of resources for our own use and benefit, thus knowledge which enables such control – these things are said to lead directly to human progress. This is to forget two things: one, that as Whorf once said 'we do not know that civilization is synonymous with rationality' (Whorf 1956, 81): it is possible that there are other measures of progress than those cherished in the dominant Western ideology; second, even if this view is accepted, it must be recognized that everywhere the actual utilization of such knowledge so as to lead to the actual control of the environment, so as to subjugate the resources depends upon labour of the kind where the agent's relation to the material base is highly localized. Given the organization of our societies, this segment is as essential for progess as those who display the more valued forms of higher mental functioning. The valuation of the variant forms of human consciousness is thus quite invidious, especially in societies such as ours whose economic structure depends upon stratification.

Before closing this paper, it should be added that Vygotsky's approach to the development of human mental functioning presents a paradigm that linguistics might well learn from. Like the elementary mental functions, it is likely that the elementary forms of human semiosis have a biogenetic foundation. The early pre-symbolic and earliest protolanguage (Trevarthen 1979; Halliday 1975; Shotter 1978; Newson 1978) might be regarded as forms of human semiosis which develop along the natural line. The complex structures of the adult language are laid on this foundation, but the emergence and evolution of human language as we know it, is inconceivable without sociogenesis. And sociogenesis takes us to the social, which is itself construed through semiosis. Herein we have in a nutshell the complexity of linguistics: Theories of language have to strive to explore this challenge.

References

Bakhtin, M. (1984) *Problems of Dostoevsky's Poetics*, trans. by Caryl Emerson (ed.). Manchester University Press.
Bakhtin, M. (1986) *Speech Genres and Other Late Essays*, Caryl Emerson and Michael Holquist (eds). Austin: University of Texas Press.
Bernstein, B. B. (1971) *Class, Codes, and Control*, Vol. I: *Theoretical Studies Towards a Sociology of Language*. London: Routledge & Kegan Paul.
Bernstein, B. B. (1982) 'Codes, modalities, and the process of cultural reproduction'. In *Cultural and Economic Reproduction in Education: Essays on Class, Ideology and the State*, Michael W. Apple (ed.). London: Routledge & Kegan Paul.
Bernstein, B. B. (1987) 'Elaborated and restricted codes: An overview 1958–85'. In *Socio-linguistics: An International Handbook of the Science*, Vol. I, Ulrich Ammon, Norbert Dittmar and Klaus J. Mattheier (eds). Berlin: de Gruyter.
Bernstein, B. B. (1990) *Class, Codes and Control. The Structuring of Pedagogic Discourse*, Vol. IV: London: Routledge & Kegan Paul.
Bottomore, T. B. and Rubel, M. (eds) (1976) *Karl Marx: On Sociology and Social Philosophy*. Harmondsworth: Penguin.
Butt, David G. (1989a) 'The object of language'. In *Language Development: Learning Language, Learning Culture. Meaning and Choice in Language: Studies for Michael Halliday*, Ruqaiya Hasan and J. R. Martin (eds). Norwood: Ablex.
Butt, David G. (1989b) *Talking and Thinking: The Patterns of Behaviour*. Oxford: Oxford University Press.
Cook, Guy, (1990) 'Transcribing infinity: problems of context presentation'. *Journal of Pragmatics*, 14, 1–24.
Dumont, Robert V. Jr (1972) 'Learning English and how to be silent: studies in Sioux and Cherokee classrooms'. In *Functions of Language in the Classroom*, Courtney B. Cazden, Vera P. John and Dell Hymes (eds). New York: Teachers College Press.
Firth, J. R. (1957a) 'Personality and language in society'. In *Papers in General Linguistics 1934–1951*. London: Oxford University Press.
Firth, J. R. (1957b) 'Ethnographic analysis and language with reference to Malinowski's views'. In *Man and Culture: An Evaluation of the Work of Bronislaw Malinowski*, Raymond Firth (ed.). London: Routledge & Kegan Paul.
Gregory, Michael (1988) 'Generic situation and register: a functional view of communication'. In *Linguistics in a Systemic Perspective*, James D. Benson, Michael J. Cummings and William S. Greaves (eds). Amsterdam: Benjamins.
Halliday, M. A. K. (1973) *Explorations in the Functions of Language*. London: Edward Arnold.
Halliday, M. A. K. (1974) *Language and Social Man*, Schools Council Programme in Linguistics and Language Teaching: Papers Series II, Vol 3. London: Longman.
Halliday, M. A. K. (1975) *Learning How to Mean: Explorations in the Development of Language*. London: Edward Arnold.
Halliday, M. A. K. (1977) 'Text as semantic choice in social context'. In *Grammar and Descriptions*, Teun A. van Dijk and Janos S. Petofi (eds). Berlin: de Gruyter.
Halliday, M. A. K. (1984) 'Language as code and language as behaviour: a systemic functional interpretation of the nature and ontogenesis of dialogue'. In *The Semiotics of Culture and Language*, Vol. I, Robin P. Fawcett, M. A. K. Halliday, Sydney M. Lamb and Adam Makkai (eds). London: Pinter.

Halliday, M. A. K. (1985) *Introduction to Functional Grammar*. London: Edward Arnold.
Halliday, M. A. K. (1992) 'How do you mean?'. In *Advances in Systemic Linguistics: Recent Theory and Practice*, Martin Davies and Louise Ravelli (eds). London: Pinter.
Halliday, M. A. K. and Hasan, Ruqaiya (1989) *Language, Context and Text: Aspects of Language in a Social-Semiotic Perspective*. Oxford: Oxford University Press.
Hasan, Ruqaiya (1978) 'Text in the systemic functional model'. In *Current Trends in Textlinguistics*, W. U. Dressler (ed.). Berlin: de Gruyter.
Hasan, Ruqaiya (1984) 'The nursery tale as a genre', *Nottingham Linguistic Circular*, 13, 71–102. (Chapter 3 of this book).
Hasan, Ruqaiya (1986) 'The ontogenesis of ideology: an interpretation of mother–child talk'. In *Semiotics, Ideology, Language*, Terry Threadgold, Elizabeth Grosz, Gunther Kress and M. A. K. Halliday (eds). Sydney: Sydney Association for Studies in Society and Culture. (Chapter 6 of this book).
Hasan, Ruqaiya (1989) 'Semantic variation and sociolinguistics', *Australian Journal of Linguistics*, 9, 221–276.
Hasan, Ruqaiya (1991) 'Questions as a mode of learning in everyday talk'. In *Language Education: Interaction and Development*, Theo Le and Mike McCausland (eds). Launceston: University of Tasmania, pp. 70–119.
Hasan, Ruqaiya (1992a) 'Rationality in everyday talk: from process to system'. In *Directions in Corpus Linguistics: Proceedings of Nobel Symposium 82, Stockholm, 4–8 August 1991*, Jan Svartvik (ed.). Berlin: de Gruyter.
Hasan, Ruqaiya (1992b) 'Meaning in sociolinguistic theory'. In *Sociolinguistics Today: International Perspectives*, Kingsley Bolton and Helen Kwok (eds). London: Routledge.
Hasan, Ruqaiya (1993) 'Contexts for meaning'. In *Georgetown University Round Table on Language and Linguistics 1992: Language, Communication, and Social Meaning*, James E. Alatis (ed.). Washington, DC: Georgetown University Press.
Hasan, Ruqaiya (1995) 'The conception of context in text'. In *Discourse in Society: Systemic Functional Perspectives*, Peter H. Fries and M. Gregory (eds). Norwood: Ablex.
Hasan, Ruqaiya and Cloran, Carmel (1990) 'A sociolinguistic interpretation of everyday talk between mothers and children'. In *Learning, Keeping and Using Language*, Vol. I: *Selected Papers From the 8th World Congress of Applied Linguistics, Sydney, 16–21 August 1987*, M. A. K. Halliday, John Gibbon and Howard Nicholas (eds). Amsterdam: Benjamins, pp. 67–100.
Hickman, Maya (ed.) (1987) *Social and Functional Approaches to Language and Thought*. New York: Academic Press.
John, Vera P. (1972) 'Styles of learning – styles of teaching: reflections on the education of Navajo children'. In *Functions of Language in the Classroom*, Courtney B. Cazden, Vera P. John and Dell Hymes (eds). New York: Teachers College Press.
Lee, Benjamin (1987) 'Recontextualizing Vygotsky'. In *Social and Functional Approaches to Language and Thought*, Maya Hickman (ed.). New York: Academic Press.
Lemke, J. L. (1992) 'Interpersonal meaning in discourse: value orientation'. In *Advances in Systemic Linguistics: Recent Theory and Practice*, Martin Davies and Louise Ravelli (eds). London: Pinter.

Luria, A. R. (1976) *Cognitive Development: Its Cultural and Social Foundations*, Martin Lopez-Morillas and Lynn Solotaroff (trans.), Michael Cole (ed.). Cambridge, Mass: Harvard University Press.

McLellan, David (1975) *Marx*. Glasgow: Fontana/Collins.

Malinowski, B. (1923) 'The problem of meaning in primitive languages', Supplement 1 in *The Meaning of Meaning*, C. K. Ogden and I. A. Richards (eds). London: Kegan Paul Trench, Trubner.

Malinowski, B. (1935) 'An ethnographic theory of language. Part IV', *Coral Gardens and Their Magic*, Vol. II. London: Allen & Unwin.

Markova, Ivana (1990) 'Introduction', *The Dynamics of Dialogue*, Ivana Markova and Klaus Foppa (eds). New York: Harvester.

Martin, J. R. (1985) 'Process and text: two aspects of human semiosis'. In *Systemic Perspectives on Discourse*, Vol. I, James D. Benson and William S. Greaves (eds). Norwood: Ablex.

Martin, J. R. M. (1991) 'Intrinsic functionality: implications for contextual theory,' *Social Semiotics*, 1, 99–162.

Martin, J. R. (1992) *English Text: System and Structure*. Amsterdam: Benjamins.

Matthiessen, Christian (1992) 'Interpreting the textual metafunction'. In *Advances in Systemic Linguistics: Recent Theory and Practice*, Martin Davies and Louise Ravelli (eds) London: Pinter.

Matthiessen, Christian (1995) *Lexicogrammatical Cartography: English Systems*, (mimeo) Department of Linguistics, Sydney University, NSW 2006.

Mertz, Elizabeth and Parmentier, Richard A. (eds) (1985) *Semiotic Mediation: Sociocultural and Psychological Perspectives*. New York: Academic Press.

Newson, J. (1978) 'Dialogue and development'. In *Action, Gesture and Symbol: The Emergence of Language*, A. Lock (ed.). New York: Academic Press.

Painter, Clare (1984) *Into the Mother Tongue: A Case Study in Early Language Development*. London: Pinter.

Phillips, Susan U. (1972) 'Participant structures and communicative competence: Warm Springs children in community and classroom'. In *Functions of Language in the Classroom*, Courtney B. Cazden, Vera P. John and Dell Hymes (eds). New York: Teachers College Press.

Shotter, J. (1978) 'The cultural context of communication studies: theoretical and methodological issues'. In *Action, Gesture and Symbol: The Emergence of Language*, A. Lock (ed.). New York: Academic Press.

Todorov, Tzvetan (1984) *Mikhail Bakhtin: The Dialogical Principle*, Wlad Godzich (trans.). Manchester: Manchester University Press.

Trevarthen, Colwyn (1979) 'Communication and cooperation in early infancy: a description of primary intersubjectivity'. In *Before Speech: The Beginning of Interpersonal Communication*, Margaret Bullowa (ed.). London: Cambridge University Press.

Ventola, Eija (1984) 'The dynamics of genre'. *Nottingham Linguistic Circular*, 13, 103–124.

Ventola, Eija (1987) *The Structure of Social Interaction*. London: Pinter.

Volosinov, N. V. (1983) *Marxism and the Philosophy of Language*, Ladislav Matejka and I. R. Titunik (trans.). Cambridge, Mass.: Harvard University Press.

Vygotsky, L. S. (1962) *Thought and Language*, Eugenia Hanfmann and Gertrude Vakar (trans. and eds). Cambridge, Mass.: MIT Press.

Vygotsky, L. S. (1978) *Mind in Society: The Development of Higher Psychological Processes*, Michael Cole, Vera John-Steiner, Sylvia Scribner and Ellen Souberman (eds). Cambridge, Mass.: Harvard University Press.

Vygotsky, L. S. (1981) 'The genesis of higher mental functions'. In *The Concept of Activity in Soviet Psychology*, James V. Wertsch (ed.). Armonk: M. E. Sharp.

Wertsch, James V. (ed.) (1981) *The Concept of Activity in Soviet Psychology*. Armonk: M. E. Sharpe.

Wertsch, James V. (ed.) (1985a) *Culture, Communication, and Cognition: Vygotskian Perspectives*. Cambridge: Cambridge University Press.

Wertsch, James V. (ed.) (1985b) *Vygotsky and the Social Formation of Mind.* Cambridge, Mass.: Harvard University Press.

Wertsch, James V. (ed.) (1985c) 'The semiotic mediation of mental life: L. S. Vygotsky and M. M. Bakhtin'. In *Semiotic Mediation: Sociocultural and Psychological Perspectives*, Elizabeth Mertz and Richard A. Parmentier (eds). New York: Academic press.

Wertsch, James V. (ed.) (1990) 'Dialogue and dialogism in a socio-cultural approach to mind'. In *The Dynamics of Dialogue*, Ivana Markova and Klaus Foppa (eds). New York: Harvester.

Wertsch, James V. and Hickman, Maya (1987) 'Problem solving in social interaction: a microgenetic analysis'. In *Social and Functional Approaches to Language and Thought*, Maya Hickman (ed.). New York: Academic Press.

Whorf, Benjamin Lee (1956) *Language, Thought and Reality: Selected Writings*, John B. Carroll (ed.). Cambridge, Mass.: MIT Press.

8 Ways of saying: ways of meaning

1 Culture and semiotic styles

1.1 Introductory remarks

Genuine dichotomies are probably rare; upon closer examination most turn out to be the by-product of some particular point of view.[1] For example, take the persistent dichotomy between the how and the what, the manner and the matter, the style and the content. When we say that **John can't swim** and its elliptical parallel **John can't** are two ways of saying the same thing, we subscribe to just such a dichotomy. The acceptance of such a view implies that meanings are immanent, with an existence independent of the expressive symbolic system, and that some kinds of meaning are matter whereas others are not. These beliefs are clearly the by-product of a particular view of human language; the opposite view underlies the belief that all kinds of meaning are matter, and that far from being immanent, meanings are the function of the relations that hold between the symbols of an expressive system. This polarization between the views is deliberate; I do not believe that the choice of one as against the other is determined by reality being thus and thus, but rather because a particular descriptive schema appeals to us as a convincing model of reality.

Having made this effort at impartiality, I wish to align myself quite definitely with the second view, in which the dichotomy between form and meaning is rejected. The text for this paper can be summed up in one sentence: different ways of saying are different ways of meaning – obviously not the same thing. How we say is indicative of how we mean. And a culture develops characteristic ways of meaning. These ways of meaning, in their totality, are specific to that culture; they constitute its *semiotic style*.

1.2 Semiotic and semantic styles

The term *semiotic style* covers not only characteristic ways of saying but also of being and behaving. I assume that these, taken together, exhaust the means by which humans can mean. To say that there is a culture-specific semiotic style is to say that there is a congruence, a parallelism between verbal and non-verbal behaviour, both of which are informed by the same set of beliefs, values and attitudes.

The assertion that specific cultures have specific semiotic styles is neither totally evident nor incontrovertible. However, if examination reveals that ways of saying, being and behaving do run largely parallel to each other in a community, then the claim is plausible that there exist some organizing principles which have the effect of producing this congruence, this parallelism. The presence of the principles is productive of a unique set of attributes which characterizes all aspects of human behaviour in the community. It is this unique set of attributes found in the ways of being, behaving and saying that defines the character of a community's semiotic style. I would suggest that the very organizing concepts which control the congruence of the semiotic style are also the ones which underly that community's world view – and there is a good reason for the suggestion.

It is widely accepted that the universe is not entirely given: humans have had to make sense of it – and in doing so, they may be said to have created it – at least in part. This universe is as much a construct of human imagination, as it is a brute, concrete reality outside of it. Here, too, there are potential irreconcilables which must be allowed coexistence without creating permanent chaos. The congruence of the semiotic style can be said to arise out of the need to construct a design for the living of human life so that aspects of it do not militate constantly against each other. Thus to understand the basis of this congruence in a particular culture is tantamount to understanding that culture, even if only partially.

Logically the notion of semiotic style subsumes that of *semantic style*; the latter can be succinctly described as the style of meaning verbally. A characteristic semantic style prevalent in a culture must logically be in keeping with that culture's prevalent semiotic style.

1.3 Culture consonance and culture conflict

The definition of the boundaries of a culture is problematic. In the first place, there is the well-recognized fact that no culture is a homogeneous, monolithic system any more than any language is. Secondly, the idea of congruence applied to culture as a whole can be misleading if one is left with the impression that congruence is synonymous with 'total lack of conflict in ideology and/or practice'. There is quite obviously an intricate relationship between these two points, but a detailed discussion of neither can be undertaken in this paper. It is, however, important to point out, first, that I believe the notion of culture to be variable in delicacy. Thus at a particular point in delicacy, we may be justified in maintaining that cultures (A) and (B) are distinct; this does not imply that at a point of greater delicacy we may not claim two distinct cultures (A1) and (A2) or (B1) and (B2). Equally, there may be environments in which the interest lies in a much more generalized comparison; if so, it would be valid to think of (A) and (B) as belonging to the same culture as opposed to (C) and (D). A recognition of the usefulness of shifting boundaries is found in such current terms, e.g. 'subculture' and 'culture-group'. It remains now to add that whatever is said here about 'culture' is applicable, *mutatis mutandis*, to 'subcultures' – and equally to distinguishable 'culture-groups'.

Turning to the question of conflict in culture, I do not believe that it could be thought of as a total rift or a complete divergence. The closest analogy that comes to mind in this respect is that of the linguistic relation of antonymy, which – as is well known – involves opposition between two terms. However, the assertion of opposition has significance only in an environment of a large degree of congruence. Thus the items **buy** and **sell** are opposites as are **long** and **short**, while it would be nonsense to make this claim with regard to **sell** and **throwaway** or **short** and **narrow**. It seems to me that conflict in culture – or between its subcultures – can be a meaningful concept only if the opposite of conflict, i.e. consonance or congruence, is also applicable to some other area(s) of the culture in focus.

Nor is there an insurmountable problem in relating the present view of semantic style with such a view of culture-with-conflict. Language is not a strait-jacket constraining its speakers into one invariable mould – indeed the notion of semantic style would be empty of significance in that case. The interest lies in the fact that while within the range of its systemic options each language provides a very wide set of resources for meaning, distinct subsets of its speakers characteristically select only a particular subset of the options permitted by the overall system. In comparing two languages we are thus concerned with two questions: one, how do the overall systems differ from each other; and secondly, what resources of the system are characteristically deployed by which section of the speakers. To talk about a characteristic semantic style is to imply the possibility of other semantic styles which are *not* characteristic. Style presupposes option; but the frequency of the selection of a particular set of options is itself a significant fact. It is this aspect that I particularly wish to explore in this paper.

1.4 *Semantic distance*

As cultures differ from each other in their characteristic semiotic styles, so do languages in their characteristic semantic styles. Fairly competent bilinguals often find themselves in a position so well described by Wittgenstein (1921) as: 'we cannot find our feet with them'. This is not because the sounds and the wordings are unfamiliar but more because the ways of meaning are not familiar – the manner in which the universe is made meaningful is not fully apprehended.

Semantic distance across languages is created by the differences in characteristic ways of meaning. This distance across two languages cannot be measured by counting lexical gaps or by examining the difference in the relative referential domains of individual lexical items, e.g. cup or camel. Rather it would be far more profitable to study the basis for the organization of meanings – as I understand Whorf to have suggested – than to ask if two languages have an equal number of words for colours, camels, or snow – as Whorf is often reported to have said (Bolinger 1968; Brown 1970; Lenneberg 1971; Leech 1974). What is relevant to the exploration of the semantic distance between two languages is an account of the principles which govern and systematize their meanings. Asking whether the English physical eye perceives the same colour distinctions as the Hopi eye would be totally beside the point, as Whorf would have been the first to point out. The stoneness of the stone and the cloud-ness of the cloud are both real and evident to human physical senses. However, this physical apprehension of the real and concrete does not bar the Indian from seeing the stone as divinity, or the Hopi from taking the cloud as animate. To me there seems to be no reason why the stone cannot be both that thing against which the toe may be stubbed painfully and that god which grants the wish of the heart. After all, 'seeing as' is no less real an experience than that of 'seeing'; and reality is neither stone nor god, but the concrete and the symbolic are definitely two major modes of reality. I certainly do not object to the fact that linguists pay attention to the unitary lexicogrammatical categories, or that they enquire into the literal referential relations; the point of my criticism is that they stop short of the goal, converting the means into the end of the enterprise and finishing with the atomistic examination which should have been no more than the bare start. Then, by some sleight of hand, the evidence regarding the concreteness of the stone is made to appear weightier and more decisive than the evidence regarding its symbolic status as divinity – as if what one should understand by the expression 'world view' is actual, physical viewing of concrete phenomena.

To develop the above themes, I shall examine two characteristic ways of saying; the *explicit* and the *implicit*, with particular emphasis on the latter. I shall try to show how a particular kind of implicit style is related to certain aspects of social structure, and how the latter affects the style of non-verbal behaviour, creating a congruence that extends over the entire semiotic domain. Using middle-class English and Urdu as comparable varieties of two distinct languages, I shall attempt to show how the semantic distance across these languages is in the last resort relatable to cultural differences between the two communities.

2 Implicit and explicit styles

2.1 Implicit and explicit ways of saying

The difference between explicit and implicit styles can be stated most conveniently in terms of what a normal person needs in order to interpret an utterance as it is intended by the speaker. Where explicit style is concerned, the correct interpretation of a message requires no more than a listener who has the average working knowledge of the language in question. When, however, the message is in the implicit style, its intended more precise meanings become available only if certain additional conditions are met; the average working knowledge of the language is necessary but not sufficient. Consider for example:

1. Dill will.

The fact of simply knowing English does not equip one to provide the correct more precise interpretation of (1). This does not mean that the English speaker will fail totally to understand (1) or regard it as a non-sentence; however, what could be understood by (1) as it stands in isolation is something highly general, such as perhaps: **dill will be implicated in some process**. The precise nature of this process and the other participants and/or circumstances attendant upon it – if there are any – cannot be known, unless some clue is provided by a source that lies outside of (1). If, for example, we know that the full textual context for the occurrence of (1) is:

1a. Phlox
   Won't grow on rocks.
   Dill
   Will.

We have no difficulty in arriving at the correct interpretations: **dill will grow on rocks**.

The two sentences of this 'poem' are examples of the two styles. While (1) exemplifies the implicit style of saying, the example below:

2. Phlox won't grow on rocks.

exemplifies the explicit style. The intended interpretation of (2) is available to a normal speaker without reference to any source of information extrinsic to the string itself. This, then, is the basic difference between the two styles: the explicit string is semantically self-sufficient; by contrast, the implicit string involves a semantic dependence. The precise meanings of the latter are not contained within itself but must be retrieved from some source extrinsic to the string.

2.2 Implicit devices

The distinction between implicit and explicit encoding is present most probably in all human languages. The construction of texts as we know them requires their presence side by side (Halliday and Hasan 1976; 1980; Hasan 1981). Still to refer to an entire string either as implicit or explicit could be inaccurate for the simple reason that it is seldom exclusively either the one or the other. Instead while some of the units in a string are implicit, others may be explicit. For example in (1), it is only the interpretation of the elliptical verbal group **will** that involves semantic dependence; the precise meaning of **dill** does not have to be retrieved from anywhere else any more than that of any of the units in (2).

From this point of view, implicitness in strings is variable, some being more implicit than others. The degree of implicitness, in this sense, is determined purely quantitatively, by comparing the proportion of the explicit units to the implicit ones. Compared with (1):

3. They will.

would be more implicit. In fact it is maximally so, since there is no unit in the string that is not implicit. The two ways of saying can be seen, then, as ranged upon a continuum, with the totally explicit and the totally implicit forming the two endpoints, each exemplified by (2) and (3) respectively, with (1) somewhere between the two.

An encoding unit which involves a semantic dependence for its precise interpretation will be referred to here as an *implicit device*. In the construction of texts such implicit devices play a major role because of the semantic links they establish with those segments by reference to which they may be interpreted. The implicit devices are, thus, a category of cohesive devices (Hasan 1981); however, the present paper is not concerned with the cohesive potential of these devices as such. The focus is largely upon how the interpretation of the implicit devices becomes available. For English these devices may be discussed under the familiar heading of *reference, substitution,* and *ellipsis* (Halliday and Hasan 1976; 1980; Hasan 1981).

2.3 The interpretation of implicit devices: endophora

Consider **dill will** again. The source of the interpretation of the elliptical verbal group **will** lies in the co-text, i.e. in a part of the accompanying text. When some part of the co-text forms the interpretative source for an implicit device, the interpretation is described as *endophoric*. **Will** in (1) is an implicit device, interpreted endophorically.

The interpretative source in the co-text may either precede the implicit device or follow it, as in (4) and (5), respectively:

4. Phlox won't grow on rocks. Dill will.

5. You won't believe it but they have accepted the entire scheme.

The interpretative source is underlined with broken lines; the implicit device itself with a solid line. When the source precedes the device, the interpretation is said to be *anaphoric*, as in (4) above. Where it follows the device, as in (5), the interpretation is said to be *cataphoric*.

2.4 The interpretation of implicit devices: exophora

The implicit device is not always textually interpreted; on occasions the source for its interpretation lies in the context, i.e. in the relevant situation in which the utterance is embedded. An example would be:

6. Don't!

called out to someone who is engaged in some activity that the speaker wishes to put an end to. When the interpretation depends upon the situationally provided clues, as it would in (6), then the interpretation may be said to be *exophoric*. **Don't** in (6) is an exophorically interpreted device; its intended precise meanings are situationally mediated.

In the following sections, I may refer to an implicit device as an anaphoric, a cataphoric, or an exophoric one. It is important, therefore, to state here quite clearly that the phoric status of the devices is not inherent; rather, it is determined from occurrence to occurrence of a device by reference to the location of the relevant interpretative source (Halliday and Hasan 1976; 1980). In itself, the implicit device **don't** is neither endophoric nor exophoric; its phoric status is variable. In (6) it is interpreted exophorically while in (7) the interpretation is endophoric:

7. Do elephants like Coca-Cola?

   No, they don't.

3 Endophoric and exophoric interpretation

3.1 Endophoric interpretation and implicit style

The endophoric device is interpreted by reference to some part of the cotext. Although co-text is variable in length, normal speakers have little or no difficulty in locating the interpretative source and in retrieving the intended meanings. This is because the intended meanings of the endophoric devices are not randomly sprinkled anywhere, anyhow in the text. The nature of the device itself often provides some specification of the nature of the interpretative source. This point can be demonstrated by a consideration of the implicit device **the**.

Speaking somewhat informally we may say that the function of **the** is to indicate definiteness for the (group of) thing(s) named by the noun that it modifies. But **the** is not the only device which renders its modified definite. What distinguishes **the** from other Modifiers is the fact that underlying it are only the following options: [specific:neutral].

So while the presence of **the** indicates definiteness for the modified Thing, the item **the** itself has to be considered implicit because information regarding parameters relevant to definiteness are not built into the meaning of **the** itself. They must be retrieved from some other source. However, crucial properties of the interpretative source can be clearly stated, showing that the retrieval of the intended meanings is as much 'system-governed' as other productive patterns of the language.

When **the** is cataphoric, the interpretative source forms part of the same nominal group in which the cataphoric **the** occurs; and its structural function is normally that of Qualifier as in:

8. At dinner Mihrene sat opposite the old gentleman who was Papa's business friend.

The clause **who was Papa's business friend** functions as a Qualifier in the nominal group **the old ..... business friend**; the more specific intended meaning is located within the Qualifier. The definiteness of the old man consisted in the fact that he was Papa's business friend. There are languages in the world, Urdu included, where this nominal group could be literally ordered as **Papa's business friend old gentleman**.

When **the** is anaphoric, a semantic link exists between the noun it modifies and the interpretative source which provides the parameter for definiteness. These semantic links may be those of synonymy or hyponymy or meronymy. Under synonymy, we may include reiteration and scatter as special cases. Each of these relations is exemplified below:

9. John's car was badly damaged. The rear left door was completely bashed in.
[aforementioned car's rear left door; modified door is a meronym of car.]
10. He bought pearls, each one separately, each one perfect. He bought fragments of mother-of-pearl. He bought moonstones.... He bought jade and crystals and collected chips of diamonds.... He kept the jewels first in a small cigarette box. [aforementioned types of jewels; modified jewels is superordinate to pearls, mother-of-pearl, jade, crystal, and diamonds.]
11. The wind blew, the hat flew, hither and thither, in loops and hoops and landed at last on the bald head of Benito Bedaglio, a penniless veteran. 'Don't shoot, I surrender', shouted the bewildered old soldier.
[aforementioned veteran; modified soldier is synonymous to veteran.]
12. She was wearing last year's dress and choker of false pearls.... Ephraim saw the false pearls and suffered.
[aforementioned pearls; modified pearls lexical reiteration.]
13. As you are aware, the Committee has recommended a cutback in research funds. We are gathered here today to protest against the recommendation.
[product of aforementioned act; modified recommendation related to recommend as lexical scatter.]

While the formal criteria for the recognition of the interpretative source from the co-text are clearly statable – as demonstrated above – there is no reason to suggest that the normal listener is aware of a search for such bits of the co-text. Subjectively the entire processing of meaning appears to be a simple act, performed painlessly in one single step. On hearing **Phlox won't grow on rocks. Dill will.**, normal users of English know how the elliptical verbal group **will** needs to be interpreted by the time they come to the item; they are not conscious of engaging in a search for its precise meaning.

In understanding the complexity of the process of interpretation, the linguist must consciously analyse many meaning relations; it is such conscious analyses which form the basis of viable hypotheses about the location and nature of the interpretative source in the co-text. The linguist's findings have to be phrased in terms of the formal attributes of the implicit device and/or the interpretative source; but so far as the normal speaker is concerned, the operation is simply one of establishing correct relevances – that is, of being able to understand. This is demanding no more than that speakers know their language; for knowing a language is, in Halliday's excellent phrase, only 'knowing how to mean' (Halliday 1975).

It follows from the above observations that so far as access to the more precise, intended meanings of the endophoric devices is concerned, there is no significant difference between the implicit devices and the explicit ones. While the correct interpretation of the explicit devices demands a working knowledge of the language, that of an endophoric device demands not only such knowledge but also the presence of the relevant part of the co-text. If both these conditions obtain, the normal speaker may not even be aware of the occurrence of such implicit devices. Not many of my readers will have taken a special note of **both these** and **such** in the previous sentence; but they will become aware of a qualitative difference between these items and others, e.g. **aware**, **occurrence**, if the sentence preceding the last one is not made available.

3.2 Exophoric interpretation and implicit style

It is not possible to make the same claims about the interpretation of the exophoric implicit devices. Here, the intended more precise meanings are mediated through the relevant extra-linguistic situation. This implies that the most natural environment for the use of exophoric devices is in face-to-face interaction, where the channel of discourse is spoken and visual contact between the speakers is present.

However, situation is a large word and covers different types of factors. If the interpretation of the exophoric device depends upon the situational factors, we need to be more precise about the specific nature of these factors. In the following discussion I shall suggest criteria for the subclassification of the exophoric devices; these criteria themselves would be based upon the type of situational knowledge that is needed for the correct more precise interpretation of the exophorics.

First, we need to be more precise about the interactant relations. In the discussion of both the explicit and the endophoric devices, it was possible to operate with the neutral term 'listener'. I refer to this term as neutral because it makes no distinction between a casual hearer and the intended addressee. Both are assumed to be able to interpret equally successfully, which is, incidentally, a good indication of the fact that endophoric relations are as system-governed as the relations in the lexicon.

However, in discussing the interpretation of the exophorics, the first important distinction is that between the intended addressee and the casual hearer. The speaker *intends* the former to hear; the latter may just *happen* to overhear. The speaker's wording is fashioned for the former; the needs of the latter are in no way relevant to the interaction. Obviously, then, the speaker would assume that the more precise meanings of the exophoric devices are available to the intended addressee. This assumption is based on no more than the common-sense observation that, in natural language use, one talks so that one's addressee can make sense of what one is saying (Firth 1950; Grice 1975). Nothing proves so cogently the fundamentally interorganic nature of human language (Halliday 1975) as the frequency with which the speaker's expectation is fulfilled regarding his addressee's ability for correct interpretation.

The relatively peripheral status of casual listeners can be exploited in considering the interpretation of the exophorics. Since speakers' wording is not fashioned with their needs in mind, they can be used as a test case. We may postulate that if casual listeners are able to interpret an exophoric correctly, then it is highly probable that such an exophoric would be correctly interpreted by the intended addressee as well. Thus in discussing the various types of exophorics the question I shall ask each time is: what do casual listeners need in order to be able to interpret this type of exophoric?

3.3 Instantial exophorics

Consider the following examples:

14a. Don't –   [don't what?]
  b. I'll need to get up a bit high<u>er</u> –   [higher than what?]
  c. Do have some –   [some what?]
  d. Which <u>one</u> would you like?   [which what?]

Let us assume that each example (14a–d) represents a complete text; i.e. the possibility of endophoric interpretation does not exist. So, the question arises: how can we answer the queries in the left column?

If (14a–d) are complete texts, then the implicit devices within them can only be interpreted by their relation to some aspect(s) of the material situational setting which also bears relevance to the text (Hasan 1981). The distinction implied between the material situational setting and the text-relevant context is necessary because the two are not synonymous. For example, the material situational setting surrounding the composition of this paper bears little or negligible relevance to the status of this paper as text. By contrast, for (14a–d) we must assume a large degree of overlap between the material situational setting and the relevant context, which is another way of saying that aspects of the former constitute a part of the latter.

It follows then that casual listener will be able to interpret the exophoric devices correctly so long as he has visual contact with the material situational setting. This is made all the easier for two reasons: first, the internal make-up of the message wherein the implicit devices occur provides a general indication of the essential nature of the relevant aspect of the material situational setting. For example, (14a) can only relate to a 'doing' of some sort; (14b) can only relate to three-dimensional objects that can serve as base for something or someone, while (14c–d) can only be said in relation to some concrete object. In other words the total semantic structure of the message provides a 'clue' as to where the listener's attention should be focused. In addition to this, the speaker's own body cues reinforce the listener's perception of the relevant bits of the material situation. So in order to arrive at a correct interpretation of (14a–d), the casual listener should be able not only to overhear but also to see what is going on that engages the speaker and who or what else is implicated in these goings-on. Given this, the interpretation provided by the casual listener will be significantly close to that which the intended addressee will provide. However, the meaning of these same devices will become opaque to the casual listener, as soon as visual contact disappears. It can be concluded therefore that the precise meanings of the exophoric devices in (14a–d) are mediated by relatively concrete 'bits' of the material situational setting, such as are amenable to perception.

I shall refer to this type of exophorics as *instantial exophorics*; an instantial exophoric is an implicit device whose precise meaning is mediated in a given instance only through some concrete elements of the goings-on surrounding the utterance in which the device occurs.

3.4 Intermediate exophoric

Superficially the following example appears to belong to the same type as (14a–d):

15a. Don't touch the books. [which books?]

but there are some interesting differences. If casual listeners are able to both hear and see, they will know what actual objects **the books** refers to in the material situational setting. However, being able to see the concrete entities does not necessarily imply that they will also know for certain what the the-ness of **the** in the nominal group **the books** consists of. This happens because of the nature of the definite article in English.

The simply indicates definiteness without actually providing any clue whatever about the nature of the parameters relevant to the definiteness. Clearly one source of definiteness can be the presence here-and-now of the entities to which the modified noun refers. Wherever the total semantic structure of the clause permits this interpretation, it can be employed as in the case of (15a). But it is not impossible that the speaker of (15a) has some parameter of definiteness in mind which goes beyond that of here-and-now. This might very well be the case in (15b):

15b. Don't touch the books. Mummy will be cross.

It seems highly plausible that in saying (15b) the speaker intends and is interpreted as saying **don't touch these-here-and-now books which in some way pertain to Mummy (or she will be cross)**. In this case, the intended precise meaning of **the** is not that of situational deixis only; it involves the relation of books to Mummy.

And yet such an interpretation is not necessarily guaranteed by the presence of the second clause as a comparison of (15b) with the following will show:

15c. Don't play with the stones. Mummy will be cross.

Presumably the stones in question do not pertain to Mummy; they are far more likely to be just these-here stones. And by the same token, it is just possible that **the books** in (15b) do not pertain to Mummy – she may simply be against children touching books. There appears to be no way that we can be privy to such information except through knowing the life circumstances of the various protagonists involved. Thus there appears to be a genuine indeterminacy of intended meaning in the exophoric **the** of the type under consideration. The ability to see and hear does not necessarily guarantee the retrieval of all the intended meanings of the implicit device. Moreover, casual listeners have no means of finding out if they have understood all that there was to understand.

This genuine indeterminacy can be counterbalanced by certain other factors. Imagine that our casual listeners are not able to see the goings-on for (14a–d) or (15a–c). Under this condition, they are likely to have a clearer idea of what is being talked about in (15a–c) than they would in (14a–d). This is for two reasons, and one of these has already been discussed above. The total semantic structure of the clauses in (15a–c) is such as to affirm the presence of books on the interactive scene. Thus casual listeners know at least something about the books and stones being talked about. Note this is not simply because **the** occurs, but it is primarily because the semantics of the verb and the agreement between time of speaking and temporal reference within the clause permit such an interpretation. This can be indicated by a comparison of (15a–c) with the following:

15d. Go and fetch the man immediately.
15e. We played with the doll yesterday, didn't we?

The second reason for a clearer idea of what is being talked about in (15a–c) lies in the formal functioning of **the**. **The** is one of the very few Modifiers which cannot be 'pushed up' to function as Head in an elliptical nominal group (Halliday and Hasan 1976); it must be followed by some other nominal word(s). The degree to which the meanings of the nominal group with the exophoric **the** become available to the listener then depends partly on what follows **the**. If the exophoric **the** occurs in an elliptical group, e.g. in:

15f. I'll have **the other** as well.
15g. I'll take **the bigger two**.

the access to meaning would be as restricted in the absence of visual contact as it would in (14a–d). If, on the other hand, the exophoric **the** occurs in a non-elliptical nominal group, the access to meaning is affected by the status of the modified noun. This can be seen from a comparison of the following:

16a. Look at the silly **thing**.
16b. Look at the silly **creature**.
16c. Look at the silly **fellow**.
16d. Look at the silly **boy**.

Here the four nouns are graded on the cline of specificity (see §4.3 below), with **thing** being the least specific and **boy** the most. If we assume that the situational referent of each one of these four items is the same entity, then the non-seeing casual listener knows most clearly what is being talked about in (16d), and least clearly in (16a). It is my impression that the characteristic environment for the occurrence of the exophoric **the** is as in (16d), i.e. in a non-elliptical nominal group where the modified noun has fairly high specificity. Thus in the light of the above discussion we find that although in (15a–c) there is a genuine indeterminacy in the precise meaning of **the**, it is also true that the casual listener is able to understand a good deal, though his understanding may be somewhat less complete than that of the intended addressee.

When an implicit device is genuinely indeterminate so that its intended precise meanings can vary in scope, so that casual listeners cannot be sure whether or not they have missed some significant information, then such an implicit device will be referred to as *indeterminate exophoric*. The only implicit device in English that is capable of being used in this manner is **the**.

3.5 *Restricted exophoric*

Consider now the following example:

17. Did **the** man come?

It is obvious that some parameter of identification renders **the man** definite. However, unlike (15a–c), this definiteness cannot consist in the presence of **the man** in the material situational setting. The total semantic structure of this clause as that of (15d–e) prevents such an interpretation. (17) thus presents a complete contrast to (14a–d) and a partial one to (15a–c). Access to the material situational setting would render the former totally transparent; such access would also provide some information regarding **books** and **stones** in (15a–c) to the extent that their physical presence on the interactive scene can be affirmed, although there may be some other parameter of definiteness which does not become accessible to the casual listener. In (17) the casual listener has no interpretation, as the meanings intended by **the** go completely beyond the here-and-now of the discourse. Whoever is able to supply the correct intended meanings here must possess knowledge that goes beyond this interactive situation and this particular text – it is knowledge that is mutually shared through common past experience. The nature of this knowledge is such that it precludes casual listeners completely. Thus the correct retrieval of the intended meanings of **the** in (17) argues for the existence of interaction in the past, and for a consequent rapport between the speaker and the addressee. This is not a public form of discourse.

When the interpretation of the implicit device depends upon the above type of shared knowledge, excluding 'outsiders' from the circle of communication, it may be referred to as *restricted exophoric*. Other examples of this type would be:

17a. **Has** she already left?
   b. Let's hope we have a bet**ter** holiday.
   c. I can't find **the** book.

3.6 *Formal exophoric*

The three types of exophorics discussed so far all differ from that exemplified below:

18a. What was John on about?
     Tell you later.

The second clause – functioning as response – contains the implicit device of ellipsis – more accurately that of Subject-ellipsis (from now on S-ellipsis). The environments in which S-ellipsis can occur in English are formally identifiable; further, the location of their interpretative source can also be specified by reference to formal criteria. Here are a few examples of endophoric S-ellipsis:

19a. John will put off the lights and **lock up the door**.
  b. Where's Agnes?
     Finishing her homework.
  c. My dad can't come today.
     Can't come! Whyever not?

The second clause of each example contains S-ellipsis. Endophoric S-ellipsis occurs only in the second member of a pair of clauses, such that the pair either constitutes a co-ordinate clause complex (Halliday 1982) or it acts as an adjacency pair. The S-segment for the elliptical clause is always interpreted by reference to the S-segment of the clause to which it is co-ordinated or which functions as its initiating pair-part. An associated feature of S-ellipsis is that no other clause may intervene between it and the clause that contains its interpretative source unless the intervening clause can act as a mediate link (Halliday and Hasan 1976). Thus in (19c) the third clause **whyever not?** can be interpreted as **whyever can't your dad come?** through the mediation of **can't come** which is itself interpreted as **your dad can't come!** by reference to the initiating pair-part **my dad can't come today**.

When S-ellipsis is exophoric, as in (18a), the intended S-segment cannot be retrieved by reference to the first member of the adjacency pair, even when such a member is around. The non-elliptical version of (18a) is not **John will tell you later** but **I will tell you later**. How is such an interpretation arrived at?

It is not that **I** is the only item which could function as the intended S-segment, and is therefore supplied automatically by the listener. This is evident from:

18b. Like an apple?
     Yeah, thanks.

Here the non-elliptical version of the first member in the adjacency pair would be **would you like an apple?**

In English, the more precise meaning of the exophoric S-ellipsis is either the first or the second person pronoun – either **I** or **you**. There is a strong tendency to interpret such a clause as 'needing' a first person pronoun if the contextual function of the clause is some variety of statement. If, on the other hand, the elliptical clause has the contextual function of question, the tendency is to interpret the S-ellipsis as second person pronoun. (For further discussion and rationale see Halliday 1985.) These tendencies for the interpretation of exophoric S-ellipsis are so strong that even if a clause with such an ellipsis were encountered in an uncharacteristic environment – i.e. in isolation from its situational setting – the normal speaker would interpret the ellipsis in the manner indicated above – unless there is good reason for doing otherwise.

This qualification is required for two reasons. First, complications arise due to the peculiarities of monologue and such text forming strategies as rhetorical questions. Secondly, the possibility of a third person pronominal as the intended S-segment cannot be ruled out entirely.

The possibility of a third person pronoun functioning as the intended S-segment in exophoric ellipsis, I regard as a marked state of affairs. There are three reasons for holding this view. If the intended S-segment is indeed a third person pronoun, then:

(a) whatever this pronoun refers to situationally must be present on the interactive scene;
(b) the speaker must accompany the utterance with some body cue, e.g. eye-movement, to directly pin-point the situational referent;
(c) unless the semantic structure of the clause prohibits, in isolation from the material situational setting, the clause would be assigned **I** or **you** as the intended S-segment.

These points can be illustrated from a consideration of the following:

20a. Met Harry.
  b. Met Harry?
  c. Met Harry, I believe.

There is nothing in the lexicogrammatical form of (20a–b) which prevents it from being interpreted as **she met Harry**. However, the formal convention for the interpretation of the exophoric S-ellipsis is so strong, that in isolation (20a) would be interpreted as **I met Harry** and if question-ness can be indicated in some way for (20b) it would be interpreted as **did you meet Harry**? In (20c), however, the insertion of **I believe** renders improbable the interpretation of the S-ellipsis as either **I** or **you**. Thus it is almost by default that (20c) may be interpreted as **some one other than the interactants met Harry as the speaker believes**.

In discussing how our casual listener would arrive at the interpretation of exophoric S-ellipsis, we must make a distinction between the marked and the unmarked variety. When S-ellipsis is unmarked, the intended meaning of the implicit device is available to all normal speakers of English. To know English is to know how to 'fill out' the ellipsis in such clauses as **tell you later** and **like an apple?**. So, even without access to the material situational setting, the casual listener would know that the former clause means **I will tell you later** and the latter, **would you like an apple?**. True that in this case the casual listener would not know the identity of the interactants; even so the general meaning is clear enough – the pronouns concern the maker and the receiver of the text in question.

It is implied in the above account that unmarked S-ellipsis is largely a formal matter. In the first place the recognition of ellipsis itself is purely formal. In English there is a formal requirement that a major clause with the feature 'indicative' must have the function Subject. It is this requirement which forces us to consider **like an apple?** as elliptical; after all, we do not need to have **you** as the liker of apple any more than we need to have **you** as the minder of your own business for the clause **mind your own business!** The argument that **you** in both may be said to be understood and therefore necessary to the interpretation of both appears an irrelevance. In the fairly common utterance **someone's at the door**, the nominal group **the door** is normally understood as **the front door**. However, this does not permit us to treat **the door** as an elliptical nominal group. There is no formal requirement in English that every nominal group must have the element Classifier in it. The recognition of ellipsis is not based on the perception of implied meanings for if this were the case every linguistic string produced would be elliptical, since implication is a constant condition of encoding. Metaphorically speaking, implied meanings are like the proverbial coming events whose shadow is cast before by the actually occurring linguistic units. The reason for insisting upon an element Subject for (18a–b) and (20a–b) is not that if there is any liking or minding to do then there should be a mention of someone who does this liking and minding; it is rather that all indicative clauses in English must have the element Subject. The element itself is an output of the Mood system (Berry 1975–77; Halliday 1970; Young 1980); and appropriately enough the clue to the interpretation of the ellipsis is provided by reference to the options in the same system. Both the ellipsis and its interpretation are thus formulaic in nature, permitting no really true variation; and both are controlled by the system of English language almost right down to the last detail. For this reason I shall refer to such ellipsis as *formal exophoric*. A formal exophoric device is one whose interpretation is predetermined by the language system and permits no true variation in wording.

Marked S-ellipsis presents a contrast to the above situation, although there are several points in common. For a casual listener with access to the material situational setting, the interpretation of this ellipsis is as easy as that of the unmarked one. But once visual contact with the material situational setting is removed, the casual listener is likely to fare worse in the case of marked S-ellipsis. In the last resort, this happens because marked S-ellipsis is not a formulaic thing; and moreover, the third person pronominals are very much less determinate in meaning than the first and second person ones. These points can be elaborated by using (20c) as the text in focus.

A casual listener, who simply overhears but cannot see the goings-on, will deduce from the total semantic structure of (20c) **met Harry, I believe** that someone other than the speaker or listener met Harry. Whereas being able to see would have rendered the ellipsis quite transparent, the inability to see leaves the casual listener with a far more diffuse interpretation of (20c) than that of (20a–b) under the same circumstances. This is because marked S-ellipsis is not formulaic; so there exists the possibility of true variation in its interpretation. When the intended S-segment is **I** or **you**, although one may not be certain of the identity of the situational beings to whom these pronouns refer, a generalized meaning *speaker of text* and *addressee of text* are readily available to the casual listener. When, however, the intended S-segment is neither of these, then in the first place selection must be made from the paradigm **he, she, it, they**. And once this selection is made, there still remains the fact that the semantics of the third person pronoun is expressible only negatively by reference to the speech roles; thus members of the paradigm refer to some entity which does not have a speech role in the text in focus. This leaves the field wide open, even when the semantic structure of the text might be such as to favour one single selection from the paradigm. For example, if we overhear:

20d. Doesn't look ripe.

we know that the only pronoun capable of functioning as S-segment here would be **it**. But unlike **I** and **you**, it can be given no definite general meaning. Marked S-ellipsis is then very much like those implicit devices exemplified by (14a–d). With full access to the material situational setting, the casual listener will find it totally transparent; when such access is withheld, it renders the implicit device opaque.

4 Degrees of implicitness and explictness

4.1 Encoding devices and degrees of implicitness

The discussion above (§§3.1–3.6) has demonstrated an important fact. When the question is asked: how easy is the access to the intended meanings of an implicit device?, the answer cannot be given simply in terms of formally defined categories to which the various implicit devices belong. Not all pronominals are equally easy to interpret, nor all S-ellipsis. The definite article **the** can function differently depending upon the environment in which it occurs. Thus the classification presented above cross-cuts the classification of implicit devices as belonging to the categories of reference, ellipsis and substitution (Halliday and Hasan 1976). The total set of encoding devices so far discussed can be presented as a taxonomy, the various categories of which differ from each other in respect of what is needed for their precise interpretation (see Figure 8.1). Earlier I suggested (§2.2 above) that the implicitness of strings is variable; in that context, I used a purely quantitative method for grading the degree of implicitness in a string: the larger the number of implicit devices in proportion to the explicit ones, the more implicit the string would be. In the light of the above remarks, it should be obvious that such quantitative grading is not the most reliable method. A more valid criterion for the grading of implicitness would be by reference to the requirements for interpretation. The greater the ease in interpreting the speaker's intended meanings, the less implicit the device. In using this criterion, the taxonomy in Figure 8.1 would be helpful.

WAYS OF SAYING: WAYS OF MEANING 209

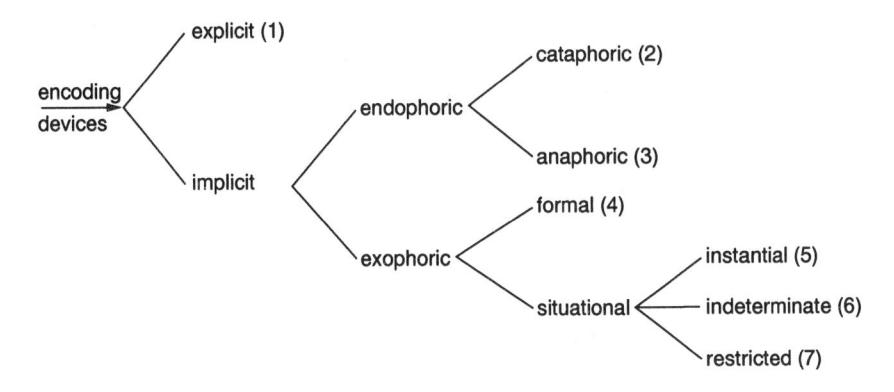

```
                    explicit (1)
                                              cataphoric (2)
encoding                     endophoric
devices                                       anaphoric (3)
                    implicit
                                              formal (4)
                                                              instantial (5)
                             exophoric
                                              situational    indeterminate (6)
                                                              restricted (7)
```

Figure 8.1 Taxonomy of encoding devices

The terminal nodes of this taxonomy yield a series (1–7). This series represents a cline of implicitness. On this continuum, the lowest number represents the least implicit device and the highest the most implicit ones, as shown in Figure 8.2.

least 1 —— 2 —— 3 —— 4 —— 5 —— 6 —— 7 most
implicit   implicit

Figure 8.2 The cline of implicitness

Assuming normal speakers, the move from (1) to (7) is a move in the direction of an ever-narrowing circle of potentially successful interpreters; this is because the resources needed for such interpretation are increasingly more restrictive. Thus, the meanings of explicit devices (1) are available to every normal, mature speaker of English: the circle is the widest. With endophoric devices (2, 3), this circle is reduced; it now covers only those who have access to the relevant part of the discourse. For (2), the relevant part of the discourse is expected to be more contiguous with the device than it would be with (3). With formal exophoric (4), this circle is further reduced; although the knowledge of language itself allows a partial interpretation, its precise intended meanings become fully available only when the listener has access to the material situational setting. This circle is likely to be much narrower than that for (2) and (3). Where instantial exophorics (5) are concerned, unless the listener has access to the material stituational setting, the devices would remain opaque; the interpretation that the casual listener might provide under such a situation would be far more diffuse than that for (4). So the circle of successful interpreters is rendered narrower still. In the case of indeterminate exophorics (6), access to material situational setting will permit some interpretation, but it is not necessary that even with such access the casual listener has understood all that there was to understand. Restricted exophoric (7) logically implies the narrowest circle; neither the knowledge of language nor the knowledge of the material situational setting is sufficient for a correct interpretation. As Bernstein puts it, one must be keyed into the relevant context; and this can happen through shared experience such that it generates a considerable amount of empathy.

4.2 Inherent grading of implicit devices

A new dimension can be added to the above grading of implicitness, by enquiring how far an implicit device provides clues about the area in which its more precise intended meaning may be located. The greater the detail with which this area can be stated, the narrower and better defined it is, the less implicit the device would be.

As a starting-point we may consider the first and second person pronouns. It is justifiable to claim the lowest degree of implicitness for these since their own semantic specification explicates them fully; the only element of uncertainty is the particularity of the situational referent. In fact, the same claim can be made for all those implicit devices which involve 'textual deixis' by taking the text and its setting as their point of departure. Thus **here, there, this, that, now** have the lowest degree of implicitness.

The above situation contrasts with that of the third person pronouns (see also §3.6 above). The area from which the meaning of the third person pronoun may be retrieved is not as narrow as that for the above. Yet the semantic specification of **he, she, it** provides clues about the possible referents for these devices; under normal conditions **he** can only be coreferential with some item whose underlying semantic configuration includes [human; male; one; non-interactant]. Thus, inherently, the three singular third person pronouns are more transparent in their meaning than **they**, whose own semantic specification is much reduced as it contains [one+; non-interactant].

In fact the inherent implicitness of **they** is greater than that of the nominal substitute **one/ones**. Any substitutable noun must have the underlying options [countable; non-unique] in addition to the two mentioned for **they**. Thus **I'll take these ones** cannot be said of **milk, tea**, and **sugar** though it may be said of cartons of milk, packets of tea, and bags of sugar. Similarly we can't say **here are John, Jim and Stanley. I'll take these ones with me** with **these ones** referring to **John, Jim, and Stanley**, though it is fine to say **I'm not worried about these three boys; I can take these ones with me – it's the others I can't find room for**. The inherent implicitness of the verbal substitute **do** is much greater by comparison, as there are only a few verbs that it cannot substitute (see Halliday and Hasan 1976).

The definite article **the** surpasses all the above-mentioned devices as in its inherent implicitness (see §§3.1, 3.4 and 3.5). However because it cannot occur by itself, the modified noun itself can function as a clue-provider (see example 16a–d).

WAYS OF SAYING: WAYS OF MEANING 211

Perhaps the inherent implicitness is the greatest in the case of non-formulaic ellipsis. This claim is based on two observations. First, there can be instances, especially at the rank of clause, where simply by looking at the syntagm one cannot decide whether or not it is elliptical. I am not suggesting that in normal language use this creates any problem, since obviously here there is the entire dynamics of discourse to assist the listener. But this is not less true of **she, he, they**, etc. as implicit devices in normal language use. In talking about the inherent implicitness of the device, I am examining each as an isolate. And from this point of view there can be little doubt that by itself a clause such as **turn off the lights** does not appear elliptical. It would however be elliptical if we perceive it in relation to **John can tidy up, turn off the lights, and lock the doors**. Secondly, the general area from which the intended meanings might be retrieved is indicated by the internal properties of the elliptical string itself. Just as in the case of **the**, the modified noun is potentially a provider of clues to interpretation, so also in ellipsis, the rest of the syntagm assists in locating the intended meaning. This can be seen clearly from the following example:

21. If it had pleased them they would have told you. It didn't – so, naturally, they didn't –

Keeping the above discussion in mind, we can construct a cline of inherent implicitness. On this cline, the lowest degree of implicitness would be represented by the first/second person pronoun, and the highest by non-formulaic ellipsis. Using one item as representative of each category in question, the cline of inherent implicitness may be presented as in Figure 8.3.

least implicit	1	2	3	4	5	6	7	most implicit
	you	she	one	they	do	the	φ	

Figure 8.3 The cline of inherent implicitness

4.3 Inherent grading of explicit devices

It seems necessary to draw attention to an aspect of explicit devices if only to provide a reason for not discussing them any further. These devices can be ranged on a continuum from general to specific; that is to say, explicit devices vary in the degree of specificity of meaning. This attribute is the recognized basis for the construction of lexical taxonomy. The terms 'implicit' and 'explicit' run parallel to 'general' and 'specific' in one important respect: the more implicit a device, the less precise the meaning it conveys; equally, the more general a device, the less precise the meaning it conveys. The line between the lowest degree of implicitness and the highest degree of generality is blurred; none the less, there is a qualitative difference between the two.

There can be no doubt that as we move along the series **thing, creature, animal, horse, foal, colt, yearling,** there is a reduction in generality and a proportionate increase in the specificity of meaning. **Thing** being the most general item in English even forms part of a composite implicit expression, e.g. in **the silly thing**; here I am concerned with its other uses. The basic difference between **thing** and an implicit device, e.g. **it** is that when speakers use an implicit device, at least they themselves are quite clear about the more precise intended meaning; also, they expect their addressee too to perceive this meaning. The same claim cannot be made about the use of **thing**. Compare:

22a. Do you see that thing over there? What is it?
  b. Do you see it? What's that thing over there?

In (22a) the nature of whatever is being pointed out is not clear to the speaker; this is shown by the generality of **thing**, which commits the speaker to no more than the pointed-out being an object. Thereafter it can be used with the meaning: the aforementioned object. (22b) is odd because the use of **it** creates an effect of the speaker knowing more than the following clause gives him credit for; as the text stands **it** and **that thing over there** are co-referential. If the same two clauses are read with an **and** between them, which negates the co-referentiality, the text would be quite normal.

The cline presented by **thing, creature ..... yearling** can be related to the

$$A \underline{\quad 7 \quad 6 \quad 5 \quad 4 \quad 3 \quad 2 \quad 1 \quad}B \quad C\underline{\quad 1 \quad 2 \quad 3 \quad 4 \quad 5 \quad 6 \quad 7 \quad}D$$

Figure 8.4 The relation between least specific and least implicit

cline as shown in Figure 8.4. The continuum between (A–D) represents all the encoding devices, (A) being the implicit end, and (D) the explicit one. (A–B) represent only the implicit devices ranging from (A): most implicit to (B): least implicit; (C–D) represent only the explicit devices, ranging from (C): the least specific – i.e. general – to (D) the most specific. The gap between (B) and (C) indicates the qualitative difference between the two categories of encoding devices. Hopefully Figure 8.4 shows clearly that despite the nearness between the notions of implicitness and non-specificity, the two are not identical. However, as example (16a–d) showed, the occurrence of general devices can affect access to meaning.

4.4 On establishing degrees of implicitness

It may be concluded from the discussion in this section that to talk of implicit and explicit ways of saying as if it were a simple binary distinction would be to create yet another non-existent dichotomy. The three variables

WAYS OF SAYING: WAYS OF MEANING 213

– quantitative, based on the proportion of implicit to explicit devices; qualitative, based on resources for access to the intended meanings; and the inherent implicitness and generality of the devices – operate together to produce what we impressionistically describe as highly implicit, somewhat implicit, or entirely explicit. In the comparison of ways of speaking between middle-class English and Urdu speakers, only the latter two qualitative variables will be considered in determining the degree of implicitness. The quantitative criterion will be ignored since it can only be employed on the basis of a systematic analysis of a large amount of corpus.

5 English semantic style

5.1 The semantic style of English

If semantic style is a characteristic way of saying and meaning, then the defining attributes of this style should be present in most natural verbal interaction. Exceptions, where the characteristic semantic style is not used, will be significantly fewer; moreover it should be possible to state clearly how these exceptions can be defined.

On this definition of characteristic semantic style, I would suggest that the predominant semantic style for the educated middle-class English speaker is the explicit one. This claim is based on two observations: first, the system of English itself does not permit the possibility of using the logically most implicit means of encoding; secondly, such implicitness as is permitted by the system can be used only in few and well-defined environments, thus indicating that it is a departure from the norm. These points are developed below.

5.2 Degrees of permissible implicitness in English

In the discussion of the significant degrees of implicitness, we need not concern ourselves with devices other than those functioning exophorically. The endophoric devices are only temporarily implicit, so much so that the listener is typically unaware of their occurrence so long as the relevant co-text is available. And even among the exophorics, the formal exophoric is a borderline case (see §3.6). The logically highest degree of implicitness would be reached if ellipsis could function as a restricted exophoric. (See Figures 8.2 and 8.3.) If my analysis is correct, English does not permit such ellipsis – when ellipsis is not endophoric, it is typically instantial exophoric. Thus the logically highest possible degree of implicitness is not permitted to occur in English.

The next degree would be represented by **the** functioning as a restricted exophoric. The occurrence of such **the** is permitted. Thus this could be regarded as the highest permissible degree of implicitness in English. Since the substitutes do not function as restricted exophoric, we are left with **the** and the third person pronominals that can function in this way. These same devices can also function as instantial exophoric.

I have argued that the instantial exophoric is rendered quite transparent to anyone who happens to have full access to the material situational setting. We can claim then that in English there are only two significant degrees of implicitness: the optimal and the non-optimal. The optimal is achieved with the functioning of the device as a restricted exophoric. However, a large proportion of the implicit devices are prevented from functioning in this manner. The system of English language does not favour the optimal degree of implicitness. The non-optimal degree of implicitness is fairly low, and it is open to all implicit devices. Thus the system of English language may be said to favour this kind of implicitness.

These generalizations hold for all varieties of English. The degree of implicitness that can be achieved in English is much lower for all varieties, not just middle-class English, than that which could logically have been possible. This is partly what would be meant by the claim that the predominant semantic style of English is explicit. It isn't simply that English speakers *would* not, but rather that they *could not*, speak as implicitly as Urdu speakers, even if they tried – the system of their language will not permit them to do so.

5.3 *Environments for the operation of implicit styles*

That the implicit style is the marked style for most speakers of English and particularly for the middle-class members is also borne out by the fact that the environments in which implicit style may be employed appropriately are few and very clearly specifiable.

Let us take the non-optimal degree – that where the devices are used as instantial exophorics. This kind of implicitness occurs characteristically in face-to-face encounters. This, it might be argued, is quite logical: the instantial exophoric is rendered transparent if one has access to the situational setting. In their setting the meanings of **don't** and **have some more** are quite obvious; divorced from this setting, their meaning is opaque. It is, therefore, quite appropriate that their higher occurrence should be associated with an environment which gives total access to the material situational setting.

The frequency of the instantial exophorics is higher still in a face-to-face encounter where the relationship between the interactants is intimate. Thus we can say that the more informal the tenor, the more likely the middle-class English speaker would be to use this kind of implicitness. However, this aspect of the correlation cannot be said to be logical in nature. If it is true that the casual listener with full access to the material situational setting would be able to interpret the instantial exophorics almost as successfully as the intended addressee, then it cannot be maintained that intimacy between the interactants is a logical requirement for its more frequent occurrence. It seems to me that an understanding of the semiotic control on the optimally implicit style might provide a rationale for the correlation between informal tenor and higher frequency of instantial exophorics.

The optimal degree of implicitness, where the devices are used as restricted exophorics, can be employed only in those environments where the social distance between the interactants is minimal (Hasan 1973; 1978; 1980). A relationship of intimacy, if not necessarily that of informality, is logically required, since the interpretation of meanings rests on shared knowledge which is a product of consistent past interaction. It is this aspect of the restricted exophorics which excludes strangers and casual listeners.

It is probably useful to separate the assumptions that accompany the use of restricted exophorics from the conditions favourable to its successful interpretation. Speakers employing such a style of speaking assume that their addressees are 'keyed into' the discourse, that their mental set is the same and that there is no danger of ambiguity or misunderstanding – in short, speakers assume that addressees know what they are talking about. Such expectations cannot be entertained regarding every member of one's speech community over a wide range of contexts. Obviously, then, the circle of potential addressees is likely to be limited to those in-group members with whom a certain degree of empathy is experienced. This assumption of the close mental set, of empathy, is a logical necessity to the sensical use of restricted exophorics. Their successful interpretation depends upon the correctness of these assumptions; if the assumptions were not well founded, the implicit style would be a constant source of frustration to both parties. There can of course be occasions when although the assumption of empathy is correct in principle, the interpretation is not successful because the addressee's attention is being claimed by some other matter. I do not think that this affects the points being made here; such sporadic failures of communication are likely to occur in any style of communication, not just the implicit one.

Social distance itself is variable in degree (Hasan 1973; 1978; 1980); there are intermediate degrees of intimacy felt for an utter stranger or for one's own mother, wife, or close friend. It is, however, best to talk of social distance in comparative terms without referring to a relationship as the measure for the degree; this is because across the cultures the kind of intimacy that may exist between spouses, parents and children, or friends can be qualitatively different (Hsu 1971a; 1971b). It can be claimed that the more minimal the social distance between the interactants, the more likely the occurrence of restricted exophorics. Thus a frequent use of such exophorics is indicative of the fact that the interactants habitually interact in wider areas of the living of life. This style of speaking is, then, indexical of a qualitatively different social relation (Bernstein 1971).

It is my tentative suggestion that the correlation between the higher frequency of instantial exophorics and informal tenor is a symbolic means of construing closeness of relationship. The efficacy of this symbolism depends upon the semiotics of the optimally implicit style. Because of the logical relationship between the restricted exophoric and the closeness of social ties, the former tends to be seen as the outward manifestation of the latter. Instantial exophorics are an attempt to create the semblance of this reality. There are many ways in which language makes up our world for us – not simply naming existing objects, processes and states, but actually creating them. Despite the long philosophical tradition, the primacy of the onomastic function of language is highly suspect. Language is useful to social man not because it names all the pre-existing phenomena in the world, but because it actually creates the most significant ones. 'The limits of my language mean the limits of my world' (Wittgenstein 1921).

5.4 Concluding remarks on English semantic styles

I conclude from the above discussion that the characteristic semantic style in English is the explicit one. The very fact of speaking English forces one toward explicitness rather than implicitness. Further, this is even more so with regard to the educated middle-class English speakers. To say that one is a middle-class English speaker is to say that for the most part one talks so that one's meanings are easily available to anyone present at the interactive scene. The assumption of shared knowledge and reliance upon it, which is a logical necessity for the successful operation of implicit style, is not encouraged in the majority of interactive environments. Ambiguity is an ever-present threat, therefore; explicitization is an imperative. There are very few contexts in which the middle-class English speaker is free to assume complete rapport with others of his kind. The similitude of beliefs, attitudes, and values (Durkheim 1947) which would make each one of us as like the other as possible, despite our physical discreteness, is not to be taken for granted. So, to put it sentimentally, the universe is a lonely place, where each one of us is an island unto himself.

If in a background such as I have described above – especially with reference to the total language system – we find a section of the speech community whose predominant orientation is to the implicit style of speaking, we must ask *why*. What conditions obtain for this section of the community which guide the speakers' options to paths in the language system, which are not favoured by the members of other sections of this same speech community. The variation is not a matter of shame; nor does it call for an indignant championship of the variant section (Labov 1970). To me it seems that there is just as much condescension in saying that 'they' are like 'us', as there is in maintaining that 'we' are better than 'them'. 'Us' and 'them' are culturally created realities, as are also the standards of good, bad, and better. They cannot be altered by a simple denial of their existence; they must be analysed and understood, if we are to redress the balance in the monopoly of cultural values. To recognize with Bernstein that the various styles of speaking are socially created phenomena, which further the status quo of an established power structure, is to be pointed in the direction of exposing the sources of cultural monopoly. Thus it is meaningful to ask: what creates this assumption of rapport in 'them' which is so conspicuously missing from 'our' own social universe? I propose to throw some light on this problem by comparing the dominant middle-class English semantic style with the Urdu one.

6 Urdu semantic style

6.1 Implicitness in Urdu

I have developed the categories of implicitness and my main arguments by reference to English, in the hope that it may lead to an easier understanding of facts relating to Urdu. In talking about the patterns of implicitness in Urdu, I shall have to make statements regarding its lexicogrammatical structure. Such statements are incidental to the main purpose of this chapter and it will not be possible to include justification for my claims at each point.

My strategy will be to start with an examination of the logically highest degree of implicitness – that which would arise from a substantial use of restricted exophoric ellipsis. If I can show that this type of implicitness is permitted in Urdu, and that it is not counter-balanced by turning ellipsis to either formal or instantial exophoric, then I shall have shown that the potential for implicitness is higher in Urdu than it is in English. The system of Urdu language itself could then be said to allow a higher degree of implicitness to its speakers than that which is permitted by the system of English language.

My second step would be to enquire into the range of environments where this higher degree of implicitness might be employed by Urdu speakers. If I can show that such a style of speaking is characteristically employed by Urdu speakers over a wide range of contexts, I shall have proved that not only does the system permit a higher degree of implicitness, but also the speakers make wide use of it; and therefore the dominant Urdu style is the implicit one.

Finally I shall raise two questions: first, how does this style relate to the prevalent semiotic style and what organizing concepts may be at work in maintaining this parallelism; secondly, what do these findings say about that subsection of English speakers who are orientated to the implicit style of speaking?

6.2 S-ellipsis in Urdu

It would be useful to compare the patterns of S-ellipsis across the two languages, but there is the initial problem of determining what, if anything, the element S of English corresponds to in Urdu. The traditional accounts of Urdu grammar are not very clear on this issue; thus in the traditional description of the grammar of the language there appears to exist no category with the exact value of the English Subject. The term closest to Subject appears to be '*məsnəd yləh*' (Fateh Mohammad Khan 1945, 195f.) which together with '*məsnəd*' renders a clause potentially a 'complete unit of discourse'. 'Məsnəd' is defined as that which is related to – or pertains to – something; the thing to which it pertains is defined as 'məsnəd yləh'. We are further told that while the latter is always realized by a nominal unit, the former can be realized by a nominal and/or verbal unit. This makes it sound as if 'məsnəd yləh' and 'məsnəd' correspond exactly to the distinction made by Subject and Predicate, respectively. However, such an interpretation would not be quite accurate. The two categories recognized in the traditional Urdu grammars are said to apply only to that class of clauses, regarding which the question of truth or falsehood could be sensibly raised. So, reasonably enough, not only the imperative but also the interrogative – among many other clause classes – are specifically excluded from this category.[2] In

23. **twm** kəb ləndən gəĩ?
    you when London went?
    when did **you** go to London?

twm (you) is not a 'məsnəd yləh'; nor is there a 'məsnəd' in this clause. Rather than being diverted into a lengthy discussion of this issue, I shall follow modern grammatical descriptions in affirming that a category comparable to the English Subject can be recognized usefully for Urdu as well (Kachru 1966; Verma 1961; Hasan 1972). First, I shall stipulate which segment of the clause is in question when we use the term Subject to refer to it. The statement would read as follows:

> That segment of the Urdu clause is comparable to the S-segment of the English one, which has the privilege of number–gender–person concord with the verbal group realizing the element Process in the clause. The sole exception to this, are clauses where a nominal group with post-position 'ne' is either actually present or is potentially insertable. In this latter class of clauses the nominal group with the post-position 'ne' is comparable to the S-segment.

Here are a few examples; the S-segment in each case is underlined both in Urdu and the English clause-rank translations:

24a. ləRki   dal   pəka   rəhi   həy
     girl   lentils cook   ing   is
     (the) girl is cooking (some) lentils
  b. ləRki   cavəl   pəka   rəhi   həy
     girl   rice   cook   ing   is
     (the) girl is cooking (some) rice
  c. dal   pəkai   ja   rəhi   həy
     lentils cooked go   ing   is
     lentils are being cooked
  d. cavəl   pəkaya ja   rəha   həy
     rice   cooked go   ing   is
     rice is being cooked

e. ləRki   ne   dal   pəkai
      girl   lentils   cooked
      (the) girl cooked (some) lentils
   f. ləRki   ne   cavəl   pəkaya
      girl   rice   cooked
      (the) girl cooked (some) rice
   g. admi   dal   pəka   rəha   həy
      man   lentils cook   ing   is
      (the) man is cooking (some) lentils
   h. admi   cavəl   pəka   rəha   həy
      man   rice   cook   ing   is
      (the) man is cooking (some) rice

Although the above examples represent only a very small subset of the total paradigm, they substantiate the points made above, especially if the information is added that in (24 e–f), **ləRki** could be replaced by **admi**, without causing any change in the meaning except that resulting from the lexical difference between the two items.

It is, of course, comparatively easy to establish which segment of the Urdu clause is most like the S-segment of the English one; it is quite a different matter to validate the recognition of Subject as a descriptive category in Urdu grammar. Yet such motivation must be present if we claim S-ellipsis as a significant fact in Urdu. If there is such an element of structure in the Urdu clause, what is its function? What systemic options is it related to? And how may its semantic value be determined? To begin with we may state clearly that neither in English nor in Urdu is the element S an output of the transitivity system; for Urdu this should be obvious from a comparison of (24a) and (c). In agreement with Halliday, I have argued that S in English is the output of the Mood system; and although there are crucial differences, I would propose that the same is true of Urdu. Before stating the evidence for this conclusion, it is important to add that there are two separate aspects to be examined: first, the justification for the recognition of the element S; and secondly, the actual presence, absence, and position of the S-segment in the syntagm.

Essentially the function of S in Urdu is the same as that in English; it acts as 'something by reference to which the proposition can be affirmed or denied' (Halliday 1985). In English, this is what underlies the systematic behaviour of tag questions. In Urdu, there is only one invariable tag **həy na** (is not: isn't it), however the principle that 'the subject is responsible for the success of the proposal' (Halliday ibid.) holds good. It is certainly the 'resting point of the argument', so that it always functions as the point of reference for raising any queries about the message. A consideration of the following examples will illustrate the above points:

25a. hamyd   nəwkrani   nəhĩ   laya
     Hamid   maid-servant not   brought
     Hamid didn't bring the maidservant

220   PART THREE: LANGUAGE AND SOCIETY

   b. nəwkrani   <u>hamyd</u>   nəhĩ laya
      maid-servant Hamid   not   brought
      the maid-servant <u>Hamid</u> didn't bring (i.e. it was not Hamid who brought her)

   c. hamyd   se   <u>nəwkrani</u>   nəhi laĩ   gəi
      Hamid   by   maid-servant not brought went
      <u>the maid-servant</u> was not brought by Hamid

   d. <u>nəwkrani</u>   hamyd se nəhĩ lai   gəi
      maid-servant Hamid by not brought went
      <u>the maid-servant</u> was not brought by Hamid

The S-segment in each clause is underlined; that neither order nor participant status affects Subject-ness is also obvious. However, since S is the resting point of the argument, if the propositions are to be debated then S must serve as the point of reference. Suppose one wishes to contradict the statements (25a–d), then the contradiction for (25a–b) will be as follows:

26 i. laya to
      brought   emphatic particle
      did bring (i.e. he did)

  ii. kəhā   nəhĩ   laya
      where   not   brought
      where didn't bring (i.e. of course he did)

  iii. kəyse   nəhi   laya
      how   not   brought
      how didn't bring (i.e. of course he did)

  iv. laya   kyõ   nəhi
      brought   why   not
      why didn't bring (i.e. of course he did)

(26i–iv) can all function as contradictions of (25a–b), although with some differences in emphasis. This latter point need not concern us here; but it should be noted that in each case, the concord pattern of the contradiction quite clearly shows **Hamid** to be the central reference point. If this is compared with the contradictions for (25c–d), we find that the pattern of concord 'picks up' **nəwkrani** as the resting point of the argument. Compare (26i–iv) with (27i–iv):

27 i. lai   to   gəi
      brought   emphatic particle   went
      did get brought (i.e. she did (get brought))

  ii. kəhâ   nəhî   lai   gəi
      where   not   brought   went
      where didn't get brought (i.e. of course she did (get brought))

iii. kəyse nəhĩ lai gəi
    how not brought went
    how didn't get brought (i.e. of course she did (get brought))
iv. lai kyõ nəhĩ gəi
    brought why not went
    why didn't get brought (i.e. of course she did get brought))

Although the experiential meanings of (25a–d) are the same, therefore contradicting one of these is experientially tantamount to contradicting the others, these patterns of contradiction are not exchangeable. Thus while (25c–f) make a good exchange, (25g–h) are definitely odd:

25e. -hamyd nəwkrani nəhĩ laya (see (25a) for translation)
     -laya to   (see (26i) for translation)
  f. -hamyd se nəwkrani nəhĩ lai gəi (see (25c) for translation)
     -lai to gəi   (see (27i) for translation)
  g. -hamyd nəwkrani nəhĩ laya
     -lai to gəi
  h. -hamyd se nəwkrani nəhĩ lai gəi
     -laya to

Clearly this pattern obtains because S is the point of reference. When the contradictions are switched around, the alteration in the concord pattern indicates a segment as S which cannot so function for **g** and **h**; hence the oddity of the latter two exchanges. The point is brought out even more dramatically if we consider a clause where the S-segment is a pronoun referring to one of the interactants, as in:

28. həm ytna kam nəhĩ kərte
    I so much work not do
    I don't do so much work (i.e. I don't work so hard)

Imagine that the **I** here refers to the author. The relevant properties of the S-segment then would be: first person, singular, feminine. Its ordinary contradiction would be:

28i. kərti to ho
     do emph.part. are
     do do (i.e. (you) do)

Here the verbal group through its concord points to an S-segment whose properties are: second person, singular, feminine. Given the nature of the exchange, this is exactly how it should work.

It is significant that even in clauses where the S-segment is a nominal group with post-position **ne**, if the natural context permits, the pattern of concord will change to point to the S. Consider the following:

29. -ap   ki   ləRki   ne   ye   drama   nəhĩ   dekha nə?
    you   of   girl   this play   not   saw   no
    your daughter didn't see this play, did she?
    -nəhĩ   kəl   dekhe   gi
    not   tomorrow   see   will
    no, tomorrow will see (i.e. no, (she) will see it tomorrow)

In the initiating turn the concord is not with the ne-group – as it never is – but in the second turn, where the tense of the verbal group permits this, the person, number and gender concord is with **ləRki**. We also find such 'switching' of concord in co-ordinated pair with ellipsis:

30. kwlsum   ne   bəRi   mətanət   se   mwjhe   dekha   əwr   phyr
    Kulsoom   very   seriousness with   me   looked-at and   then
    Kulsoom looked at me very seriously and then

    əpni   kapi   pər   jhwk   gəi
    her   note-book at   bent   went
    bent (her head) over her note-book

                                            (Ishfaq Ahmed n.d., 181)

It appears then that the concord which ties the elements S and Predicator in Urdu is not simply an empty formalism, but is semantically motivated. In English the centrality of the element S to the clause is reflected in the significance that must be attached to its actual presence and its position in the syntagm; in Urdu, the reflection of this centrality is the pattern of concord, which points to the identity of the S (see below, for further remarks). Hopefully, this discussion shows that despite differences between the English and Urdu Subject, there exists sufficient similarity between the two to permit valid comparison.

Although the element S is the output of the Mood system in Urdu, the actual presence, absence and position of the S-segment in the clause is not determined by the Mood system. The presence or absence of the S-segment is largely a realization of the options in the Information system, while its position in the syntagm is related to the Key system and to the Theme system. I shall not concern myself with problems relating to the position of the S-segment, but I do need to say something about the conditions which control its appearance in or absence from the clause. The discussion will be largely in terms of the Information system, though the system of Theme too affects aspects of this.

Two elements which are the output of the Information system are Given and New; together they make up a structure called 'information unit'. Under normal conditions, the information unit is coextensive with one clause. As elaboration on these statements it is best to quote from Halliday:

> The information unit is what its name implies: a unit of information. Information, as ... used here, is a process of interaction between what is already known and what is new or unpredictable.... It is the interplay of new and not new that

generates information in the linguistic sense. Hence the information unit is a structure made up of two functions, the New and Given.

In the idealized form each information unit consists of a Given element accompanied by a New element. But there are two conditions of departure from this principle. One is that discourse has to start somewhere, so there can be discourse initiating units consisting of a New element only. The other is that by its nature the Given is likely to be 'phoric' – referring to something already present in the verbal or non-verbal context; and one way of achieving phoricity is through ellipsis, a grammatical form in which certain features are not realized in the structure. (1985, 274–275)

One of the conditions of departure from the ordinary structure of the information unit is met with quite frequently in Urdu: it is the achievement of phoricity through S-ellipsis as a (partial) manifestation of the element Given. S-ellipsis in Urdu is the output of this systemic option, though it should be noted that the S-segment of a clause is not always realizationally associated with the element New, since it could be the (partial) realization of unmarked Theme, especially when it precedes both Complement and Predicate. The fact that S-ellipsis in Urdu is controlled by a systemic option does not weaken the ground for its comparison with S-ellipsis in English. This is obvious from the true meaning of the elements Given and New. To quote Halliday again:

> The significant variable is: information that is presented by the speaker as recoverable (Given) or not recoverable (New) to the listener. What is treated as recoverable may be so because it has been mentioned before; but that is not the only possibility. It may be something that is in the situation, like I and you; or in the air, so to speak; or something that is not around at all but that the speaker wants to present as Given for rhetorical purposes. The meaning is: this is not news. Likewise, what is treated as non-recoverable may be something that has not been mentioned; but it may be something unexpected, whether previously mentioned or not. The meaning is: attend to this; this is news....
>
> (1985, 277)

These are precisely the possibilities of interpretation we have been considering for the implicit devices: either they are interpreted endophorically or exophorically; if exophorically, either through some bit of the situational setting or through shared knowledge. Urdu S-ellipsis does not present any contrast in these respects. It acts like an implicit device; it is quite beside the point that it is itself (partially) motivated by the options in the system of Information.

Endophoric S-ellipsis is far more frequent in Urdu than it is in English. In the latter case, the environment can be enumerated very simply (see §3.6 above); for Urdu, it is easier to formulate the principle negatively: S-ellipsis cannot occur wherever the S-segment would form part of New or contrastive information. Although endophoric S-ellipsis is not my primary concern here, an extract from a short story is presented below just to give an idea of how frequent this pattern is in Urdu:

31. təbyət   ke badshah   the <u>thwmhare nana</u>; dyl mẽ
    temperament   of king   was your grand-dad; heart in
    by temperament he was a king, <u>your grand-dad</u>; if (<u>he</u>)

   kysi ciz   ki Than   li to phyr wse pura kər
   any   thing of determine take then it   finish do
   made up his mind to do something then (<u>he</u>) would draw breath

   ke hi dəm   lia. <u>həm</u>   lakh   sər   marẽ,
   after breath took I   thousand head beat,
   only after finishing it. <u>I</u> might try my utmost,

   mənnətẽ xwshamdẽ kərẽ, tane uləhne dẽ, məgər
   prayers flatteries do   taunts   give but
   (<u>I</u>) might cajole or pray, (<u>I</u>) might even taunt, but

   <u>vo</u> vəhi kwch kərte <u>jo</u> wnhe pəsənd hota.
   he   that some do   which him   liked was
   <u>he</u> only did <u>whatever</u> pleased him.

   gəRh shənkər mẽ nayb təhsildar the; ytni bəRi
   Garh Shanker in deputy collector was; such big
   (<u>He</u>) was deputy revenue collector in Garh Shanker; such a big

   həveli   do bhə̃yse   ek ghoRi car kwtte
   residence two buffaloes one mare four dogs
   residence, two buffaloes, one mare and four dogs [it carried].

   <u>kysi ne</u>   a   kər shəgufa choR dia kə KəŋgaRe
   someone   came did flower leave gave that Kangara
   <u>someone</u> just brought a tempting tale that <u>a holy man</u> has

   mẽ <u>ek dərvesh</u> ae hẽy.   jo   kəhte hẽy vəhi kər
   in a holy man   come is. whatever say   is that do
   come to Kangara. Whatever (<u>he</u>) says (<u>he</u>) actually

   dykhate hẽy; kysi   se   mylte nəhi; kysi ko   mwrid
   show   is; anyone with meets not; someone disciple
   brings about; (<u>he</u>) doesn't meet anyone; (<u>he</u>) doesn't take

   nəhı̃ bənate.   <u>vo</u> to əysi batõ   ke dyl   se   xwahã
   not makes.   he   such things of heart with desirous
   any disciples. <u>he</u> of course was very keen on such things

   the; jhəT   ystifə   lykh bheja   ...
   was; at once resignation wrote sent
       ;straight away (<u>he</u>) sent off his resignation ...
                                        [Ishfaq Ahmed n.d., 27]

The extract in (31) consists of 17 major clauses with 17 finite verbal groups. So, potentially, there could be 17 S-segments. However, only seven of these have an S-segment; the remaining 10 display S-ellipsis which is indicated by

WAYS OF SAYING: WAYS OF MEANING 225

putting the intended S-segment in round brackets in the English translation.

6.3 Formal exophoric S-ellipsis in Urdu

The question may be raised whether S-ellipsis in Urdu does not simply function as formal exophoric, when it is not endophoric; after all, if there is concord between Subject and Predicator, then the latter must provide clues for the correct interpretation of the former. However, the situation is not as simple as this – and for several reasons.

First, there are clause types in which the concord obtains not between S and P but between P and Complement (as in 24e–f above). Thus if we have an example, such as the second and the third clauses of the following:

32. mə̃y   ys   tərəh ke   khane se   bylkwl   ajyz   a   gəya;
    I   this   kind   of   food with   absolutely   sick   come went;
    I am absolutely sick of this kind of food;

    dal   pəkai   to   cavəl   nəhĩ,   cavəl   pəkaya to
    lentils cooked   then   rice   not,   rice   cooked then
    if (–) cook lentils then no rice, if (–) cook rice then

    dal   nəhĩ.
    lentils   not
    no lentils.

No clues are provided regarding the nature of the S-segment from the form of the P **pəkai** and **pəkaya**.

Even when concord obtains between S and P, as in the majority of cases, the form of the P-segment is not entirely unambiguous; thus it may permit not just one single invariant possibility but a range from which choice must be made. This is obvious from a comparison of the following two examples:

33. kəl   ja   rəhi hũ   pətə nəhĩ kəb vapəs aũ   gi   əb
    tomorrow   go   ing   am   know not when back come will now
    (I) am going tomorrow, God knows when (I) will be back again now

34. kəl   ja   rəhe hə̃y pətə nəhĩ kəb vapəs aẽ   ge   əb
    tomorrow   go   ing   am   know not when back come will now

In (33), the P-segment is entirely unambiguous; it permits one single invariant interpretation, pointing to an S-segment which must have the following properties: first person, singular, feminine, formal. These requirements are met only by one item in the language – the pronoun **mə̃y**. Thus casual listeners have no problem in understanding the speaker's meanings; further, note that the amount of information they would have on simply hearing (33) is more detailed than that they would have for (18a): **tell you later**. By contrast, it is not possible to provide one single translation for (34); the P-segment permits more than one option, and further complications arise from the nature of the Urdu pronominal system. Thus the following S-segments are permissible for (34):

34 i. ap kəl   ja rəhe hẽy ......
   <u>you</u> are going tomorrow
                              [ap = you: 2nd person, sing., masc., honorific]
   ii. həm kəl   ja rəhe hẽy....
   I/<u>we</u> am/are going tomorrow....

                              [həm I: 1st person, sing., fem./masc., informal]
                              [həm we:1st person, plural, fem./masc., informal]
   iii. <u>vo</u>   kəl   ja   rəhe   hẽy....
   he/<u>they</u> is/are going tomorrow....
                              [vo he: 3rd person, sing., masc., honorific]
                              [vo they: 3rd person, plural, masc., hono./non.hono.]

In (34), it is possible to insert any of the three pronouns **ap**, **həm** or **vo** as the S-segment. Urdu pronouns are unambiguous only with regard to the speech role (i.e. person) information; their number and gender is projected by the P-segment. Since in (34) this segment is not unambiguous, alternative possibilities of interpretation for **həm** and **vo** exist. Casual listeners who simply overhear (34) are not likely to be able to interpret it without some additional clues.

Finally, unlike English it is not the case in Urdu that exophoric S-ellipsis must be interpreted as **I** if the clause has the function of statement and as **you** if the clause has the function of question. The discussion of (34) has hopefully demonstrated that clauses with the function of statement can be interpreted, at least in some environments, as having a first, second or third person as their intended S-segment. To consider clauses with the function of question, compare the following:

                          ii. zərə   ydhər   ao!
                              little here   come
                              come here for a minute!

35i. kəhã   cəli   gəĩ?
     where   walk   went
                          iii. zərə   ydhər   bwlao!
                               little here   call
                               call (–) here for a minute!

(35i) may be interpreted as (a) **where have you got to?** in which case (iii) cannot follow it; the addressee of both (35i) and (ii) is the same person. It is also possible to interpret (35i) as (b) **where has/have she/they got to?**; in this case (35iii) is not addressed to the same person, whose absence is the

WAYS OF SAYING: WAYS OF MEANING 227

subject of comment in (35i). In other words, the clause with question function is not necessarily to be interpreted as if its intended S-segment is a second person pronoun.

For these reasons the stating of environments where exophoric S-ellipsis would simply belong to the category 'formal' is not as simple for Urdu as it is for English. Space does not permit a detailed discussion, but some general tendencies may be noted about the kind of indications provided by the P-segment for the interpretation of S-ellipsis:

(i) The P-segment provides a clearer indication to the nature of the intended S-segment, if the number selection is singular; greater neutralization of person and gender occurs when the number is plural.
(ii) Even with a singular selection, the gender of the S-segment is indicated unambiguously more frequently than its person status; second person status is indicated invariantly with greater frequency than the first or third person status.
(iii) An invariant S-segment is indicated more frequently if the primary tense selection is present, rather than future, rather than past.

By implication, then, the optimal environment for the functioning of S-ellipsis as formal exophoric is where the P-segment of the clause unmistakably displays a singular number and a primary present tense. This possibility will be considerably reduced if the tense selection is future, and even more reduced where the tense is past. Irrespective of tense, S-ellipsis is less likely to be formal exophoric if the number selection is even potentially plural. These predictions can be checked from Table 8.1, where the lexical verb is **become** (hona) and **walk** (cəlna). This table relates only to the P-segments in indicative clauses where the verbal group is positive. A great deal of neutralization results when the verbal group is negative and/or the tense system applicable is a non-indicative one. A further source of neutralization is to be found in the distinctions made by reference to the systems of 'formality' and 'honorifics' which are applicable to the Urdu pronouns. This invariably has the effect of rendering the P-segment with a potentially plural selection more ambivalent with regard to person, gender and number (see the discussion of example (34) above).

It was important to go into this degree of detail in order to bring home the realization that in Urdu, exophoric S-ellipsis *cannot* function as formal exophoric in a wide variety of environments. If then, S-ellipsis *is* exophoric, it must function as some variety of situational exophoric, much more often than as formal exophoric. This situation is qualitatively different from English, where S-ellipsis is either endophoric or predominantly formal. The fact that exophoric S-ellipsis may have an intended S-segment which refers not to the interactants but the third person – appropriately referred to in Urdu as **Gaeb** (absent) – adds greatly to the opacity of this implicit device.

Table 8.1 Partial paradigm of verbal groups

singular (I: m ə̃y; you: twm; he/she/it: vo)
plural (we: həm; you: twmlog; they: vo)

		(i) M	(ii) F	(iii) M	(iv) F	
First person	present	hota	hoti	hote	hoti	(a)
		cəlta	cəlti	cəlte	cəlti	(b)
	future	hũ	hũ	hõ	hõ	(c)
		cəlũ	cəlũ	cəlẽ	cəlẽ	(d)
	past	hua	hui	hue	hue	(e)
		cəla	cəli	cele	cəle	(f)
Second person	present	hote	hoti	hote	hoti	(a)
		cəlte	cəlti	cəlte	cəlti	(b)
	future	ho	ho	ho	ho	(c)
		cəlo	cəlo	cəlo	cəlo	(d)
	past	hue	huĩ	hue	huĩ	(e)
		cele	cəlī	cəle	cəlī	(f)
Third person	present	hota	hoti	hote	hoti	(a)
		cəlta	cəlti	cəlte	cəlti	(b)
	future	ho	ho	hõ	hõ	(c)
		cəle	cəle	cəlẽ	cəlẽ	(d)
	past	hua	hui	hue	huĩ	(e)
		cəla	cəli	cəle	cəlī	(f)

First person:
(a) hə̃y / hə̃y, (b) hə̃y / hə̃y, (c) ga / gi, (d) ga / gi, (e) (tha) / (thi), (f) — (columns i, ii)
(a) hə̃y / hə̃y, (b) hə̃y / hə̃y, (c) ge / ge, (d) ge / ge, (e) (the) / (the), (f) — (columns iii, iv) — I

Second person:
(a) ho / ho, (b) ho / ho, (c) ge / gi, (d) ge / gi, (e) (the) / (thĩ) — II

Third person:
(a) hə̃y / hə̃y, (b) hə̃y / hə̃y, (c) ge / gi, (d) ge / gi, (e) (the) / (thĩ) — III

6.4 Restricted exophoric ellipsis in Urdu

Operating again with the optimal and non-optimal degrees of implicitness (see §§ 5.2–5.3), let us examine exophoric S-ellipsis in Urdu. If such ellipsis functions as instantial exophoric – i.e. at a non-optimal degree of implicitness – then casual listeners are likely to interpret the message quite correctly as long as they have access to the material situational setting. When however such ellipsis occurs as restricted exophoric, access to the material situational setting is of no consequence, since the clues needed for the interpretation are in the knowledge shared by the interactants.

If we can find examples of restricted exophoric S-ellipsis where the semantic structure of the message(s) indicates quite clearly that the intended S-segment must refer to some absent third person entity, then we have a case of the highest degree of implicitness – such as is not found in English, since here only **the** of the third person pronoun might function as restricted exophoric. However, as I have argued above (§4.2) ellipsis is inherently more implicit than either of the latter mentioned devices. It remains then to find examples of extended discourse which would be acceptable to Urdu speakers and which contain the above feature; below I present two such examples:

36. – səlam-o-ləy-kwm sahyb!
    salam-o-laikum Saheb
    Greetings   Sir!   (i.e. Good morning/afternoon/evening)

    – valəykwməssəlam bhai! ys dəfə bhi ghər pər nəhĩ hə̃y?
    walaikum-as-salam brother! this time too home at not are
    Greetings! is/aren't (–) at home this time, either?

    – nəhĩ ji. əbhı əbhi bahər gəe   hə̃y.
    not sir   now now   out   went are
    no, sir! (–) just went out a minute ago.

    – to   kya xəbər həy? dehli ja rəhe hə̃y ky nəhĩ?
    then what news is?   Delhi go ing is that not
    what's the news then? Is/are (–) going to Delhi, or not?

    – ji əpən ko to kwch pətə nəhĩ;   kəl   teliphun kiya tha.
    sir me   to   some know not; yesterday telephone did was
    I don't know sir! (–) did telephone yesterday.

    – əccha ãe to bətə dena ky həm ae the.
    o.k. come then tell give that I   came was
    o.k. when (–) come(s), then tell (–) that I called.

37. – kyõ bhəi əb kys lie ae ho?
    why   now which for come are
    Now then, why are (you) here again?

230   PART THREE: LANGUAGE AND SOCIETY

> – sərkar   vəhi pəreshani həy; tin məhine se   tənxah
>   master   the same worry   is; three months since   wages
>   Sir, it's the same worry; for the last three months (my) wages
>
>   rwki   həy; mə̃y soca ap bol dẽ to shayd jəldi   kər
>   stopped are;   I   thought you speak give then perhaps quickly do
>   have been withheld; I thought if you tell (* –) then perhaps
>
>   dẽ;   bəcce bhuke həỹ.
>   give kids   hungry are
>   (–) might hurry. (my) kids are going hungry.
>
> – pucha twm ne kyõ   roki   həy?
>   asked you   why stopped is
>   did you ask why (–) have stopped (*your wages)?
>
> – ji sərkar bole ki tin   həfte ki   jo   chwTTi bimari
>   yes sir   said that three weeks of that leave sickness
>   yes Sir, (–) said that because of the three weeks' sickness
>
>   ki li thi to ws me kəT gəi.
>   of took was then that in cut went
>   leave that (–) took, (–) will have to make up for it.

In the above examples ellipsis is indicated by round brackets in the English translations. Not all of these represent S-ellipsis; and not all brackets are unfilled. There are two examples of Complement ellipsis, indicated by placing a star * in the bracket. One of these is filled (37; turn 3; **your wages**); the evidence for this comes from the co-text directly, as the only thing stopped is the wages of the first speaker. Note that the entry is not underlined; underlining is used only to indicate exophoric ellipsis. The other filled bracket is in the same example at Turn 1 (**you**); this is a case of formal exophoric; the form of the P-segment permits one invariable selection **twm**. In the last line of the last turn of this example, we have a borderline case. The semantics of the rest of the message in text (37) makes it quite obvious that the penultimate bracket could only have **I** as the intended S-segment; the form of the P-segment remains opaque since in this clause the concord is with Complement **chwTTi** and not with the intended S-segment. The nature of the dialogue in both examples (36), (37) is such that the referents of the other exophoric S-ellipsis could not possibly be present on the interactive scene. The dialogues are however quite extended, showing that communication is taking place without any problem. Further, the social distance between the interactants is quite different in the two examples: in (36), the first speaker is a friend/relation of the family whose servant of considerable standing is his addressee; the social distance is near minimal. In (37), this distance is much greater: the first speaker is likely to be an employee of a fairly low standing, the second must be a superior with considerable power. This points to the fact that the occurrence of exophoric ellipsis does not correlate with a particular tenor

WAYS OF SAYING: WAYS OF MEANING 231

selection. I shall return to the question of the environments in which restricted exophoric ellipsis is less frequent, but before this let us look at an additional source of greater implicitness in Urdu.

6.5 Complement ellipsis in Urdu

I have argued that the implicitness of ellipsis is so great because the area in which the intended meanings may lie can only be stated by reference to the elliptical string itself (4.2 above). It follows that the less implicit the rest of the syntagm, the easier it would be to retrieve the intended meanings. If, then, a clause with S-ellipsis were to contain also Complement ellipsis, I think we would be justified in claiming greater implicitness for that string. The question of Complement ellipsis was not raised in the discussion of English, because the constraints on such ellipsis are even stronger. For example, its exophoric functioning is not permitted at all. We cannot say **read**? in English to mean **have you read it**? However, Urdu very often makes use of C-ellipsis along with an S-ellipsis, so that the translation equivalent of **read**? i.e. **pəRh lia**? is a fairly normal and common pattern in Urdu.

There are, of course, some conventionalized, non-productive specimens of exophoric C-ellipsis in English, e.g. **finished?**. However, one cannot, by analogy, ask **knitted?** or **made?** or **typed?**. In Urdu, C-ellipsis is a productive pattern; sentences such as **bwn lia?** (knitted), **bən gəya** (made?) or **mil gəya?** (found) and dozens like these occur all the time. I am certainly not implying that Urdu speakers talk in one word sentences as children are supposed to in the holophrastic stage. None the less it is amazing to what extent one finds oneself talking thus to members of one's family, friends, colleagues, and of course one's servants. Here is an example of such an exchange:

38. – pəka lia?
    cooked?   (i.e. have you finished cooking it?)

   – hã
    yes.   (yes)

   – cəkhao zəra
    give a taste   (let me have a little taste)

   – lijie
    have   (here you are)

   – bəhwt məze ka həy; tez āc pər əb nə rəkkho;
    very taste of is high flame on now no keep
    is very tasty; don't put on high flame now.

    xərab ho jae ga; bəlke mere xyal se ys pyale
    bad become go will rather my thought with this bowl
    will get spoilt; I'd say take out in this bowl.

mẽ nykal lo.
in turn out take
(it's very tasty; don't put it on high flame any more; it will get spoilt; I'd say perhaps you should take it out in this bowl)

I doubt if any normal speaker of Urdu will find this exchange either extraordinary or incomprehensible, even though without the situational clues the precise meaning of C-ellipsis is not available.

6.6 The semantic style of Urdu

As planned earlier (§6.1) I have started by an examination of the logically highest degree of implicitness in Urdu – that which arises from a substantial use of exophoric ellipsis, in particular of restricted exophoric ellipsis. I hope that the previous discussions have established beyond doubt the fact that the system of the language permits a much higher degree of implicitness than that permitted by the system of English. Of course Urdu has other implicit devices than those of ellipsis; but since we can make this point of greater implicitness simply through an examination of the patterns of ellipsis, there is no need to describe these other implicit devices, though it is my impression that comparable differences will be found in other areas too.

Let us now turn to the second question: what is the range of environments in which the optimal degree of implicitness might be employed by the Urdu speaker? The claim that the system permits a very high degree of implicitness is not tantamount to the claim that therefore every speaker of that language *must* exploit this potential. In English the clause pattern exemplified by **would that they offered me a million pounds** is permitted, but it could not be described as offering a resource which is typically and regularly exploited by any members of the contemporary English-speaking community. Similarly, being permitted to use a high degree of implicitness is not equal to being forced to use it. Otherwise the case for arguing cultural control on semantic styles would be weaker; nor could we explain how the same system of language can serve the differing needs of different subcultures, sharing the same language. Because of this, there is a significance to the claim that not only does the system of Urdu language permit a much higher degree of implicitness than English does, but also the speakers of the language employ this same degree of implicitness in a wide range of contexts.

We can claim without hesitation that the dominant semantic style in Urdu is the implicit one, because the range of environments in which this style can be used appropriately without raising communicative problems is much wider than that where it could not be used so. This latter range can be specified very simply as those contexts where the access to the language is through the written channel and the field is (semi)technical, for example textbooks on history, chemistry, etc. will not display the use of exophoric ellipsis. For the remaining range of contexts, it is my impression that neither class membership nor social distance affect the frequency of restricted exophorics.

To say, then, that one is an Urdu speaker is largely to discount the possibility of being misunderstood. It is to believe that your addressee knows what you are on about; it is to assume that the chances of ambiguity are so low as to be almost negligible. This raises a fascinating problem: how do we decide what can be ambiguous? How can we decide what is or is not universally grammatical? If in English it is grammatical to say **must be cooked** in the presence of a pan of rice on the stove, it surely cannot be ungrammatical to say the same sentence in the absence of the pan. Grammars may or may not be pot-boilers, but the question of grammaticality cannot be made to depend upon the presence or absence of a pan of rice on the stove! The environment can only be taken into account in a systematic manner if the boundary between language and non-language is not watertight, if grammar is seen as a mode of meaning, and meaning itself as fundamentally the use of language in the living of life. Without such systematic relations, one can only invoke *ad hoc* rules. Thus pragmatics will tell us that the speaker's communicative competence consists in avoiding ambiguity and that ambiguity in this case is avoided if the pan is physically present on the interactive scene; clearly this is 'natural logic'.

These assumptions and modes of descriptions would be quite harmless but for the fact that normally along with them goes the assumption that the natural logic of situations is the same the world over. If you are a rational being you know what is 'obvious', what is not; what is given, what is new. The comparison of English and Urdu does not support these assumptions. The invariant natural logic of the situation does not prevent an Urdu speaker from saying:

39. zərə dekho to bavəprci-xane mẽ! pək gəya ho ga.
    little look   kitchen   in   cooked gone become will
    just take a look into the kitchen! must be cooked.
    (i.e. go to the kitchen and take a look at the thing you know
    I am talking about because I rather think it must be cooked.)

Subscribing to the tenet of a universal natural logic, we must either see the Urdu speaker as maddeningly illogical – primitive, perhaps? – or we must cook up a romantic hypothesis about all members of the culture possessing a sixth sense that allows them to ESP the more precise intended meanings: such sentimental adulation of the politico-economically underprivileged groups is not entirely absent from the sociolinguistic literature. But clearly there is little to choose between these two science fiction views. Nor do I wish to give the impression that if understanding meanings in English is a miracle – as some theories of semantics would have us believe – then it is a well-nigh impossible feat to perform in Urdu. Unlike many American Indian cultures (Benedict 1935), the culture here is not a silent one; nor is there any reason to believe that communication suffers more breakdowns in Urdu than it does in English. What all this means is that somehow the addressee must be able to retrieve the information which the speaker refers to only implicitly because he expects the addressee to know. This successful transaction of meaning is 'neither a miracle nor a mirage' (Geertz 1971); it is something made possible through participation in the same culture.

Sources of ambiguity cannot be defined in isolation from specific cultures. What we perceive as a universally applicable natural logic because it applies invariably in our own linguistic universe might be simply a culturally specific way of saying, being and behaving. Meanings and ways of meaning are a function of human ability to construct symbolic systems – perhaps the only species-specific innate attribute. But there is no conclusive evidence that the meanings meant by humanity are entirely derived from and predictable as a result of the brute aspects of the physical world in which man lives. To understand language at its deepest level, we must see it primarily as a cultural phenomenon wherein systems of meaning appear not because the 'real' world is thus and thus, but because the world has been construed thus and thus by specific subgroups of humanity; and this construed world *is* their real world. But what does it mean to say that sources of ambiguity must be defined by reference to a culture?

7 Language and social systems

7.1 *Social factors in the interpretation of implicit styles*

If it is true that interactions of the type exemplified by (36) and (37) are fairly normal, what allows an ordinary Urdu speaker to operate on the same wave length as the speaker? We cannot invoke a high degree of intimacy between the specific interactants (cf. 37), so the answer appears unavoidable that in some sense the Urdu speaker's world must be a fairly well-regulated place in which persons, objects and processes have well-defined positions with reference to each other, and the speakers know the details. Let me make this point by reference to a familiar situation.

If **has he already left?** when addressed to my boss's secretary would normally be interpreted by her as **has my boss left?**, this is largely because there is a routine, a well-defined set of relationships whereby the secretary is expected to know about my boss, who is expected to be in that particular place at certain times of the days of the week and the secretary expects to be asked about the boss but not about scores of other males that might be milling around in that same building. These expectations are not 'natural' in the way that mountains are natural; they were constructed by groups of men and women. Their construction created a set of roles; culture consists of a socially created, mutually recognized set of rights and obligations centring around systems of roles.

However, role systems can vary in respect of how well defined their boundaries are: i.e. how clearly established the rights and obligations

WAYS OF SAYING: WAYS OF MEANING

accruing to the role are. Obviously the more determinate these boundaries, the less likely it is that ambiguity will arise in social interaction. I am suggesting that the role system for the community of Urdu speakers is considerably more determinate than it is for the middle-class English speaker. It is only this kind of social structure which will explain why the optimally implicit style has such wide currency in the community. We must postulate that the set of expectations regarding who does what, when, where, why and in relation to whom must be fairly well established.

I am well aware that emphasis on highly determinate role systems is liable to be misunderstood – there is a danger that one is treating 'individuals' as if they were marionettes. Let me add, then, that individuation is not the strong feature of the Indo-Pakistani cultures; or rather, the conception of individuality is fundamentally different. Secondly, a role system can be highly determinate at one level without being so at another. Thus there is a much greater consensus in the 'picture' of the rights and obligations of the various roles than there is adherence to this picture in the actual practices of every member of the community. So, even in the presence of divergent cultural practices in the modern era, the picture associated with each role remains largely intact. A role in the Indo-Pakistani cultures is a sharply defined object with hardly any fuzziness to its boundaries so far as its popular picture is concerned; how that role is enacted today and what consequences it might have on the total culture is a different matter. It is by postulating a large consensus in the picture of the role that we can explain the lack of ambiguity in the following examples:

40. əy-həy! dekho to Gwsəlxane ki kya halət həy!
    gosh   look <u>do</u>   toilet   of what condition is
    Gosh look what condition the toilet is in!

    barə bəj gəy əbhi   tək nəhĩ ai.   zərə dekho
    twelve ring went up-to-now not came   little look
    it's twelve o'clock and (she) is still not arrived. Just

    kəhã   Gaeb   ho gəi
    where disappear become went
    find out where (she) has disappeared to.

41. əre bhəi kəhã cəli gəĩ? mere kəpRe tək nəhĩ nykale.
    hello   where walked went? my clothes   not taken-out.
    hello, where have (–) got to? (–) not even taken out my clothes.

    nəhane ko bəyTha hũ,   der ho   jae gi.
    bathe   to sitting am, late become go will.
    (I) am sitting waiting to have my bath. (–) will get late.

Any reader who truly knows the subcontinent will understand these two examples qualitatively differently from those who do not have a picture of the roles involved. In (40), the **she** will be understood as referring to **bhəngən** (a woman whose job is to clean the toilet); further they will understand the sentences to have been addressed to a servant; the speaker, on the other hand, must be a woman of the house. In (41), the speaker has to be a husband and the addressee his wife. This degree of specificity comes as a result of having a picture of the role of a wife; note that the P-segments **cəli gəi** and **nykale** provide no unambiguous clue about the intended S-segment.

7.2 Role systems and their non-verbal manifestations

Interesting though the question is, I shall not ask here what gives rise to such determinate role systems. The answer could be offered in terms of religion creating an overall 'ethos' (Geertz 1973), or types of social solidarity (Durkheim 1947; Bernstein 1971) arising from the distribution of labour, or affective structures which are the product of dominant kinship dyads (Hsu 1963; 1971a; 1971b) or by some other hypothesis (Benedict 1935; Douglas 1972). The parameters that are important to the definition of determinate roles consist of ascribed attributes (Bernstein 1971). Thus the inherent attributes of sex, age, age-relation, and other inherited factors, e.g. caste, religion, and family's social status function as the determiners of the roles. The centrality of all these factors to the roles on the subcontinent is indisputable. What are the non-verbal ways of 'legitimizing' these attributes, so that they do not lose their hold in the definition of the role system?

Consider the construction of social hierarchy. Despite determined efforts in recent years, caste remains an important vector in determining hierarchy. In 1981, an entire colony of scheduled caste were burnt out of home and house because some of them had dared to pass lewd remarks about an unmarried girl of the upper caste. This is all the more significant if we remember that males passing lewd remarks about females is not an entirely extraordinary happening on the subcontinent; quite the contrary. Within the family, hierarchy is strictly determined by age-relation and sex. Thus both caste and kinship operate as definers of roles (Mayer 1960; Dumont 1966; Mandelbaum 1970).

Turning to the socialization of the young, we shall find that much emphasis is laid on categories of behaviour which are defined by reference to sex, age, kinship relation, and family status (Hsu 1963; Strodtbeck 1971; Hasan 1975). The patterns of how leisure might be used are different for the two sexes; the behaviour of the sister to the brother is not one of 'equality', and so on.

The institution of marriage again upholds the sanctity of these boundaries. The choice of a marriage partner is a process of delicate balancing of caste, class – economic and social – and prestige status of the two families. To marry into a family below one's own in any of these respects is to be subjected to shame; and the shame is greater if the woman moves below the status of her father's family.

I hope it is apparent from these brief remarks that the entire weight of behaviour in the community is orientated towards sensitizing members to the rights and obligations of others – where in the last analysis these rights and obligations accrue from their hierarchic location in the social structure. Despite the slow and constant introduction of a conflicting view of social relations, I believe I am right in suggesting that the Urdu speakers' world remains to a large extent a world in which everyone's place is well known in respect of anyone they could possibly come in social contact with.

It is just possible that this description arouses either a sense of claustrophobia in my reader or a feeling of womb-like security. However, I am concerned neither with denigrating the suffocating impersonality of existence nor the warm security of knowing who you are. The moon has a dark side to it, as I believe Douglas remarked (1972), whether it is the lonely individuation of the middle-class English speaker or the public communality of the Urdu speaker. My concern is simply to establish that the two cultures are qualitatively different; and that this difference is reflected in their characteristic semantic styles. Further, the peculiarities of the social structure are essential for explaining the peculiarities of the semantic style.

7.3 Social structure and language system.

Summing up my position on the semantic style of Urdu, I would say that the optimal degree of implicitness in style is a function of the social structure of the speech community; moreover, the consideration that appears to be the regulating principle is that of creating clear role boundaries. This highly implicit style is capable of surviving because the role system maintains highly determinate boundaries, regarding which there is a great deal of communal consensus. It is certainly not a part of the communal expectation that 'you are free to do your own thing'. As the language puts it proverbially, even God cannot be worshipped in a mosque built of your own private brick and a half. The verbal style is in keeping with patterns of non-verbal behaviour, which again support the same maintenance of clear boundaries. The case for this dialectic between the social structure and the semantic style is strengthened if it can be shown that the system of Urdu language possesses other attributes directly relatable to the characterizing attributes of the social structure.

In this respect the first characteristic of Urdu that comes to mind is that which has often been described as 'levels' of speech in sociolinguistic literature. Often the contrast is presented of the pronominal system in the language, where the pronouns are said to be formal or informal (Khubchandani 1975), but the matter goes far beyond the pronominals, if we are concerned with the relation between wording and meaning. The obsession with hierarchy that Geertz (1960) finds among the Javanese does not seem to be specific to the Javanese alone. The Urdu-speaking community too strikes a delicate balance between age, sex, status of the family, and degree of acquaintance to decide what level of speech is to be used, how a person is to be addressed or referred to. It is this concern which finds its expression in the appropriate use of the honorific forms of speech – which again transcend the boundary of the pronominal system, even at the level of wordings.

The use of the honorific form is determined by reference to kinship relation, age-relation, socio-economic status, and prestige status – the latter is not always determined by the socio-economic status. In the pronoun system, the option honorific vs. non-honorific is not applicable to the first person pronoun: the speaker acts as a point by reference to which the lower and the higher is measured along the various attribute scales mentioned above. Even where a non-honorific term, e.g. **xadym** (servant) is used to refer to self, this selection is conditioned by the status of the addressee *vis-à-vis* oneself. The attributes, themselves, are capable of being ordered with regard to their relevance. Kinship and age take precedence over all considerations: no matter how poor, how ill-to-do one's uncle may be, he deserves the honorific form. The middle-class Urdu speaker will not say **mera cɔca aya** but **mere cɔca ae**. This is, in effect, a way of showing one's estimate of the family status. If the families are equal in prestige and economic status, then age takes on significance; someone older than oneself from a family of equal or higher status, deserves an honorific form.

When the interaction of the system of formality with that of honorifics is examined, we find that formality of speech level always goes with the honorific form. To put it more accurately, the distinction is neutralized. This makes sense in view of the semantics of formality. The choice of formal/informal is applicable only to the interactant roles, since formality is clearly the product of interactant relationship. The actual choice is determined by the degree of social distance: the wider the distance between the two, the more formal the level. In effect, social distance itself is a function of the degree of familiarity, but this familiarity is a meaningful notion only in the environment of family parity. The less intimate one is with an interactant who is one's equal the more likely it is that he is deserving of the honorific form – also that he should be addressed with the formal speech level. Thus the various social vectors for the classification of roles in the society find their expression in the verbal system; and they do this not only through the specific forms associated with the verb or the pronouns but also in the selection of the level of lexicon.

The congruence between the verbal and non-verbal behaviour of the Urdu speakers appears to be such as to justify the statement that the semiotic style of the community is characteristically implicit, that both verbal and non-verbal modes of behaviour are governed by a consideration of the maintenance of clear boundaries. This obsession with the maintenance of clear boundaries appears to act as one of the regulating principles in the social life of the community, and it finds its expression in the ways of being, doing and saying – in other words it exercises a control on the style of meaning.

Compared with this, the regulating principle in the social universe of the middle-class English speaker is indeed very different. Instead of clearly defined ascribed role systems, his social universe contains a challenge – the roles must be achieved (Bernstein 1971) and individuation functions as one of the regulating principles. Whereas the ascribed roles create a secure identity (Hsu 1971a; 1971b; Bernstein 1971), the achieved roles demand the creation of one's identity. The freedom to define one's identity and one's role relation with others carries with it the penalty that nothing much can be taken for granted; ambiguity can therefore exist and must be guarded against. The world is not necessarily a well-regulated, stable place; one's own self has to act as the catalyst. This is not a social environment in which a high degree of implicitness could be tolerated – and it is not.

7.4 *Implicit style in English-speaking community*

If the above explanations of the social genesis and function of the implicit style of meaning is accepted, it would follow that the English-speaking subcommunity whose characteristic semantic style is implicit – i.e. Bernstein's restricted code users – must experience a social relationship qualitatively nearer that of the Urdu speaker than that of its middle-class counterpart. It is at this point that the question cannot be avoided: why and how do these social relations arise? What changes them? The Durkheimian explanation in terms of forms of social solidarity is one such effort. It seems to me that approaching the problem as I have done raises many interesting questions. What attributes does a social structure have to have to contain within itself two such subcommunities? What kind of relations can exist between these two subcommunities? The comparison with the Urdu semantic style is interesting from another point of view: to speak highly implicitly is no more looked down upon in the Urdu-speaking universe than r-lessness would be frowned upon by the Queen. Not so for the subcommunity orientated to implicit style in the English-speaking community. Why not? Is it because there is some attribute inherently undesirable in this way of saying and meaning, or is it that by contrast with the privileged it presents a dead end? To this, we may provide an answer if we examine the environments both in Urdu and in English communities where the orientation to the implicit style would be inappropriate. I would suggest this examination will allow a basis for stating the direction of cultural change.

7.5 *Conclusions*

I have deliberately chosen the distinction between the implicit and the explicit ways of saying and meaning for the simple reason that so far as the referential content – the experiential meaning – of the message is concerned, it could plausibly be claimed that **John can't swim** and its elliptical version **John can't** mean exactly the same thing. The difference between the two is often treated as a matter belonging to performance, therefore lying in pragmatics – not in semantics – or it is seen as simply concerned with surface structure matters, hence not worthy of serious consideration. I would suggest that both these views are wrong. These dichotomies do not serve any useful purpose. On the other hand, if one treats the ways of saying as being necessarily the ways of meaning, as I have attempted to do, it seems quite plausible to suggest that the relationship between language and social life is deep indeed. Different ways of saying reveal different orientations to orders of relevance – their examination shows how the semantic universe of two communities may not be identical.

Today it is normal to claim equality by claiming identity. But identity is not a necessary condition of equality. The readiness to assert that what 'we' can mean, the 'others' can mean too is often associated with liberal egalitarianism. I would suggest that it could in fact be the result of a harmful lack of sensitivity to differences which are possibly as important for the true appreciation of the 'other' as the laudable fact of their being just like us. After all this latter fact follows from our humanity; but the differences are our own creations through which we manage to maintain our monopolies and our interests.

Notes

1. This paper is a revised version of a talk presented at the Bourg Wartenstein Symposium No. 66, 8–17 August 1975.
2. The conventions used here are borrowed from Firth in Harley (1944), with the following alterations: vowel nasalization indicated by diacritic above vowel thus aũ; sh for ʃ; G for γ; capital letters for retroflexion, e.g. T for t and R for r, etc.

References

Benedict, R. (1935) *Patterns of Culture.* London: Routledge & Kegan Paul.
Bernstein, B. B. (1971) *Class, Codes and Control,* Vol. I, London: Routledge & Kegan Paul.
Berry, M. (1975–77) *Introduction to Systemic Linguistics,* Vols. I and II. London: Batsford.
Bolinger, D. (1968) *Aspects of Language.* New York: Harcourt Brace & World.
Brown, R. W. (1970) *Psycholinguistics: Selected Papers.* Chicago: Free Press.
Cole, P. and Morgan, J. L. (eds) (1975) *Syntax and Semantics,* Vol. III; *Speech Acts.* New York: Academic Press.
Douglas, M. (1972) 'Self-evidence'. Henry Myers Lecture given for the Royal Anthropological Institute, 4 May: reprinted in *Implicit Meanings.* London: Routledge & Kegan Paul, 1975, pp. 276–318.
Dumont, L. (1966) *Homo Hierarchicus: The Caste System and Its Implications,* trans. Sainsbury. London: Weidenfeld and Nicolson.
Durkheim, E. (1947) *The Division of Labour in Society,* trans. Simpson. Chicago: Free Press.

Fateh Mohd. Khan (1945) *Misbah-ul-Qawaid, Hissa Doem.* Rampur: Nazim Barqi Press.
Firth, J. R. (1944) 'Introduction' to A. H. Harley, *Colloquial Hindustani.* London: Kegan Paul, Trench, Truber & Co., pp. ix–xxx.
Firth, J. R. (1950) 'Personality and language in society', *Sociological Review* (Journal of the Institute of Sociology), 42, section 2. Also in *Papers in Linguistics.* London: Oxford University Press, 1957.
Geertz, C. (1960) *The Religion of Java.* Chicago: Free Press.
Geertz, C. (ed.) (1971) *Myth, Symbol and Culture.* New York: Norton.
Geertz, C. (1973) *The Interpretation of Culture.* New York: Basic Books.
Grice, H. P. (1975) 'Logic and conversation' in Cole and Morgan, (eds) (1975).
Halliday, M. A. K. (1967–8) 'Notes on theme and transitivity in English'. *Journal of Linguistics,* 3.1, 37–81; 3.2, 199–244; 4.2, 179–216.
Halliday, M. A. K. (1970) 'Language structure and language function'. In Lyons, (ed.) (1970), 140–165.
Halliday, M. A. K. (1974) *Language and Social Man.* London: Longman.
Halliday, M. A. K. (1975) *Learning How to Mean.* London: Edward Arnold.
Halliday, M. A. K. (1985) *An Introduction to Functional Grammar.* London: Edward Arnold.
Halliday, M. A. K. and Hasan, R. (1976) *Cohesion in English.* London: Longman.
Halliday, M. A. K. and Hasan, R. (1980) *Text and Context: Aspects of Language in a Semiotic Social-Perspective,* Sophia Linguistica VI, Sophia University, Tokyo.
Hasan, R. (1972) 'The verb BE in Urdu'. In J. M. W. Verhaar (ed.) *The Verb BE and Its Synonyms,* Part 5. Dordrecht: D. Reidel.
Hasan, R. (1973) 'Code register and social dialect'. In *Class, Codes and Control,* Vol. II. London: Routledge & Kegan Paul.
Hasan, R. (1976) 'Socialization and cross-cultural education'. *International Journal of Social Linguistics,* 8.
Hasan, R. (1978) 'Text in the systemic functional model'. In W. U. Dressler (ed.) *Current Trends in Textlinguistics.* Berlin: de Gruyter.
Hasan, R. (1980) 'What's going on: a dynamic view of context in language'. In *The Seventh LACUS Forum.* Columbia: Hornbeam Press. (Chapter 2 of this book).
Hasan, R. (1981) 'Coherence and cohesive harmony'. In J. Flood (ed.) *Understanding, Reading, Comprehension.* Newark: International Reading Association.
Hsu, F. L. K. (1963) *Class, Caste and Club, Princeton,* N.J.: Van Nostrand.
Hsu, F. L. K. (1971a) 'Psychosocial homeostasis and Jen: conceptual tools for advancing psychological anthropology' *American Anthropologist.* 73.1.
Hsu, F. L. K. (ed.) (1971b) *Kinship and Culture.* Chicago: Aldine.
Ishfaq Ahmed (n.d.) *ek mohəbbət səw əfsane.* Lahore: Latif Publishers.
Kachru, Y. (1966) 'An introduction to Hindi syntax', University of Illinois, mimeo.
Khubchandani, L. (1975) 'Toward a selection grammar: fluidity in modes of address and reference in Hindi'. Honolulu: East-West Centre, mimeo.
Labov, W. (1970) 'The logic of non-standard English'. In F. Williams (ed.) *Language and Poverty.* Chicago: Markham.
Leech, G. (1974) *Semantics.* Harmondsworth: Penguin.
Lenneberg, E. (1971) 'Language and cognition'. In Steinberg and Jakobovits (eds) (1971), pp. 536–557.
Lyons, J. (1970) *New Horizons in Linguistics.* Harmondsworth: Penguin.
Mandlebaum, D. G. (1970) *Society in India,* Vols. I–II. Berkeley: University of California Press.

Mayer, A. C. (1960) *Caste and Kinship in Central India: A Village and Its Religion.* London: Routledge & Kegan Paul.

Steinberg, D. D. and Jakobovits, L. A. (eds) (1971) *Semantics: An Interdisciplinary Reader in Philosophy, Linguistics and Psychology.* Cambridge: Cambridge University Press.

Strodtbeck, F. L. (1971) 'Sex-role identity and dominant kinship relations'. In Hsu (ed.) (1971).

Verma, S. K. (1961) 'A study in the systemic description of Hindi grammar and comparison of the Hindi English verbal group', University of Edinburgh doctoral thesis, unpublished.

Wittgenstein, L. (1921) *Tractatus Logico-Philosophicus.* London: Routledge & Kegan Paul.

Whorf, B. L. (1956) *Language, Thought and Reality, Selected Writings,* J. B. Carroll (ed.). Cambridge, Mass.: MIT Press.

Young, D. J. (1980) *The Structure of English Clauses.* London: Hutchinson.

Index

Aarsleff, H. 20
abstract objectivism 175–6
abstract thinking 161–5
abstraction, orders of 174, 181
academic study of language 3
acculturation 1, 43–4, 115, 158
actualization 164, 167
adjacency pairs 56, 205
advertising 41–2
agnation 110, 112, 115
ambiguity 232–5
anaphoric interpretation 196–8, 209
animal communication 104–5
antonymy 101, 193
attribution 60–4, 66–7
Australia, research in 134, 165–6
autonomy *see* individual autonomy
Awdry, Revd W. 28, 55, 63

Bakhtin, M. 9, 152–3, 166–80, 182–5
Barthes, R. 144–5
behaviour
   language as 181
   non-verbal 191–2, 237–8; *see also* gesture
   normal and abnormal 43–5
Berger, P.L. 21
Bernstein, Basil B. 2, 4–5, 7–10, 34, 46,
   113–16, 144, 152, 154, 180, 182–4,
   210, 217
biogenetic influences 159, 165, 186
Black English 33–4
body cues 201, 206
Brown, R. 17–18
Butt, David G. 14, 113, 134

Capture (of attention in text) 41
Cartesian concepts 15–16, 20, 159
casual listeners, comprehension by 200–9,
   214–15, 225–6, 229
cataphoric interpretation 196–8, 209
categorical thinking *see* abstract thinking
categorization 8, 19, 161, 164
character particularization 58–60, 62–7
children
   cultural development of, 8, 158, 165
   language of 24, 104, 119; *see also* mother–
      child talk
   perceptions of work at home 143
   questioning by 136–9
   view of death *see* death

choice paths 106–8, 115
Chomsky, N. 20, 77, 112
civilization 17, 186
clause 107, 117–19, 205–6, 210
Cloran, Carmel 113, 117–18, 134
code
   language as 181
   semiotic *see* semiotic codes
   verbal *see* verbal codes
codified patterns of language 147, 149
coding orientation 9, 162, 179, 183
Cole, M. 18–19
common-sense knowledge 147
communication
   adult 165
   animal 104–5
   children's *see* children
   extra-linguistic 174; *see also* gesture
   ideologically-based 166–7, 178, 181
   language as 19, 21–3, 38
community values 18, 23–6, 32, 34, 38, 42,
   52, 62, 66, 104, 115, 133–4, 140, 166,
   176, 192, 237
companionship between women and
   children 137, 143
Complement ellipsis 230–2
concrete thinking *see* situational thinking
configurative rapport 8, 10, 148–9
conjunct entry points 108
conscious realization 155–8
consciousness
   forms of 9, 152, 158–9, 179–80, 183–6
   valuation of 185–6
   of speakers 175–7
constellations of linguistic patterns 148–9
content and form *see* form and content
context
   of creation 52
   of culture 9, 184
   of situation 9, 37–46, 51, 105–6, 111,
      113–17, 184
context-specific and contextually-open
   networks *see* semantic networks
contextualization 164
convergent semiotic codes 47–8, 51
conversation 56, 134; *see also* mother–child
   talk
correspondence theory 21
co-text 197–9
Coulthard, M. 41, 56

244 INDEX

cryptogrammar 182

death, children's view of 28–32, 135–6
decontextualization 164–5
definite article *see* 'the'
definiteness 197–8, 201–2, 204
delicacy, degrees of 6–7, 74–5, 85, 92, 99, 101, 107–8, 115, 192
design of language 18, 100
detachability 21–3
dialectical materialism 160
dialogue *see* turn-taking
dictionary definitions 17, 139–40, 144
discourse semantics 118
discrete and non-discrete Placement 65–8
disjunct entry points 108, 121
disruptive behaviour 44
dissonance 104
dogs and ideology 104
Douglas, J.D. 26
Douglas, Mary 104
dynamic nature of semantic systems 124–5

economic independence of women 144
elaborative semantic properties 62–3, 66
elementary mental functions 155–6, 186
ellipsis 148, 196, 211; *see also* Complement ellipsis; Subject ellipsis
emotional support of children 137, 142–3
empathy 215
encoding devices 208–9, 212
endophoric and exophoric interpretation 9, 196, 199–205, 209, 213
  in Urdu 217–231
English speakers *see* middle-class English
entry conditions 74–5, 88, 94–7
entry point 108, 119, 121
environment 106–8, 123
equality and identity 240
ethnic communities 33
ethnocentricity 16
everyday experience 8, 153, 158, 185
exchange structure 56, 124–5
exophorics, types of 200–4; *see also* endophoric and exophoric interpretation
experiential semantic component 73, 99
explicit style *see* implicit and explicit styles
explicit and inexplicit Placement 65–8

face-to-face interaction 199, 214; *see also* interpersonal interaction
Fahey, R. 117
fashions of speaking 5, 8, 10, 145–7, 149, 179, 183, 216–17
fathers, image of 138
Fawcett, R.P. 7–8, 20
feminist discourse 144

field of discourse 45–6, 116
filtered reality, 37–9
Firth, J.R. 37, 74, 102, 112, 149
Fishman, J.A. 16
form and content 18, 144, 191
formal exophorics 204, 207, 209, 213
  in Urdu 225, 230
Foucault, M. 145
frame 68–70, 117
free regulation 157–8
freedom *see* individual autonomy

generality *see* specificity
generic structural potential 6, 53–7
genetic theory 154–5
genre theory 173
genres, literary 6, 51–7, 60, 62
gesture 24, 38–9, 51, 146
Goffman, E. 13, 37, 56
grammar, traditional 19, 22, 107, 119
  in Urdu 217–18
grammaticality 233
GSP *see* generic structural potential

habitual forms of communication 144–5, 147
habitude 60–4, 67
Halliday, Michael 6–8, 13, 20–6, 37–40, 53, 60, 70, 73–4, 77, 81, 110–21, 146–9, 153–4, 177, 222–3
handkerchiefs, knots in 156–7
hierarchic relationships 47–8, 148, 236–7
higher mental functions 8, 152–67, 181–6
  empowering nature of 160
Hjelmslev, L. 7, 14, 20, 21–2, 74, 100–1, 112, 146–7, 149
Hoijer, H. 18
honorific forms 148, 227, 237–8
Hubley, P. 21, 24
Hudson, Richard 106
human activity *see* social situation
hyponymy 101–2, 198
hypotheses in linguistics 106–7, 113–14

ideas, formulation of 19
ideologically-based communication *see* communication
ideology 104–5, 125, 138, 143–5, 149
  inevitability of 133, 144
  of woman's work 133–6, 144, 148
  social construction of 133–4, 146–9
impersonalization 59–60, 62–4
implicit and explicit styles and devices 9, 194–6, 199–216, 232–9
implicitness
  degrees of 9, 208–15, 232, 237, 239
  in Urdu 217, 227, 229–31
  inherent 201–11, 213

INDEX

permissible 213
implied meanings 207
Inciting Moment 69
'incompletions' in Bakhtin's work 180
indeterminate exophorics 203, 209
'individual, the'
　concepts of 159
　uniqueness of 216
individual autonomy 5, 44–5, 48
individual subjectivism 175
Information, system of 222–3
Initiating Event 54–5, 61, 65, 67–71
inner speech 164
instantial exophorics 201, 209, 213–17
instantiation 107, 110, 112, 114–16, 181
institutionalization 5, 46–8
instructor role of women 136–9
intellectualization 156–7, 160, 169
interaction *see* face-to-face interaction; interpersonal interaction; social interaction
internalization 158, 165
interpersonal interaction 73, 119, 170, 184–5; *see also* face-to-face interaction
interpretation, types of 196–7
interpretative sources 195–9, 205
intersubjective objectivsm 176
intersubjectivity 38, 45, 21–3, 113, 165
intertextuality 65, 166–8, 179–83
intimacy 214–15
isomorphic semantic features 120

Jacobs, J. 61–2, 64–7, 69
Johnson, N.S. 58

Kipling, Rudyard 60
'knowing how to mean' 199
knowledge structure *see* world knowledge

laboratory experiments 18
labourer role of women 136, 139
Labov, W. 34, 43, 69–70
langue and *parole* 7, 100–1, 149, 154, 167, 175
Lenneberg, E.H. 17–18, 24–5
lexical items 74–5, 98–9, 102
　unique identification of 84–5, 93, 98
lexicogrammar, role of 73–4, 90, 100, 105–6, 110
linguistic patterning 10, 148–9
literary genres *see* genres
living of life 1–2, 10, 105, 134, 136, 233
logic *see* natural logic
logical component of semantics 73
Longacre, R.E. 57, 69, 71
Luckman, T. 21
Luria, A.R. 159, 161–6, 179–81, 183, 185

McGregor, William 107

Macquarie Dictionary 139–40
main act (in Initiating Event) 68–70
Maley, Y. 117
Malinowski, B. 37, 100
Mandler, J.M. 58
marriage 46–7, 236
Martin, J.R. 118
Marx, Karl 133, 159, 186
material situational setting 10, 39, 47–8, 51, 200–1, 204–10, 214, 219, 229
material social conditions 5–6, 154, 162, 182–3, 186
mathematics, language of 15
Matthiessen, Christian 111
Mead, G.H. 22–3
meaning
　theory of 21, 24, 26, 149
　see also ways of saying, etc
meaning of words, exact 92
meaning potential 9, 114–17, 124–5, 146, 149
meanings
　construal of 181–2, 185, 234
　construction of 100, 102
　extra-linguistic 105–6
　see also semantic networks; semantic units
means to an end, language as 4, 14
mediation, concept of 156–8
memory 155–8
mental functions, human *see* higher mental functions
meronymy 198
message semantics 117–20, 125
metafunctional hypotheses 115–16, 118, 120
metalanguage 55
metaphor 77, 95, 145, 207
Michaelis, A. 58
middle-class attitudes 116, 166
middle-class English 194, 213–17, 234, 237–8
Milne, A.A. 60, 66
mind, human 14–15, 153–4, 160
mirrorites 14
monologue 206
Mood, system network of 109, 111, 121, 207, 219
　in Urdu 222
Moral (in stories) 54–5
mother–child talk 4, 8, 25–32, 116, 124–5, 134–45, 150, 166
mother tongue, use of 125
multifocal realization 111
music 146
myths 54, 60, 62–3, 65–6

naming 20, 216
natural language 15, 24

natural logic 19, 233
Natural Rationality 20
nature, language of 15
need for language 24
negotiation of context 5, 45–8
Nesbitt, Chris 111
networks *see* systemic functional model
Newson, J. 21
norms of behaviour 42–4
nuclear semantic properties 62–3, 66
nursery tales, 6, 51–71

objectification 77, 148
one-to-one relations 120–1, 123
'onion' of culture 145
onomastics *see* naming
ontogenesis 8, 143, 145, 155
Oxford Learner's Dictionary 27

paradigm and syntagm 6–7, 73–4, 99, 101, 107, 112, 119, 141, 149, 161, 186, 208, 211, 219, 222, 228, 231
paralinguistic codes 51
parole see *langue*
parsing 58
particularization *see* character particularization
Peirce, C.S. 16
person particularization *see* character particularization
philosophy 15, 33
phonology 73, 105
physical reality *see* reality
PI *see* systematic path inheritance
pictures 146
Placement 6, 54–70
plasticity 104
point of entry 8
point of origin 108, 113–14, 117
power relations 33, 42, 183–4, 186, 216
Predicator 118–19
  in Urdu 222, 225
privileging of language 157
progress, human 186
protolanguage 24, 104–5, 119
psychological autonomy 159–60
psychology, animal and human 160
purpose of language 22, 25, 146, 149, 181; *see also* use of language

Qualifier 198
quasi mythology 63, 65
questioning children's 136–9

Ramsey, F.P. 22
rational thinking 162–3
rationality 16–17, 20, 186
reality
  filtered *see* filtered reality
  in relation to language 17, 146–7
  modes and models of 191, 194
  physical 16, 18, 20–1, 37
  'raw' and 'sensed' 21
  relative 16
  socially constructed 4–5, 16–22
  ultimate *see* ultimate reality
realization 73, 107, 110–12
  dialectical nature of 105–6
  of Initiating Event 68–71
  of Placement 54–68
realization statements 7, 74–84, 87, 111
reasoning *see* natural logic; thought processes
Recipient role 82–3
reference, concept of 100, 196
register studies 114
religion 16, 146, 236
renewal of language 184
resource, language as 13–14, 181, 185
response 173, 177–8; *see also* validation
restricted exophorics 204, 209–10, 214–17, 232
  in Urdu 228–31
rhetorical questions 206
rhetorical units 117–18
role systems 47–8, 120, 122, 234–9
Rorty, R. 14, 16, 32
Royce, J.R. 14
Rumelhart, O.E. 58, 69–70
RUs *see* rhetorical units

Saussure, F. de 7, 10, 21, 74, 100, 146, 149, 154, 175, 177
scientific method 15–16, 164, 185
Scribner, S. 18–19
SE *see* selection expressions
secretaries expectations of 234
selection expressions 7, 84–99, 108–12
semantic distance 193–4
semantic inheritance 75, 101
semantic (system) networks 5, 7–8, 104–25
  context-specific 7, 114–15, 120
  contextually open 8, 115–16, 119–20, 124–5
  uses of 124–5
semantic potential *see* meaning potential
semantic properties of text 57–70
semantic style 9, 192–3, 213, 216, 237
  characteristic 213, 216
  in Urdu 217–34, 239
semantic units 117–18
semantic variation 115–16
semantics as stratum of language 73
semiosis 18, 20–1
semiotic codes 38, 40, 43, 45–8, 51
semiotic mediation 8–9, 152–67, 171, 178–86

INDEX

semiotic potential 146
semiotic style 9, 191–3, 238
  in Urdu 217, 232–4
semiotic systems *see* sign systems
Sequent Event 54–5
SFL *see* systemic functional linguistics
shaping
  of reality 14, 18, 22–3, 25, 33–4
  of utterance 168
shared knowledge 9, 216, 223
shopping 47, 53, 55
short stories 55
Shotter, J. 21
SI *see* semantic inheritance
sign systems 21–2, 24, 28, 100–1, 104, 145–6
signification *see* value
'silly mummy' 137–9, 149
Sinclair J. McH. 41, 56
situational thinking 162
social class 4, 7, 40, 232, 236
  see also socio-economic differences
social distance 5, 47–8, 215, 230, 232, 238
social interaction 5, 45–8, 152, 168–70, 179–84, 234
social language 166–7, 178–9
social nature of linguistic meanings 115; *see also* community values
social positioning 104, 114–16, 136, 138, 144, 158, 164–5, 170, 183, 194, 215, 230, 238–9
  of children 145
  see also hierarchic relationships
social processes 26, 40, 46–8, 145, 238
social situatedness of speakers 9, 6, 166, 178
social situation and milieu 167–74, 180, 184
socialization 25–6, 52, 67, 114, 125, 184, 236
socially constructed reality *see* reality
societal organisation, theory of 154, 184
socio-economic differences 33–4, 237; *see also* social class
sociogenesis 157–62, 165–6, 181, 186
sociolinguistics 237
sociological input to semantic networks 80, 114, 117
sociological theory 8, 116, 184
SP *see* generic structural potential
specificity 203, 211–13
speech
  levels of 237–8
  nature of 17, 19
'speech', meanings of 171
speech act analysis 125
speech genre 9, 152–3, 166–71, 174
speech process 175–8
stratification of communities 174, 179, 186
structural potential of text 42

structure of text *see* text structure
subcultures 193
Subject (function) 56
Subject ellipsis (S-ellipsis) 9–10, 204-8
  in Urdu 217–31
surface phenomena 144–5
surface structure 71, 239
suspension of disbelief 3, 16, 20, 23, 26, 33–4
syllogisms 162–4
synonymy 99, 101, 198
syntagms *see* paradigm
system networks *see* semantic networks
systematic path inheritance (PI) 75, 101
systemic functional linguistics 1–2, 5–7, 9, 74, 101, 106–7, 110–11, 115, 123, 152–4, 173

talking *see* speech
tape-recording 8, 134
teleology 24
temporal distance 59–60, 62–4, 66
Temporal Adjunct 69
tenor 45–7, 116, 214–15, 230
text and context 4–5, 41–2, 44–6, 48, 166, 173–4, 185, 200–1, 210
text radicals 117–18
text structure 6, 41, 51, 53–7, 62, 118
textual component of semantics 73
'the', interpretation of 197–8, 201–3, 208, 210–11, 213
Theme 56
thinking
  and language 18
  by women 138
  see also abstract thinking; rational thinking; situational thinking
thought materials 17–18
thought processes 18–20
time, concept of 15, 147
tools 154, 157
Transitivity 74–6, 98
translatability 145–6
Trevarthen, C. 21, 24
trinocular perspective 110, 114
truth *see* reality
Turner, Geoffrey J. 113
turn-taking 45–6, 171–3

Ultimate Client 82–3
ultimate reality 14–16, 23, 33, 144
understanding, nature of 177–9
units
  of information 222
  of language or speech 8, 167, 171–2, 174, 177, 218
unuttered assumptions 123
Urdu 1, 9–10, 100, 148, 194, 198, 213–14, 217–34, 236–9

use of language 13–14, 23–6, 34, 41, 104, 114–15, 164–7, 177, 181, 183–4; *see also* purpose; instantiation; semiotic mediation
utterance 167–80
  type of *see* speech genre
  wholeness of 172–5
Uzbekistan, research in 161, 165, 181, 183

validation 22–5, 27, 43, 119; *see also* response
value and signification 7, 100-1
values
  attached to human actions 143–4
  cultural 18–19
  personal 14
variation
  in behaviour 43–5, 48
  in use of language 105
verbal codes 38–41, 45–7
Vincent, John 138
visual contact between speakers 199, 201–3, 207

Vološinov, V.N. 145–6, 159, 167–70, 175–80, 185
Vygotsky, L.S. 8, 152–60, 163–7, 178–81, 183–6

ways of saying, meaning, being and behaving 191–3, 213, 234, 238–9
Weiss, P. 16
Wertsch, J.V. 8, 154–5, 164–7
Whorf, B.L. 3, 5, 7–8, 10, 14–20, 33, 74, 77, 92, 146–8, 193–4
Wilkes, Y. 101
Williams, Geoffrey 113, 117
Wittgenstein, L. 20, 22, 216
woman's work 8, 134, 136–44, 148, 235
  and non-work 139–40, 143–4
work, paid 144
world knowledge 101
world view 192, 194

Yeats, W.B. 31